UNDERSTANDING AMERICAN POLITICS

R. V. DENENBERG is a writer and lecturer who specializes in constitutional and legal issues. Educated at Cornell and Stanford Universities and the University of Cambridge, he has been a lecturer in Political Theory and Government at the University of Wales in Swansea. He has also served as a member of the Adjunct Faculty at the Columbia University Graduate School of Journalism. He has been the United States Supreme Court Correspondent for *Newsday*, an editor on the staff of the Week in Review Section of the *New York Times*, and a contributor to the *Guardian*. He is the author of articles in the International and Comparative Law Quarterly, the Modern Law Review and the Cambridge Law Journal. Mr Denenberg has been the recipient of fellowships and grants from the English Speaking Union, the American Political Science Association, the Ford Foundation and the Alicia Patterson Foundation. He lives in the state of New York.

D0595833

R. V. DENENBERG

Understanding American Politics

Third Edition

FontanaPress
An Imprint of HarperCollins*Publishers*

First published in 1976 by Fontana
Second Edition published 1984

This Third Edition published in 1992 by Fontana Press,
an imprint of HarperCollins*Publishers*,
77–85 Fulham Palace Road, London W6 8JB

1 3 5 7 9 8 6 4 2

ISBN 0–00–686239–X

Printed and bound in Great Britain
by HarperCollinsManufacturing Glasgow

Contents

Preface to the Third Edition

In an era when the making of democratic federations preoccupies much of the world, the American experience with federal government has particular resonance. Resolving to form an 'ever closer union among the peoples of Europe', the twelve nations that met at Maastricht in 1991 echoed the goal of 'a more perfect union' enunciated in 1787 at the constitutional convention in Philadelphia. A spirit of compromise pervaded both occasions. Like the architects of European integration, the framers of the American constitution strove to reconcile disparate visions of the community. The overarching lesson of the American experiment is, perhaps, that the need for compromise persists; sharp differences – and an urge to tinker with the fundamental framework – have lingered long after the founding.

The questions most likely to harry The Twelve on the road to unity parallel issues that have been central to American politics for two centuries. Concepts like 'subsidiarity' – ensuring, in the words of Maastricht, that 'decisions are taken as closely as possible to the citizens' – find their counterpart in doctrines apportioning power between Washington and the state capitals. Whether to make decisions unanimously or by 'qualified majority voting' is a quandary analogous in many respects to that faced by eighteenth-century delegates seeking optimal formulas for representing the states in Congress, overriding a presidential veto of legislation, and adopting constitutional amendments. European debates about a 'single market' and common currency replicate those that took place across the Atlantic when a band of autarkic colonies formed a continental economic space, governed by uniform rules of commerce. The invention of European citizenship is a reprise of the formal affirmation, at the end of the American Civil War, that no state might abridge the 'privileges or immunities' of a United States citizen – a moment, in the words of historian James M. McPherson, that 'marked a transition of the United States to a single noun'.

For modern constitution writers, America's epic struggle to live within the limits set by a bill of rights is particularly apposite. It demonstrates that the innate tension between the citizen and the state is not resolved in perpetuity by making a list; the competing values of freedom and order must be balanced pragmatically, often amid hysteria, from day to day.

Whether the bill can provide shelter from the insidious threats of the current era remains to be seen. Through official chicanery and subterfuge, the accountability of government can be silently subverted, as covert operations of various sorts have demonstrated. Sectarian dogma, moreover, is increasingly transformed into coercive regulation by triumphant electoral majorities. Addressing the acts of government exclusively, the bill may afford inadequate protection against abuse of privatized power – such as that exercised by a computer data bank. And, venerable as it may be, the bill is by no means regarded as immutable; whenever a momentary advantage might be gained by chipping away at this monument to individualism, exceptions are mooted.

Despite these perils, the longevity of the bill should set an impressive example for fledgeling democracies. It has been neither suspended nor revised formally in two hundred years. To that extent, the fears of framer James Madison about the durability of mere 'parchment barriers' have proven unfounded.

Global economic and demographic changes also pose significant challenges to the American model. The New Deal of the 1930s endowed Congress and the Presidency with finely honed instincts for economic intervention, regulation and distribution. But in the post-Cold War era of neo-mercantilist rivalries, industrial and technological competitiveness has become a primary national objective. Pursuing that goal may stress the natural fault lines of the federal structure. Uncoordinated attempts by each state to manage growth and maximize its allure to entrepreneurs could lead to restrictions on free movement within the country and a domestic variant of 'social dumping'. The drive to improve educational standards and work force skills may founder if left to local school-governing bodies more committed to instilling traditional social values than ensuring intellectual accomplishment. A constitution that lacks explicit provision for cities, moreover, may deny succour to bankrupt municipalities, struggling to keep peace among contentious ethnic groups and sustain a seemingly permanent urban 'underclass'.

The attractiveness of American institutions is marred, no doubt, by their association with a flimflam brand of politics, vivid and exuberant – but increasingly shallow and tawdry. Consultants, lobbyists and media strategists, supported by the thriving interstate traffic in political funds, influence the outcome of elections, legislative deliberations and administrative policy-making. Candidacies whose appeal rests on personality rather than party or principle often implode abruptly in spasms of prurient scandal. The survivors tailor their views to the poll results, engaging in euphoric sloganeering, moral posturing and emotional symbolism. The nation's feckless political style could preclude effective responses to its more pressing, albeit less diverting, issues. Already much of the electorate has lapsed into non-voting apathy. America's future as a paragon of democracy hinges upon its success in infusing a sense of political efficacy and integrity into its remarkably resilient constitutional order.

R.V.D.
February 1992

CHAPTER ONE

Introduction

The American system of government has always held a peculiar fascination for the foreign observer. The New World symbolized regeneration, and to its political institutions the Old World turned for a glimpse of the future. After visiting the United States in 1832, Alexis de Tocqueville, a French aristocrat, declared: 'I saw in America more than America . . . it was the shape of democracy itself which I sought; its inclinations, character, prejudices, and passions; I wanted to understand it so as at least to know what we have to fear or hope there from.' In 1888, a British traveller, Lord Bryce, gave his fellow Europeans a progress report on America, which by then had quadrupled in population from the fifteen million of de Tocqueville's time. American institutions, said Bryce, intrigued the world because 'they represent an experiment in the rule of the multitude, tried on a scale unprecedentedly vast, and the results of which every one is concerned to watch . . . [They] are believed to disclose and display the type of institutions towards which, as by a law of fate, the rest of civilized mankind are forced to move . . .'

Although it is now more than 200 years old, rather a long time for an experiment, the American adventure in democratic government still excites a certain curiosity. America, obviously, is not quite like any other country. Its geography, economy, demographic profile, mores and customs are so distinctive that, arguably, any lessons about self-government that might be learned would be of little practical importance beyond its borders. But to many, America is a metaphor for humanity; if a country with so many natural advantages cannot make a go of it, no nation can. Even its endemic social problems seem to have universal meaning. The Swedish sociologist, Gunnar Myrdal, predicted that if America succeeded in fully integrating the black man into democratic society 'all mankind would be given faith again—it would have reason to believe that peace, progress and order are feasible'.

Of course, other democracies might serve as paragons, but all of them were derived from feudal or monarchical states. America was a *tabula rasa*. As the 'first new nation', the first colony to forcibly break with the motherland, it established a state where no state had existed before. To the scores of new nations that have been born since then, America remains in some sense the model of a colonial revolution brought to fruition.

America, in addition, was founded in the name of a set of ideals: democracy, political and legal equality, and individual freedom. How true a nation remains to its founding ideals, while increasing enormously in physical size and population, and while undergoing dramatic industrialization and urbanization, is a question of unending fascination. With missionary zeal, Americans have sought to convert the world. America would be, its early settlers hoped, 'as a city upon a hill', an example which the rest of humanity would emulate. Their posterity have believed, not without some presumptuousness but nevertheless firmly, that America could teach the world to cherish these same values.

Because of the position of international leadership which fell to it at the close of the Second World War, America has had more than ample opportunity to proselytize. And, as champion of the 'Free World' during the Cold War period, it has given its friends and enemies good reason to study its political institutions. The domestic sources of foreign policy are not necessarily obscure or inaccessible to the non-American, but a sophisticated understanding requires an appreciation of the political system as a whole. A key question today—which troubles Americans as well—is whether these institutions are being corrupted by the exercise of world power. The 'imperial Presidency', as Professor Arthur M. Schlesinger has termed it, may presage the same erosion of republican institutions that Rome suffered in the acquisition of empire.

Chief among these institutions is a written constitution that serves as the oracular source of governmental power and the limits upon it. Elsewhere, constitutions have often been ignored or abolished when inconvenient. But the essential prescriptions of the US constitution have commanded obedience for two centuries. Despite domestic and foreign crises, the Bill of Rights has grown, resisted dilution and remained firmly entrenched. The endurance of this constitutional structure, based upon federalism and upon separation of legislative, executive and judicial functions, reveals much about the possibilities of establishing a government that is powerful yet unable to encroach upon the citizen's liberties.

It should not be thought, however, that the system of government is fossilized. Americans themselves are wont to regard their original political institutions as the consummation of human inventiveness and the proper object of patriotic veneration. For that reason, they are ordinarily blind to the fact that these institutions are constantly evolving, as much by usage as by design, and have been preserved by this very trait of flexibility.

A careful distinction is made in America between political institutions and those who man them. Although the institutions are worshipped, the occupational title of 'politician' often as not serves as a term of opprobrium. That the people's chosen leaders are held in such slight esteem reflects the cynicism about human motives that produced a constitutional structure of dispersed and fragmented authority. Designed more for safety than for speed or efficiency, America's governmental structure evinces a deep suspicion that the lust for power inheres in all mortals. The voters thus often trudge to the polls without enthusiasm, convinced that no man can withstand the temptations of office.

Nevertheless, since constitutions, written or unwritten, do not operate themselves, some credit for the longevity of America's political system must go to those elected officials, who have succeeded in reconciling the awesomely diverse and conflicting interests of a huge and restless nation. American politicians may be, as Lord Bryce remarked, of average intelligence and less than average virtue, but they have demonstrated a certain native genius for compromise that has kept the complex structure from tumbling down on their heads. Under the circumstances, one civil war in 200 years is not a bad record.

Geography itself places many demands on the political system. The continental United States stretches from the Atlantic to the

Pacific across 3000 miles of forest, prairie, mountains and desert. The state of Alaska, detached to the north-west, spans roughly the same distance, and the island state of Hawaii lies about 2000 miles from the mainland. The great distances and variety of environments, ranging from arctic to tropical, assure wide differences in economic activities and in social attitudes. In the past, when the means of communication and transportation were feebler, sectional loyalties fiercely rivalled nationalistic sentiment; people were more likely to think of themselves as citizens of their home states than as citizens of the United States. Even today Americans tend to identify with their regions, viewing national politics as a means of persuading Washington to do more for their local agriculture or manufacturing. Denizens of the countryside perceive their interests to be different from those of urban dwellers. Westerners suspiciously eye the 'Eastern establishment'; Southerners look warily upon the 'Yankees' to the north.

Besides geography, distinct ethnic identities separate Americans from each other. While taking second place to national loyalty, ethnic loyalties run deep. Thus does the 'nation of immigrants' betray its origins. In the hundred years before 1921, when immigration was curtailed by federal law, America absorbed about 35 million foreigners, trusting in the assimilative powers of the schools and of the burgeoning economy. In this 'melting pot' the peoples of the world were to be 'Americanized', amalgamated into a new national alloy. But out of the crucible came an unexpected product. Professors Nathan Glazer and Daniel Moynihan have observed: 'As the groups were transformed by influences in American society, stripped of their original attributes, they were recreated as something new, but still as identifiable groups.' Politically these Irish-Americans, Italian-Americans and Polish-Americans behave as interest groups, measuring their power and well-being against each other. In large cities, where the 'ethnics' are concentrated, a political party usually finds it prudent to play to this heterogeneity by running a 'balanced ticket': an Italian for mayor, a Pole for city council president, and an Irishman for comptroller.

More recently, tickets have borne many Hispanic and Asian names, reflecting intensified immigration from Latin America and the Far East. During the 1980s, the Asian-descended population of the US doubled and strode rapidly toward assimilation through educational and economic advancement, often telescoping an experience more typical of several generations into one lifetime. Newcomers who arrived on US shores from Asia as 'boat people' have departed in rockets a few years later—as astronauts. (They are sometimes referred to as 'the model minority.') The expanding immigrant mosaic foreshadows a multi-cultural society: in many states there will be no single dominant ethnic or cultural group but a melange of minorities. As a result, consensus politics is likely to become more challenging.

The one ethnic group that has benefited least from assimilation is marked off from the others by the colour of its skin. Imported as chattels since the early seventeenth century, blacks gave up most of their African heritage and identity in the long night of slavery that ended with the Civil War of 1861–65. They received very little in return. The failure of the north to 'reconstruct' southern society and government after the war left the blacks to toil as share-croppers (small tenant farmers) in the cotton and tobacco fields, a subsistence which recreated some of the worst features of medieval serfdom and none of the better ones. 'Jim Crow' laws excluded blacks from the franchise and segregated them from whites in schools, trains, shops and churches. The 'Second Reconstruction', the civil rights movement of the 1950s and 1960s, removed the shackles of legal segregation and gave southern blacks access to the ballot box. But the practical results so far have not kept pace with the expectations raised by legal equality. Blacks remain the poorest, worst-educated segment of the population. Having effected since the Second World War a mass migration to the northern and western cities, they remain largely isolated there in ghetto slums. In the south, the schools had been segregated by law, but in the north they were—and still are—segregated *de facto* by residential patterns reflecting white prejudice, a distinction in which blacks find little solace. Attempts to integrate the schools have provoked opposition just as intense as in the south. However, blacks, who now compose about 12 per cent of the nation's population and a much larger proportion of the urban population, have at least begun to capture the reins of city government.

Against this background of sectional and ethnic loyalties, the politics of class plays a relatively small part. Other attachments remain more salient than income level, even though the gap between upper and lower income groups in America is certainly increasing and many obstacles encumber the ladder of social mobility. Class consciousness has not solidified in America, and socialist or workers' parties have never found a mass base. The integration of workers into democratic politics before industrialization created a true proletariat may help account for this attenuated sense of class. Property qualifications for voting disappeared early in the nineteenth century, while in Europe the working class typically had to force its way into the franchise through collective effort.

A pervasive belief in economic opportunity and the absence of a distinctive working-class culture, furthermore, has sustained the notion that it is possible to become rich through hard work and luck. The lure of the 'big break', epitomized by the occasional celebrated success story, induces a person to rely more on individual effort than on class solidarity in the pursuit of happiness. The general availability of higher education—since the establishment of state universities in the 1860s—has given some substance to this dream by affording relatively broad access to the better-paying occupations.

Moreover, Americans are comforted by the knowledge that to vault into the upper strata requires only money. There are no proper accents, only classless regional intonations, and one may become a thoroughly acceptable member of the elite by attending Texas Agricultural and Mechanical University as well as by attending Harvard—if one has a bank account to lend respectability. Even those who, in the despair of late middle age, abandon the hope of 'success' may confidently project their aspirations on to their progeny. As sociologists have discovered, most Americans, even quite poor ones, tend to identify themselves as 'middle class' or at worst 'lower middle class', convinced that they hover on the brink of being 'comfortably off'. There is, really, no alternative to this striving for social mobility. One cannot take shelter in being a staunch member of a working class that does not believe it exists.

The trade union movement, therefore, has played a tactical rather than a strategic game. Although American trade unions are often described as 'non-political', that is true only in the sense that they, unlike European unions, make no pretence of leading the workers towards socialism. Trade unions in America accept capitalistic free enterprise, upon whose continued robust health their wages depend. The unions do, however, participate avidly in electoral politics and lobbying, considering themselves interest groups not very different from those of businessmen. Their object is to win by legislation practical benefits for the workforce. Samuel Gompers, a founder of the American labour movement, summed up the ideology of the trade unions in three words: 'More and more.' Politics is a way to get more, such as minimum wage laws, social security pensions and unemployment benefits. For the unions, in fact, political power preceded and made possible economic power—the reverse of the European experience. It was federal legislation of the 1930s which secured for unions the legal right to employer recognition, a bargaining position that they were unable to win by industrial action alone. But the decline in its membership—only about one eighth of the work force is still 'organized'—has made the labour unions much less powerful than they once were.

Underlying the instrumental attitude towards politics is the fact that Americans are, in historian David Potter's phrase, a 'people of plenty'. The abundance of the American continent, as exploited by technology, furnished even the bottom of society with a standard of living undreamed of in many other countries, and the continuing dynamism of the economy made opportunity for all more than a remote aspiration. Working-class ideology in Europe assumed that social justice entailed expropriating wealth from the rich and distributing it among the poor. The pie was fixed, and the only issue was how big a slice each segment of society would consume. The upper and lower strata retreated behind formidable barricades of class ideology to protect their claims to the national income. But America has always relied upon boundless resources to ameliorate incipient social discontent. Quarrelling about the just size of each slice was unnecessary when the pie was consistently being enlarged. The poor might achieve material well-being by sharing in economic expansion rather than by seizing the portion of the rich. Equality of result would not be assured, but there was at least a reasonable prospect of well-being. Even those with a modest share of the national treasure would still be well-off, by world standards. Symbolic of the cornucopia was the nineteenth-century western frontier. While arable land was a finite and scarce resource in Europe, it was in America virtually free for a time to anyone with the fortitude to claim and work it. The 'frontier myth'—that pioneer life made Americans individualistic, independent and economically self-reliant—has been re-examined in recent years. Historians have pointed to the substantial role played by government in building the infrastructure that made settlement of the arid west possible—the railroads and large-scale water supply projects. Indeed, the west has been compared to the highly structured 'hydraulic societies' typical of Asia. Nevertheless, it is clear that the west represented a vast exploitable endowment to which there was fairly free access.

During most of the twentieth century there has been an expanding industrial economy and a rising level of real family income. Poverty became the predicament of a minority, rather than the fate of the majority. By the 1960s the government could aspire to relieve even that minority, by waging a 'war on poverty' that would eradicate material deprivation as if it were the vestige of a formerly dread epidemic disease.

Freed from the pressure of acute scarcity, America has been spared the tensions of a left and a right confronting each other with totally incompatible notions of the good, the true and the beautiful. All have in common the value of maximizing their own dividends, and they view politics as merely a mechanism for allocating the profits. Politics is thus sometimes described as about 'who get what, when and how'.

The modern prospect of chronic energy shortage and resource depletion—of reduced economic growth, that is—raises the question of how well the American system would function without abundance. The necessity for prolonged rationing, conservation and austerity could impose strains with which the usual politics cannot cope. A system whose legitimacy depends on giving access to wealth may be unable authoritatively to parcel out more meagre portions.

So far American politics has been a struggle not between left and right but among myriad organized interest groups competing for the rewards that government can confer. Some of these rewards are directly financial: subsidies, tax credits, contracts, jobs, public works projects, insurance schemes and social benefits. Any given taxpayer is likely to measure his political 'clout' by whether he gets more out of government than he puts into it. Other rewards may be indirectly financial, such as legislation and regulations allowing one's private economic interests to thrive. A third type of reward is government legislation that makes the world the kind one likes to live in: those who favour cleaner air or an end to capital punishment, for example, will try to translate their personal values into government policy.

In popular American political thought, as in the theory of free markets, the concept of the 'public good' is undefinable *a priori;* it is simply the net outcome of the competition among interest groups. The invisible hand of providence guides the nation's policy, much as it determines the price of potatoes. Each group, of course, strives to identify its private good with the nebulous public good as a tactic; in that context, it seems not so egregiously self-serving for the president of a car company to proclaim: 'What's good for General Motors is good for the country.'

The interaction of competing groups is commonly referred to as 'pluralism'. To many political scientists pluralism is the essence of American democracy, even though it smacks of greed and self-interest. They consider it a healthy phenomenon, provided that the groups struggle vigorously and balance each other. Pluralism implies that various facets of society have a voice in government and that decisions are founded upon compromise. Policy automatically represents a consensus. Each group leaves the arena with the satisfying feeling that it has got whatever was possible. No group is completely dominant, and none is shut out and left to smoulder with resentment. The upshot of pluralism, therefore, is contentment and stability. The evils of 'faction', so feared by the nation's founding fathers, are done away with, not by abolishing factions but by rejoicing in their multiplicity and their natural tendency to hold each other in check.

There is, however, a school of political science which doubts that reality conforms to this sanguine theoretical model. While acknowledging that many groups contend for power, the school of 'elite theorists' argues that not all groups are equal. Some groups are more powerful and more consistently successful than others. The successful groups monopolize the channels of access to government decision-makers, who tend to regard them as the embodiment of the general will. Many interests in society are not represented by an organized group, insist the elite theorists, and so their claims are never on the bargaining table. Facing no substantial countervailing force, the limited array of officially recognized interest groups constitute, in effect, governing cliques.

The elite theorists pinpoint a flaw in the optimistic model of the pluralists. It is easy to see, for example, that while well-paid lobby agents fight bravely in Washington on behalf of the National Association of Manufacturers, the consumers of the manufactured products are not similarly deployed as a compact phalanx. And while the American Federation of Labor-Congress of Industrial Organizations speaks with authority for organized labour, the majority of labourers are not heard at all. It must be conceded, however, that at least the possibility remains of organizing the unorganized into a potent interest group. Consumers, for one, are beginning to make their presence felt through lobbying. What lies behind any interest group is the voting power and the combined financial resources of its members. When public policy affects a large number of persons, or even a modest number concentrated in an identifiable collectivity, they are in a position to flex their muscles.

The elitist critique, at bottom, merely shades the basic picture of American politics as a huge distribution network, a kind of Arabian souk whose alleys are thronged with purveyors and purchasers haggling over the terms of sale. As such, the participants are not properly described as 'left' or 'right' but as arrayed along a continuum from 'liberal' to 'conservative'. What divides them is the question of how much the government should do and for whom. Conservatives claim to oppose 'Big Government', both as a dispenser of funds and promulgator of regulations. But their real objection is to particular kinds of government activity, chiefly welfare state expenditures and restrictions upon private enterprise. They do not object when government subsidizes business, through loan guarantees, for example, or uses its regulatory power to protect business from the perils of unbridled foreign competition. What conservatives desire, in essence, is government policies which heed the maxim that 'the business of America is business'.

While conservatives tend to equate every new welfare programme with squadrons of officious, bumbling bureaucrats, liberals are more willing to use government in a positive fashion to alleviate social and economic distress. The war on poverty of the 1960s was perhaps the apogee of the liberal faith that any evil could be obliterated with salvoes of money aimed by benign officials.

Periodic economic recessions illuminate the difference between liberals and conservatives. Both accept the need for government stimulation of the economy. The liberals advocate direct government intervention by spending public funds and extending unemployment insurance. The conservatives prefer indirect stimulus: tax credits and other incentives to private business expansion.

Attitudes towards the panoply of rights guaranteed by the constitution against abridgement by government also differ, depending on whether one is a conservative or a liberal. To the conservative, the right to property is all important. Liberals consider property less sacred than the personal liberties enshrined in the constitution, such as freedom of speech and religion.

That is the domestic affairs component of liberalism and conservatism, but the two creeds also had been distinguished by different attitudes towards the Cold War. Conservatives espoused the 'hard line'. Cold Warriors *par excellence*, they advocated a powerful military presence abroad and support of any 'Free World' dictator who seemed able to withstand communism, regardless of how little freedom he allowed his subjects. Liberals, on the other hand, contended that the United States should build defences against communism by reinforcing democratic processes in other countries, rather than by undermining them in favour of a strong-man. Having said that, one must take notice of the fact that American leaders tended to shift their international outlooks rather easily. The most outstanding example of this in recent memory was the transformation of Richard M. Nixon from arch-foe of the communist menace to engineer of *détente* with China and the Soviet Union. Nixon was able to persuade other conservatives to his point of view by making them realize that 'trading with the enemy' could be sound business as well as sound diplomacy.

Changing one's political complexion is made easier by the fact that the conservative-liberal distinction does not coincide with party lines. The Democratic ranks are heavy with liberals, the Republican ranks with conservatives. Each party, nevertheless, harbours an important minority of the opposite persuasion. Many Democrats, including those who have held powerful posts in Congress, are as conservative as a conservative Republican, and some Republicans are as liberal as a liberal Democrat. This intra-party heterodoxy, to some extent, resulted from historical accidents which have hardened into traditional partisan loyalties. The staunch conservative contingent in the Democratic party, for example, consists primarily of southerners, because Republicans were virtually routed from state politics in the south after the Civil War. A Republican administration had prosecuted the war for the north, and Republican congressmen were held responsible for the much resented post-war Reconstruction laws. These bitter memories have faded in the south, and the Republican party has re-established an effective two-party system there. But whether southern conservatism will fully convert to Republicanism, thereby placing most conservatives in one camp and permitting the parties to re-align along doctrinal lines, remains doubtful.

American parties would seem destined, by their very structure, to lack uniformity. At the national level, at least, each party is something of a front for a mosaic of autonomous state and local organizations that share not much more than the use of the party label at election times. The names Republican and Democrat thus mean different things in different places. Conservative sections of the country elect conservative Democrats and conservative Republicans; liberal areas produce liberal Democrats and liberal Republicans.

One consequence of this diffuse structure is weak party discipline in Congress. When the senators and representatives assemble, they organize themselves formally along party lines, but voting patterns, often as not, reflect the conservative–liberal division more closely than affiliation. Virtually every bill requires a coalition of

Republicans and Democrats in order to pass. Such an arrangement may seem impossibly confusing compared to that of the British Parliament, where two parties committed to opposing principles face each other across an abyss. A member of the Tory left might share some views with a right-wing Labourite, but he would not be expected to have much in common with a left-wing Labourite. Yet congressmen accept implicitly the similarity of the conservative and liberal wings of the parties, because each party spans a broad spectrum of opinion.

Parties exist, one might almost say, to satisfy the need for an organizing principle in the legislatures and a mechanism for nominating two candidates for elective office. A voter of any persuasion could flip a coin to choose his party without undue strain, and indeed, some interest groups do flit back and forth between parties to maximize their leverage, or support candidates of both parties simultaneously. The Tweedledum and Tweedledee of Republican and Democrat emphasizes the high degree of consensus on fundamental issues and the extent to which politics is simply a pragmatic struggle over the distribution of the booty.

By focusing on distribution, rather than on ideology, the party system properly addresses itself to a crucial issue. For although the nation is constitutionally dedicated to political and legal equality, it is not similarly dedicated to economic equality. Indeed, it is committed to an economic system that maximizes efficiency of production without much regard for the distributive effects. Yet there is no doubt that political equality can seem an empty shell in the presence of gross economic inequality. Under modern conditions and expectations, political equality is no guarantee of stability without an acceptable standard of living. Moreover, it is myopic to deny that the possession of disproportionately large economic resources can be translated into disproportionately large political privileges, for, as the economist Arthur M. Okun has said, 'dollars transgress on rights'. The law indeed forbids both the rich and poor alike from sleeping under bridges. That being so, the function of democratic politics is to relieve the tension between constitutional principles and economic principles. By redistributing part of the nation's production, politics makes economic reality correspond somewhat more closely to constitutional theory.

CHAPTER TWO

The Constitution: On Paper and In Practice

To unite thirteen sparsely settled agricultural colonies into a single commonwealth is one thing; to govern a populous, industrialized nation spanning a continent is quite another. The marvel of the United States Constitution is that it has done both. Of course, the constitution is not precisely the same document that it was originally; it has been formally amended twenty-six times, and numerous informal institutions and conventions have supplemented the actual text. But, on the whole, the system still functions according to the plan laid down in the eighteenth century.

Whether that is something to be admired or regretted depends upon one's point of view. Foreign observers often portray America as thrashing about inside an eighteenth-century straitjacket, hardly able to contain the robust spirit of the modern age. Americans, on the other hand, look upon the constitution with an uncritical acceptance that may be due more to gratitude for faithful service than to any rational calculation of present or future usefulness.

No doubt the constitution has stultified the national attitude towards government. American political philosophy begins and ends with exegesis of its holy writ, paying more attention to the intentions of the framers in 1787 than to the aspirations of the citizens who live under the document today. But Americans surely may be forgiven for treating the constitution as a totemic object, since they seek in it answers not so much about the mechanisms of their government as about the spirit that infuses it. Principles have been the constitution's chief blessing to the American people, because they are principles that have commanded and continue to command universal allegiance. No ideology, no ethnic or geographical division, no economic conflict of interest has destroyed the consensus on principles embodied by the constitution. In that sense, the constitution is no more an irrelevant relic of eighteenth-century America than the Bible is of ancient Palestine.

That the constitution lays down general principles of governmental structure and operation, rather than minute details, is not the result of the framers' prescience but of their pragmatism. The constitution was created to cope with an immediate, pressing problem: disunity. Were the thirteen colonies to be united under an effective, central government, or were they to go their own ways as separate sovereign nations? The constitution set about answering this limited question by proposing a general scheme of government. To have stipulated all details of the future government would have been imprudent; the framers hoped to win quick acceptance for the scheme as a whole, leaving the thornier problems for later. As Lord Bryce observed of the constitution a century after its drafting, it was a 'judicious mixture of definiteness in principle with elasticity of details'. Although acting from necessity, the framers' attention to the larger picture has given the constitution one of its enduring strengths. For the document was made more supple than if it had specified the functions of governments as recognized in the eighteenth century. In later generations it would be possible, within the broad restrictions imposed, to operate a government that was effective by twentieth-century standards.

Even if the framers wished to go into more detail, there would have been no occasion for it. The new nation was formed by assembling building blocks, the states, whose existence had to be accepted as a *fait accompli*. Since the states would continue to exercise many of their customary powers, it was not necessary to prescribe in the federal constitution relatively petty matters of local administration. Responding to the exigencies of the moment, the framers never lost sight of the main goal.

When the constitution was first conceived, it was by no means clear to most American colonists that they needed anything more than a few amendments to the Articles of Confederation, the loose league arrangement that bound the colonies following the War of Independence. The league, it was true, had manifested troubling defects; trade between the states was burdened by currency and tariff problems, the national legislature found itself unable to effectively levy taxes, and the states were reluctant to contribute troops to the national defence force. Yet many colonists wondered if they were destined to be a single nation. Could such imposing geographical distances be mastered, such differences in economic activity be overcome? Having just tossed off the yoke of imperium, would the states voluntarily submit to another large central government whose benign or malignant intentions they could not securely predict?

If there were any doubts, they were settled by the ominous presence throughout the hemisphere of foreign powers—Britain, France, and Spain—who, it was feared, would make short work of the divided colonies. The challenge thus presented was to devise a scheme of government that would create a unified, militarily capable nation while, at the same time, preserving the liberties that had been so dearly and so recently won. There would be other compromises as well, as the drafting proceeded, reconciling competing geographical and economic interests, but the overriding concern in the minds of the framers was for balancing liberty with order—or, looked at another way, for creating just enough government.

That the colonists perceived in government a tension between liberty and order has been attributed to the influence of John Locke. Certainly, the Declaration of Independence in 1776 had alluded to a social compact between the colonial subjects and the British monarch, and it echoed Locke's belief that the natural rights of man limited the purposes for which the state is formed. 'The community,' he had argued, 'perpetually retains a supreme power of saving themselves from the attempts and designs of anybody, even their legislators, whenever they shall be so foolish or so wicked as to lay and carry on designs against the liberties and properties of the subject.' Similar sentiments resonate through the Declaration:

> We hold these truths to be self-evident, that all men are created equal, that they are endowed by their Creator with certain inalienable Rights, that among these are Life, Liberty

and the pursuit of Happiness. That to secure these rights, Governments are instituted among Men, deriving their just powers from the consent of the governed. That whenever any Form of Government becomes destructive of these ends, it is the Right of the People to alter or abolish it . . .

Yet one should not credit unduly the influence of philosophers where there had been first-hand experience of tyrannical government. Determined to profit from the bitter memories of crown rule, the framers knew at least what they did not want in the new government.

In their minds, the basic lesson was that individual liberties are fragile when government is absolute. They did not reject the British form of government outright; they merely found it flawed in practice by the excessive power of the executive. They were impressed by Montesquieu's argument, that England enjoyed relatively great liberty because the functions of government were distributed among executive, legislative and judicial organs, each balancing the other's cravings for absolute power. That made sense to the framers because of their knowledge of events in England, and because of the political history of the American colonies, where the elected legislature often posed the only counterweight to a crown-appointed governor. As one of the framers, James Madison, remarked, 'the accumulation of all powers, legislative, executive, and judiciary, in the same hands . . . may justly be pronounced the very definition of tyranny'.

The framers were also firmly convinced of the value of the English common law in protecting the liberties of subjects. The common law showed them how limits might be placed upon arbitrary governmental actions. No one could be subjected by the state to penalties unless found guilty of previously specified offences, according to an established procedure. Limiting offences to those enunciated in the laws and binding judicial procedure by fixed rules precluded the capricious exercise of authority. Moreover, the colonists had been able to observe the common law in action; religious and political dissenters had often been saved from persecution by a sympathetic jury. The features of common law criminal prosecutions would thus be very closely copied in the

Bill of Rights, added to the constitution soon after ratification, but even more important than the imported mechanisms of indictment and jury trial was the underlying assumption: law could limit even the sovereign.

The founders' faith in the power of the rule of law to check arbitrary, hence despotic, government led them to write a document, a fundamental law, that would govern the rulers as well as the ruled. Almost alone among monarchies, England rejected the principle that the 'king can do no wrong', and in that notion of a 'higher law', binding even monarchs, lay the origin of the Americans' belief in the constitution as a guarantee of liberty.

The common law also afforded a seminal example for the framers in that it was not chiefly statute law, the commands of a sovereign, but rather emanated from the people, from their customs as 'found' and declared by the judges. Unlike statute law, which the sovereign gives and just as easily takes, the common law was deeply rooted in usage. It was a permanent fixture of national life. Although constantly evolving, it could no more be abolished at a stroke than the people could be abruptly wrenched from their daily habits by governmental fiat. The founders esteemed the common law even more because of a misapprehension that its principles, as then known, dated from time immemorial. As Professor Edwin S. Corwin observed: 'The idea was, obviously, a politically valuable one, since it proclaimed from the first the existence of a body of law owing nothing to royal authority and capable therefore of setting limits to that authority.'

The constitution would assume that same aura of imperviousness to the whim of authority. In an extraordinary act of legislation, the people as a whole adopted fundamental law. Their elected representatives could then legislate within those broad boundaries but could not change them. The people, not the government, remained sovereign. That largely accounts for the reverence which the constitution inspires, for it is not only a blueprint for a system of government, but also the authentic voice of a sovereign people.

Although the founding fathers, as their title would imply, are generally remembered as heroic law-givers, a revisionist school of historians argues that love of liberty was, at the very least, not the sole motive of those who drafted the constitution. In the document's carefully constructed safeguards against simple majority rule and in the various protections for private property the revisionists see the conspiracy of a wealthy elite. Attempts by state legislatures to tamper with the sanctity of property and the rights of creditors had left men of property feeling threatened by unbridled democracy, the revisionists contend, and convinced of the need for a national government, not easily susceptible to majority control, that would repress such expropriative urges.

The controversy between revisionist and traditional interpretations is not likely to be resolved conclusively. The constitutional convention delegates were, to be sure, members of the upper class in their respective states, and they expressed in the debates an unabashed desire for a document that would afford protection for property. One of the Virginia delegates termed it the 'principal object of government'. Political support for the finished document, moreover, was strongest in the cities and the coastal areas, the stronghold of the commercial interests, while opposition was stoutest among the small farmers of the interior. On the other hand, few men were absolutely unpropertied, since land was plentiful; the security of private property was a general concern. Although all states enforced a property requirement for voting, most adult males were eligible for the franchise. These were the voters, in fact, who elected delegates to the state conventions that ultimately ratified the constitution. Many of the leading opponents of ratification, moreover, were drawn from the same class as the drafters of the document.

Conflicts between large and small property-owners, or between agrarian and commercial interests, there may have been, but these economic rifts would hardly support a conspiracy theory because other, cross-cutting interests also influenced popular attitudes toward the new constitution. The large states, for example, favoured representation in Congress according to population, while the small states favoured equal representation, regardless of population. The framers compromised by providing equal representation in the Senate and representation according to population in the House. Another compromise resolved a sectional argument between north and south over the slave population:

three fifths of the slaves would be counted both for determining representation in Congress and for levying *per capita* taxes.

Whether it was the result of a conspiracy or a national consensus, the constitution did provide a notably salubrious environment for commercial enterprise. The federal government was entrusted with supervision of interstate and foreign commerce, thus removing the state boundaries as barriers to trade and cementing together a 'single market'. The government was also empowered to establish uniform bankruptcy laws, coin money, standardize weights and measures, and secure patent rights to individuals. The states were prohibited from interfering with the 'obligation of contract'. The debts of the states were assumed by the federal government, assuring that bond holders would not lose their investments. Direct taxation of individuals by the federal government was limited to *per capita* assessments, thereby excluding the possibility of a graduated income tax that would impinge more heavily upon the wealthy. Finally, the Fifth Amendment, adopted shortly after ratification, assured that 'No person shall be ... deprived of life, liberty or property, without due process of law; nor shall private property be taken for public use without just compensation.' Taken together, these provisions would seem to create the ideal Lockeian order, a government dedicated to promoting individual acquisitiveness. Whether this order was founded upon philosophic conviction or sheer cupidity is probably beyond our knowing; the two are often conjoined.

The constitution was wrought in the name of 'We, the people', by delegates from the states who met in Philadelphia during the summer of 1787. The constitutional convention had been called in desperation; a meeting to try to mend the defects of the Articles of Confederation concluded that the old order was beyond repair. Although the delegates at Philadelphia debated at length, they drafted a document that is, among constitutions at least, remarkably succinct.

In a total of approximately 7000 words, the document sets out the structure of government, enumerates the powers of each branch and divides the functions of the federal government from those of the state governments. It is much shorter than most national constitutions (and American state constitutions) and presents a curious mixture of sweeping generality and painstaking attention to some points that the modern reader may not think terribly important. Why, one wonders, would the framers bother to specify that trials for treason must be based on the evidence of at least two witnesses, yet forget to address a question as important as whether a state has a right to secede from the union? Fortunately for the future United States, the constitution usually managed to be vague in the right places, leaving some play in the joints for later interpreters.

The framers' attachment to separation of powers is plain from the arrangement of the articles. Article I vests the legislative power in the Senate and House of Representatives, Article II places the executive power in the hands of the President, and Article III confers the judicial power upon one Supreme Court and such inferior courts as Congress may wish to establish. Article IV discusses the relationship that shall exist among the states and between the states and the federal government; Article V prescribes methods for amending the constitution; Article VI is a miscellaneous section, whose most important provision declares that the constitution and federal laws made under it take precedence over all state enactments. Article VII announces that the constitution will take effect when nine of the thirteen states ratify it.

The basic plan is diffusion or fragmentation of power. The lines of demarcation run both horizontally, between the federal government and the states, and vertically, between the three branches of the federal government. The legislative branch itself is subdivided into two co-equal houses. In separating powers among the executive, legislative and judicial branches, however, the framers did not assign each a totally distinct function; rather they apportioned the functions of government so as to make each branch rely on the others. The system of 'checks and balances' thus presumes not independence but inter-dependence among the branches. Congress would enact legislation, but the President could veto it. The courts would construe the law, but the judges would be appointed by the President with the consent of the Senate.

The framers' suspicions, however, did not end there. What

would happen if all three branches were somehow to collude? To preclude that possibility, the framers were at pains to tie each component of the government to a different 'constituency', or base of support. The plan, in Madison's words, was to accord each 'the necessary constitutional means and personal motives to resist encroachment on the others . . . Ambition must be made to counteract ambition.' Thus, the Senate was to be elected by state legislatures, the members of the House by popular majorities in small districts, and the President by electors selected by each state in whatever way it wished.

The terms of officials, moreover, were made to vary—two years for the House, six for the Senate, four for the Presidency—and to overlap so that no popular majority of the moment would be able to seize control abruptly of the entire government. Such a majority might sweep up most of the House seats in an election but still find the President with two years remaining in his term. Should the majority work its will in a Presidential election, it would still find two thirds of the Senate firmly in place. The judges were insulated from fleeting majorities by lifetime tenure.

The plan, in brief, was to render the government incapable of action unless the various branches, representing diverse constituencies and chosen at different times, were in agreement. If that arrangement seems like a guarantee of governmental inertia, a built-in proclivity for doing nothing, such, in the framers' minds, was the price of avoiding tyranny. This diffuse form of government has never laid claim to decisiveness, but it has on the whole accomplished what it intended to do: prevent the accumulation of unfettered discretion. No arm of the American government enjoys complete or exclusive control over any policy matter. In Britain, the prime minister and cabinet, sitting as a committee of the majority in Parliament, exercise the full authority of government, but America lacks a comparable locus of power.

The constitution, of course, licenses the national government to act in a broad sphere, as well as imposing heavy impediments. More than half the text is devoted to the first article, outlining the powers of Congress and, by inference, the scope of the federal government. The key provision is section 8 of the article, which gives Congress authority to levy taxes, issue currency, establish post offices, create courts, declare war, provide a defence force and regulate commerce among the states and with foreign nations. These 'enumerated powers' appear to represent the minimum authority that must be possessed by any government; surely, they must be capable of expansion to meet changing conditions. But the tradition of constitutional interpretation has wavered uncertainly between the poles of 'loose construction' and 'strict construction'.

The loose constructionists have been mindful of Chief Justice John Marshall's admonition in the early nineteenth century that 'we must never forget that it is *a constitution* we are expounding', a broad enabling charter intended to create a competent government, not a paraplegic among nations. Such a constitution could not have authorized President Jefferson, in so many words, to purchase the Louisiana Territory from France in 1806, because no one might have supposed that it would be offered for sale. Yet to forgo the opportunity to acquire the entire Mississippi River basin would have been foolhardy. The strict constructionists, nevertheless, contended then, as they do now, that the constitution says precisely what it means and nothing more; to depart from its literal meaning, no matter how worthy the object, is to abandon the original scheme of limited government.

Fortunately for the loose constructionists, the last paragraph of section 8 authorized Congress 'to make all laws which shall be necessary and proper for carrying into execution the foregoing powers'. Never has so much been said in so few words. For this so-called 'elastic clause' suggested that while Congress could address itself only to the *ends* that were enumerated, it had a relatively free choice of *means*.

The pattern for expansive interpretation of the implied powers in the elastic clause was set by Marshall in the classic case of *McCulloch v. Maryland* in 1819. Faced with the question of whether the United States could establish a national bank, Marshall wrote: 'Let the end be legitimate, let it be within the scope of the Constitution, and all means which are appropriate, which are plainly adapted to that end, which are not prohibited . . . are constitutional.' To cope with new conditions, later interpreters have gladly heeded Marshall's dictum. Although the constitution is understandably silent on whether Congress can appropriate funds to send astronauts to the moon, the space programme is arguably a means towards the end of providing for the common defence. The alleged connection between means and ends may be even more tenuous than that. Congress, for example, financed the building of a network of interstate motorways under the pretext that they were national defence highways, even though it was unlikely that they would be needed to rush tanks to the Canadian or Mexican borders to repel invasions.

No provision of the constitution has been a more fertile source of implied powers than the 'commerce clause', because the regulation of trade naturally encompasses myriad activities. Significantly, the constitution did not say *why* commerce should be regulated or for what purpose. Congress was not charged with promoting capitalism or socialism, improving the lot of workers, eliminating health hazards or keeping stock prices bullish. From that we may infer that the framers simply desired orderly trade, under a common set of rules, regardless of what the rules were, since uncertainty is the *bête noire* of the businessman. Indeed, the profusion of state commercial codes, tariffs and currencies that had so impeded interstate trade was a primary motive for federating.

Because the commerce clause fails to specify the goals of regulation, Congress is free to exercise its power to accomplish purposes that are only peripherally economic. It is not limited to providing an arena for orderly competition, standardizing weights and measures and smoothing out the bumps in the business cycle. Virtually any evil—child labour, racial discrimination or car exhaust fumes—may be declared inimical to interstate commerce and restricted or banned. When Congress, in the Civil Rights Act of 1964, outlawed racial discrimination in hotels and restaurants, it found its authority in the commerce power; Congress could compel service to blacks in the remotest snack bar because the hamburgers had been shipped in interstate commerce. The real objection to racism was not that it burdened commerce, but commerce furnished the pretext for remedying a social injustice.

During the early decades of the republic, the struggle of the federal government to assert its hegemony over the states took the form of a battle over the extent of the commerce power. Jealous of their privileges, the states exploited the failure of the constitution to specify where intrastate trade ended and interstate trade began. The problem persisted well into the twentieth century, seriously hampering the federal government in its effort to regulate large-scale corporate capitalism. In the eighteenth century most enterprises existed wholly within a state, subject to its laws, and only the movement of goods across state lines fell under federal control. But when corporations in the late nineteenth century began establishing branches and plants in several states, Americans debated whether they fell under state or federal jurisdiction. It became clear, however, that the unco-ordinated attempts of individual states to regulate corporations would prove ineffectual. Not until the 1930s did the Supreme Court adopt a broad concept of interstate commerce that freed the government to deal with the social and economic problems of industrialization and corporate capitalism. Today the commerce clause is the textual basis for the government's inescapable responsibility to manage the national economy.

The growth of the commerce power through judicial interpretation exemplifies one important means of adapting the constitution to constantly changing conditions. Interpretation is probably a more useful, if less forthright, method than formal amendment because the judicial process is continual and incremental, whereas amending is cumbersome, abrupt and episodic. Before the process of ratification is complete, a proposed amendment may represent an idea whose time has past. But the amending process, although sparingly used, remains an important piece of auxiliary equipment for modernizing the constitution when there is a clear consensus in favour of change. To the framers, the amendment provision was a built-in self-renewal mechanism, enabling institutions to be perfected in the light of experience. Madison thought the amendment process a nice balance between precipitate change and petrification. 'It guards equally', he wrote, 'against that extreme facility, which would render the Constitution too mutable; and that extreme difficulty, which might perpetuate its discovered faults.'

The constitution prescribes two methods of proposing amendments, one leaving the initiative to the states, the other giving it to the federal government. Under the former, the legislatures of two thirds of the states may ask Congress to call a convention for the purpose of drafting amendments. That path has never been taken, owing to uncertainty about the protocol that such a convention would follow. There is also the lurking danger that the convention delegates might, like the founding fathers, propose an entirely new constitution. Whether Congress could limit the convention's terms of reference is unclear. For these reasons, the much simpler alternative of proposing amendments by a two-thirds vote of both houses of Congress has invariably been employed. Defenders of the states, chagrined to see them thus restricted to a passive role, have suggested that a mechanism be devised to permit state-proposed amendments to be considered without raising the bugaboo of an unrestrainable convention.

Amendments proposed by either route become part of the constitution when ratified by the legislatures of three quarters (38) of the states, or if Congress chooses, by convention in three quarters of the states. Convention ratification occurred only once: the representatives of 'dry' rural areas, who dominated the state legislatures, were prevented from defeating the Twenty-first Amendment, which repealed prohibition of alcoholic beverages. Usually, Congress will set a deadline of seven years for the requisite number of state ratifications, thus precluding the possibility that a long-dormant proposal might be approved decades after it had been forgotten.

The amending process has been used only sporadically. The first ten amendments were adopted in 1791, shortly after the constitution was ratified, in order to satisfy the demand for a Bill of Rights. Two amendments were added by 1804, but none during the next sixty-one years. Between 1865 and 1870, after the Civil War, the three 'Reconstruction Amendments' were passed, ending slavery, enfranchising blacks, and guaranteeing citizens of all colours 'equal protection of the laws'. The Reconstruction era, Professor James M. McPherson has observed, marked the moment when the 'old federal republic in which the national government had rarely touched the average citizen except through the post-office gave way to a more centralized polity'. Eleven of the first dozen amendments to the constitution had limited the national government but six of the next seven, beginning with the Reconstruction Amendments, enlarged national powers, diminishing the authority of the states. Emblematic of the transformation was a clause in the Fourteenth Amendment prohibiting any state from abridging the 'privileges or immunities of citizens of the United States'. This simple provision strengthened the cohesion of the federal union, in the same way that pan-European citizenship is expected to deepen the bonds of the European Community.

There was then a hiatus in the amendment process until 1913. In that year the Progressive movement reached its high-water mark with the passage of the Sixteenth Amendment, enacting a federal income tax, and the Seventeenth, which called for senators to be popularly elected, rather than chosen by the legislature of each state.

In 1919, a campaign by the temperance movement culminated in ratification of the Eighteenth or 'Prohibition Amendment' which outlawed 'intoxicating liquors'. The Suffragette Movement provided the impetus for adopting the Nineteenth Amendment, in 1920, granting the vote to women. The Twentieth Amendment, ratified in 1933, abolished the 'lame duck' session of Congress, between December and March, during which congressmen defeated in the November elections could continue to influence legislation. The same year the Twenty-first Amendment ended the prohibition (and bootlegging) era by repealing the Eighteenth Amendment.

Franklin D. Roosevelt's four terms as President raised fears of elective dictatorship that led to the passage of the Twenty-second Amendment (1951), limiting chief executives to two terms, the customary limit adhered to by Roosevelt's predecessors. By the Twenty-third Amendment (1961), the residents of Washington were given the right to vote in presidential elections; because the capital is technically the 'District of Columbia', administered directly by Congress, its residents had been denied the franchise. Among the first fruits of the civil rights movement of the 1960s was the Twenty-fourth Amendment (1964), which prohibited imposition of a poll tax as a prerequisite for voting in federal elections. Southern states traditionally had employed a poll tax as a device for disqualifying black voters.

The Twenty-fifth Amendment (1967) was prompted by the desire to assure a stable line of succession to the Presidency. It provides that when a Vice President succeeds a President, the Vice Presidency shall be filled by a nominee of the new President, confirmed by a majority of both houses of Congress. The amendment also sets out a procedure for temporary succession by the Vice President in case of presidential disability. In that case, the Vice President becomes an 'acting president'. Ronald Reagan was twice incapacitated temporarily during his presidency—once when wounded in an assassination attempt and again when undergoing cancer surgery. Yet he deliberately refrained from invoking the Twenty-fifth Amendment, explaining later that he believed the procedure was designed only for long-term disability. A privately funded, bi-partisan Commission on Presidential Disability concluded in 1988, however, that 'the best course is to make routine the use of this mechanism so that its invocation carries no implication of instability or crisis.' Before inauguration, the commission recommended, each chief executive should publish written guidelines for transfer of power to the Vice-President in various circumstances, ranging from emergency medical treatment to chronic illness.

The Twenty-sixth Amendment (1971) established the voting age for all federal and state elections at eighteen years; in most states, the voting age had been twenty-one even though young persons were becoming politically aware at a much earlier age—and males went to war at eighteen.

In 1972, Congress proposed a Twenty-seventh Amendment, dubbed the Equal Rights Amendment, which would prohibit the 'equality of rights under law' from being denied on account of one's sex. A major goal of the feminist movement, the proposed amendment was designed to supplement the equal protection clause of the Fourteenth Amendment. It failed to receive approval by three quarters of the States, however, even after the time limit for ratification had been extended by Congress from seven to ten years. The propriety of granting such an extension became an issue in itself, involving a number of procedural questions. Among them was whether a state could, during the extension period, reconsider its decision and rescind a previously voted ratification.

The amending process, obviously, has helped to keep the constitution responsive to contemporary sensibilities. The table of amendments is a geological record of seismic political forces that have shaken the nation. An amendment usually marks the culmination of a movement, the point at which its once radical ideas achieved respectability. That so few amendments in all have been adopted—most state constitutions have had many more in a shorter period—and that only one has been repealed testifies to the correctness of Madison's belief that the amendment process would achieve a balance between too much and too little change.

The conservative forces in society have been conspicuously less successful in the politics of the amending process than the liberals. Prohibition proved to be a short-lived victory; the two-term Presidency, if seen as a reaction to Rooseveltian democracy, is perhaps its only signal achievement in modern times. Many are the proposed conservative amendments, on the other hand, that have fallen by the wayside. Conservatives have pressed for amendments to restrict the treaty-making powers of the federal government and to limit the level of income taxation. Several liberal decisions of the Supreme Court provoked proposals to restrict court-ordered reapportionment of the state legislatures, to allow Bible-reading and prayer in the public schools, to prohibit bussing of students to achieve school integration, and to prevent 'desecration' of the American flag by political protesters. In each of these instances, recourse to the amending process was a last-ditch attempt to thwart changes that the conservatives had been unable to prevent by ordinary political means.

That pattern prevailed during the 1970s and 1980s as conservatives pressed for the adoption of an amendment to prohibit abortion. Their objective has been a provision that would undo the effects of the 1973 ruling of the Supreme Court in *Roe* v. *Wade*. The justices held that for a state to outlaw abortions during the first six months of pregnancy—the period in which they are medically routine—was to violate a woman's constitutional right to privacy. The *Roe* case resulted in the mobilization of fundamentalist groups, such as the Moral Majority, who objected to abortion (and other government policies) on religious grounds. When the Supreme Court turned more conservative, as a result of appointments to the bench by Presidents Reagan and Bush, it began to chip away at *Roe*, reversing the political dynamics of the abortion amendment issue. The court's new attitude set in motion a movement for a constitutional amendment that would guarantee a right to abortion, even if the decision were ultimately overruled.

During the same period, conservatives also sought to enshrine in the constitution basic elements of their economic faith. They proposed a Balanced Budget Amendment that would deprive Congress of the authority to adopt a budget with expenditure higher than income in any given year, except under certain rigidly controlled conditions. The Balanced Budget Amendment is an ideological spinoff of the 'tax revolt', the popular movement in many states to curb the taxing power of local and state government and force reductions in public spending.

The resort to 'economic constitutionalism', as it has been called, is vigorously opposed by those who do not share the economic orthodoxy of the conservatives. The proposal would, after all, make heretics of the many advocates of deficit spending as a tool for stimulating the economy. Certainly, writing a detailed economic doctrine into the constitution would deprive Congress of the flexibility that might be needed to deal with future conditions, saddling it with what in a few years might seem like an outdated theoretical fad. It would also pose obvious difficulties for the world's largest net debtor nation.

In addition to judicial interpretation and formal amendments, custom and usage help ensure the adaptability of the constitution. Beside the written document has grown up a kind of unwritten constitution, a collection of institutions that have been sanctioned by time and accorded universal acceptance. Among these customary adaptations is the cabinet. Although the constitution merely refers to a 'principal officer in each of the executive departments', Presidents have always treated these officers collectively as a cabinet, albeit lacking all the features of a cabinet responsible to a legislature. The constellation of standing committees in Congress likewise carries no constitutional imprimatur but has become firmly embedded in the legislative system.

The most astonishing of all the extra-constitutional adaptations, considering the attitudes of the framers, has been the development of political parties. The constitution does not mention parties, and their fulminations against the spirit of 'faction' signify that the founding fathers hoped parties would not develop. Indeed, the dispersion of political power among the branches and between the federal and state governments was intended to prevent any party from achieving dominance. Yet parties quickly made their appearance after the constitution was ratified and became a significant feature of the political landscape. 'Would they [the framers] be shocked or merely surprised', Professor Clinton Rossiter aptly asked, 'to learn that one of the most effective checks in our enduring system of checks and balances is the party in opposition . . .?'

CHAPTER THREE

Federalism and its Discontents

When they met in 1787, the framers knew of only two possible models for the new commonwealth: a national government, whose writ ran everywhere, or a confederation of sovereign states. It was their happy fortune to discover, by a compromise between the proponents of each, a third system, blending elements of national and confederal government. Federalism, American style, was to mean a national authority, supreme within the sphere assigned to it, and a number of states continuing to exercise sovereign prerogatives within their own sphere.

Although it was a burning issue at the constitutional convention, the federal structure of the new government was outlined by the framers in a remarkably indirect, almost off-hand fashion. The constitution nowhere states plainly 'there shall be a federal form of government'. The words 'federal' or 'federalism' do not even appear in the text. The system must be deduced by reading between the lines. The constitution deals primarily with the powers and limitations of the central government. When the states are mentioned it is most often to prohibit them from a certain activity. Powers were delegated *from* the states, whose continued existence is taken for granted, *to* the central government. The states gained no authority from the constitution that they did not already enjoy, and they surrendered much.

Lest it be presumed that the states had given up too much, a terse qualifying statement was later appended as the Tenth Amendment: 'The powers not delegated to the United States by the Constitution, nor prohibited by it to the states, are reserved to the states respectively, or to the people.' This, the only general description of the role of the states, hardly says more than that, with the exceptions noted, the states are to carry on with whatever they had been doing. Nevertheless, the Tenth Amendment serves as the chapter and verse most often cited by 'states' rights' advocates, because it seems to confirm the states' traditional prerogatives and preclude their usurpation by the national government.

Since the states would not look kindly upon any plan which contemplated their extinction, some such arrangement was unavoidable. But the spectre of tyranny was also conducive to federalism. Although many in Philadelphia believed that a government holding sway over a vast territory was incompatible with republican liberty, they were persuaded ultimately that the chances of any single faction gaining total power diminished as the size and diversity of a nation increased. The opponents of centralized authority were assured, furthermore, that the principle of balance of power would temper the relationship between the national and state governments.

But fear of centralization remains to this day. The threat of the national government overwhelming the states has been an enduring theme in American history. The dangers lurking in Washington have always been decried by champions of states' rights, who consider the erosion of state authority a threat to individual liberties. The states' rights position has attracted mainly those for whom the national government represents a threat to economic freedom or to such local customs as racial segregation. But the very persistence of the controversy reflects the steady growth in the power of national government during the last 200 years and the failure of the framers to describe the federal relationship precisely. The omission of any provision about secession of states from the union is particularly surprising. In later years, nationalists were to declare the union 'indestructible' and membership in it irreversible. If so, the framers were seriously derelict in forgetting to mention such an important abridgement of the states' sovereignty. Four years of civil war were required to finally extinguish the theoretical right to secede.

While the framers neglected to define their concept of the federal union explicitly, some general principles stand out. The national government was obligated to guarantee the states a 'republican form of government' and to protect them from invasion and domestic violence. The constitution is also careful to assure the states a crucial role in the selection of members of the national legislature. The state legislatures were empowered to choose their senators (until popular election was substituted by amendment in 1913), and the qualifications for voting for members of the House of Representatives were to be the same as those prescribed by each state legislature for elections to fill its lowest chamber. The 'times, places and manner' of holding elections were left to the states, subject to alteration by Congress. Thus, no congressional district crosses a state boundary, and the drawing of district lines—a crucial determinant in elections—is a valued privilege of the state legislatures.

A small but thorough catalogue of restrictions upon the states forms a codicil to the list of congressional powers in Article I. Among the proscribed activities are making treaties and alliances, coining money, granting titles of nobility, taxing imports and exports, and maintaining an army and navy in peacetime.

No state may enter into a compact with any other state without the consent of Congress. In practice, that has not been a barrier of much importance since the states have only rarely resorted to the formal compact as a device to accomplish some mutual goal. Some states have entered into agreements to preserve natural resources, regulate common waterways or build bridges between their territories, but the preferred method of dealing with problems that overspill state boundaries is to entrust them to the central government.

The states are also enjoined to give 'full faith and credit'—that is, recognition—to each others' laws and judicial proceedings. While a state may only reluctantly accept 'quickie' divorces granted by Nevada, court orders entered in one jurisdiction are usually valid elsewhere. No state is required to enforce the criminal laws of another under the 'full faith and credit' clause, but a separate provision requires the return of fugitives from justice (and, formerly, runaway slaves). Uniform extradition laws have been enacted, and Congress has made interstate flight to avoid prosecution a federal crime.

Each state, moreover, is required to grant persons from other states the same 'privileges and immunities' enjoyed by its own citizens. Non-residents may not be denied the right to engage in business, hold property and have access to the courts, nor may they be taxed in a discriminatory manner. However, the states have been allowed to treat them as a separate class for certain purposes; they may be charged higher tuition at the state university and prohibited from some state-licensed occupations, such as medicine. However, to become a full-fledged citizen of any state merely requires a brief period of residence. Restrictions on travel or emigration from one state to another have generally been held unconstitutional.

The capstone of the federal structure is the stern injunction in Article VI that the laws enacted by the national government 'shall be the supreme law of the land; and the judges in every state shall be bound thereby, anything in the constitution or laws of any state to the contrary notwithstanding.' In this, the 'supremacy clause', the framers served notice that when the national government acts within its sphere of competence, it sweeps incompatible state laws before it. At various times it has been contended that the states may 'nullify' the effect of federal legislation within their borders or 'interpose' their authority between their citizens and the enactments of the national government. The doctrines of nullification and interposition found particularly fruitful soil in the south, where they were espoused with great vigour in the period leading up to the Civil War. An echo of these doctrines was heard again in the 1950s and early 1960s when the national government forced racial integration upon southern schools.

But national supremacy has prevailed, in large measure because the Supreme Court, as umpire of conflicts between state and federal authority, has supported the supremacist position at crucial moments, particularly in the early decades of the republic. That the task of arbitrating such disputes should fall to the court was inevitable. The 'supremacy clause' addresses itself particularly to judges, and it soon became clear that the central government would founder if the Supreme Court could not restrain state judges from vitiating national legislation. The power of the Supreme Court to review state judicial decisions was firmly established by 1821, when Chief Justice Marshall, an ardent nationalist, averred in *Cohens v. Virginia* that nothing surrounding the framing of the constitution 'would justify the opinion that the confidence reposed in the states was so implicit as to leave in them and their tribunals the power of resisting or defeating, in the form of law, the legitimate measures of the union'. Marshall reminded the states that they were 'members of one great empire—for some purposes sovereign, for some purposes subordinate'.

The difficult question, however, was whether for any given purpose a state was sovereign or subordinate. The states and the national government shared many common purposes, exercising their powers concurrently. The national government levied taxes and regulated commerce, but so did the states. Each was within its proper sphere, yet the two levels of government might impinge upon each other. When Maryland had attempted to tax a branch of the Bank of the United States, Marshall declared that the states 'have no power, by taxation or otherwise, to regard, impede, burden, or in any manner control, the operations of the constitutional laws enacted by Congress'. The chief justice asserted that 'the government of the union, though limited in its powers, is supreme within its sphere of action.' And when New York State granted a private monopoly for steamship navigation on the Hudson River in 1808, the court invalidated it by announcing in *Gibbons v. Ogden* the principle that congressional power to regulate commerce takes precedence over any state enactment.

Although these decisions established the ascendancy of the federal government when a direct conflict arose, the boundary zone between national and state authority to tax and to regulate commerce remained a no man's land through which the Supreme Court had constantly to pick its way. As early as 1851, the court recognized that 'whatever subjects of this power [commerce] are in their nature national, or admit only of one uniform system or plan of regulation, may justly be said to be of such a nature as to require exclusive legislation by Congress' (*Cooley v. Board of Port Wardens*). Former Solicitor General Archibald Cox has observed, 'The Cooley formula had the enormously important effect of enabling the federal courts thenceforth to strike a balance, case by case, between the competing values of uniformity and diversity, thus keeping the national market free from selfish and seriously obstructive state laws while at the same time permitting the states and localities to deal with truly local problems unsuited to national regulation.' The court was, in effect, attempting to nurture a development comparable to the formation of the European 'single market' in the late twentieth century, yet it was keen to preserve an appropriate degree of state autonomy.

Striking the balance between federal and state spheres is a perplexing task to this day. In the field of aviation, uniform standards are indispensable. Yet the states often insist on exercising concurrent authority. Even though the national government has adopted comprehensive aviation regulations, some states may presume to protect their airports by means of anti-noise or anti-pollution laws.

Although the court has held that a state may not place an 'undue' burden on interstate commerce nor levy a tax on the privilege of engaging in it, a question may arise when a company that operates a federally regulated oil pipeline from New York to Texas is taxed by Louisiana, in which one of the pumping stations is located. In 1991, following a manic decade of corporate mergers, the court agreed that a state could regulate commerce to the extent of objecting to a merger within its boundaries even though the US Department of Justice and the Federal Trade Commission had already given approval.

All is not conflict, however. Some concurrent powers are shared quite harmoniously with the national government. In a single elementary school, the textbooks may be bought by state funds and the children's lunch by federal funds. The cost of an interstate telephone call is regulated by federal law, while that of a call between two places in the same state is set by a state commission. If it thus sometimes costs less to phone across the country than within a state, such anomalies are the price of federalism.

Despite national supremacy, the states play a role in the lives of their citizens that is far from inconsequential. Some states are larger in population and size than many European countries. (California has about 30 million inhabitants.) Except for foreign relations, each state exercises powers nearly comparable with national governments elsewhere. Each enacts its own criminal and civil laws and enforces them with its own police and judiciary. The vast majority of criminal prosecutions in the United States are undertaken in state courts for the violation of state laws; most prisoners in the US are incarcerated in state institutions. It is the state which solemnizes marriage and promulgates family law, which charters business corporations, and levies purchase taxes. The states bear primary responsibility for operating educational systems extending from free kindergarten through fee-charging university graduate schools. The states are the main disbursers of social service benefits and builders of roads, bridges, public housing and recreational facilities.

Whatever confusion and inefficiency fifty different legal codes may entail, the diversity of state governments is beneficial as well as merely traditional. Besides keeping government 'closer to the people', the states serve as isolation laboratories for experiments in public policy. One state may outlaw non-returnable beer bottles, another make them freely available. The results of these alternative policies may be judged without having to send the whole country precipitately down one or the other path. Individual states have provided the fertile ground from which sprang innovations, typically based on the plebiscite, to improve the responsiveness of government. In many states citizens may vote to 'recall' an unpopular elected official before his term expires, even when there are no grounds for impeachment. The recall referendum is set in motion by filing petitions that demonstrate a threshold level of support—for example, the signatures of one third of registered voters in favour of recalling a governor. In Nebraska, where the petitioners do not even need to state a reason for their dissatisfaction, attempts are made each year to recall scores of mayors and other officials. California swept away much of its supreme court bench during the 1980s because they were considered too liberal. Among those recalled was the chief judge: she was too favourably disposed to appeals against death penalty convictions. Arizonans sought to recall a governor (for refusing to declare Martin Luther King's birthday a holiday), but he cheated the voters, in more ways than one, by leaving office after impeachment on corruption charges.

California also entertains citizen 'initiatives'—proposals for statutes and amendments to the state constitution that are put forward by petition and ratified or rejected directly by the voters. The process renders the legislature and the governor otiose. When

Proposition 13, an offshoot of the 'taxpayer revolt', was approved in a 1978 referendum, it forced a drastic reduction in public spending by curbing property taxes.

California's experience suggests that maximizing participation in government has natural limits. The practice of holding referenda on many issues, supposedly an antidote to the influence of money in politics, has fallen victim to the same baleful influence. Access to the referendum ballot is virtually for sale. Well-remunerated firms of 'referendum consultants' gather the necessary signatures on the qualifying petitions, at an average cost (in 1990 prices) of $925,000 for each proposition. Canvassers are paid bounties of as much as 40 cents per signatory. The sponsors of a petition drive may sell 'shares' to other organizations, cobbling together an omnibus proposition. Propositions have been sponsored by business lobbies, such as a state-regulated insurance industry, and supported by funds from outside the state, intimating that the process of direct democracy can be manipulated by the very interests it was supposed to restrain. Heavy reliance on referenda also may leave voters bewildered. In November, 1990, Californians pored over a ballot containing 17 propositions. It required a manual of 144 pages, mailed to each household in advance of the voting, to detail the provisions and the arguments of their supporters and opponents. Even so, polls reveal, few citizens understand the often convoluted and sometimes contradictory propositions on which they are expected to pass judgement.

The upshot of this attempt to circumvent legislative gridlock may be electoral overload. A number of the propositions on California's ballot hardly seemed momentous enough to warrant going to the people—for example, measures to promote employment training of prisoners with tax credits or to discourage accidental netting of marine mammals. Only that paragon of awareness, the single-issue voter, is likely to have a strong opinion. The referendum no doubt encourages legislators eager for 'blame avoidance' to displace difficult choices onto inattentive or uncomprehending constituents. (Paradoxically, the legislators may then strive to evade the restraints imposed by direct voting.)

Despite the drawbacks, state-level efforts to achieve direct democracy are at least noble experiments, and where beneficial they have spread by force of example. In times of emergency or paralysis at the centre, state initiative can be particularly important. During the Arab oil embargo of 1973–4, Oregon devised a simple petrol rationing system, based on car registration numbers, that was widely copied. Throughout the Reagan and early Bush Administrations, when the Federal government remained passive in face of mounting social discontent, state government responded to the leadership vacuum at the centre with a burst of home-grown creativity. Massachusetts formulated a plan for state health care insurance; Michigan and Wisconsin each framed an industrial policy based on state investment in high-technology enterprise; Maine banned non-recyclable food containers to protect its environment. Other states offered novel schemes for promoting employment of welfare recipients, ensured that shoppers got better nutrition information on grocery labels, and pioneered needle-exchange programmes to combat the spread of AIDS. Even jurisdictions below the state level were swept along in the surge of activism: the County of Suffolk in New York State undertook to regulate—on health grounds—the use of video display terminals in offices

The states were innovating in order to fill a pressing need for governmental action in the face of quiescence at the federal level. Fiscally burdened and ideologically hostile to Big Government in the Reagan–Bush years, Washington was content to identify national needs, such as improved public education, and merely exhort the states to fulfill them. Eager to shift onto the states the disagreeable task of raising revenues through taxation, Washington permitted them to encroach upon its core domain—regulation of commerce and science—even though a host of fragmented state efforts may not be ideal. When California and New Hampshire decided to conduct their own safety trials of pharmaceuticals (the abortifacient RU-486), they usurped a prerogative that properly belonged to the US Food and Drug Administration, the traditional watchdog of medicinal purity. Yet that agency had failed to exercise that prerogative: it showed no willingness to consider RU-486, despite widespread interest in the drug.

Nuclear energy, too, has always seemed to demand a single standard. The rationale was inherent in the technology: only a national licensing authority can adequately control the uranium-plutonium fuel cycle. Indeed, nuclear energy has been a carefully guarded federal preserve since the atomic era began, under the aegis of the military, in the Second World War. In light of the Cooley balancing test, nuclear hazards might at first glance seem reserved exclusively to federal regulation, but it could be argued with equal force that Washington's failure to grasp the nettle, by promulgating an effective safety regime, justified a state response. Acknowledging their duty to protect the health of their inhabitants, states have prevented nuclear generating plants from opening because nearby populations could not be evacuated readily; levied fines for air and water pollution; and excluded radioactive waste produced in other states.

By adopting an idiosyncratic regulatory scheme, a lone state undoubtedly risks becoming an economic island, its businesses less competitive than enterprises located elsewhere. A single state also has difficulty funding a social service as ambitious as universal health care. Some state initiatives have been clearly impractical, even whimsical. Florida appointed a commission to devise its own foreign policy (toward Cuba). Texas undertook to derive revenue from the illegal sale of cannabis and cocaine by imposing an 'Al Capone tax' on black market transactions; dealers were supposed to purchase an official tax stamp, emblazoned with a skull-and-crossbones. (Understandably, few did.)

Confronting a Babel of disparate state regulations, various industries have sought pre-emptive federal legislation, on the theory that one standard is better than many. Congress often obliges, but it may also respond with hybrid measures that impose a basic federal standard yet leave room for state initiative. The Clean Air Act of 1990, for example, set federal maxima for pollutant automobile emissions but permitted individual states to adopt lower ceilings. The following year nine eastern states, forming a belt from Virginia to Maine, agreed jointly to opt for more stringent rules developed by California, where atmospheric pollution is acute. Since one third of the nation's population dwells in the highly urbanized states following the California code, the automobile and oil industries could do little but accede to the tougher regional criteria. Any state deviating

from the national norm on its own might have suffered from
the isolation.

Such policy triumphs have given the environmental movement
a tactic with which to outmanoeuvre the opponents of regulation
who congregate in the nation's capital. Myriad initiatives issuing
in a scatter pattern from the states present targets so elusive that
business lobbyists have difficulty training their guns on them. In
the matter of auto exhausts, Sacramento, California, leading the
way for its nine sister state capitals, supplanted Washington as the
font of regulation.

At the same time, there is a danger that a state could be
manoeuvred into becoming a testing ground for a controversial
policy. Claiming that his state had been captured by 'outside'
forces, Governor Cecil Andrus vetoed a bill enacted by the Idaho
legislature that would severely restrict a woman's ability to obtain
an abortion. The governor declared that Idaho, a largely pastoral
Western state, had been cynically chosen as a 'patsy' by the anti-
abortion movement in order to influence the national debate on the
issue. The governor—a former US Secretary of the Interior—may
have recognized the hallmarks of a Washington-calibre campaign
targeted on a relatively unsophisticated legislature.

Still other state initiatives may deviate unacceptably from the
principles of the US constitution. A number of states have
enshrined English as their 'official' language, despite doubts about
whether such a policy is consistent with the First Amendment
guarantee of freedom of speech. Proponents argue that according
the national tongue official status is merely codifying what already
exists. Yet the movement for official status has been criticized as a
nativist backlash against the influx of immigrants and the spectre
of a multi-cultural society, partitioned among foreign-language
enclaves where English speakers might feel ill at ease. The 'official
English' trend seems targeted particularly at the Hispanic minority,
which grew significantly in the decade leading to the 1990 census.
One quarter of the population of some cities speaks Spanish, and
in many places voting information is provided in that and other
languages.

If English were the official language, the use of Spanish in
dealings between state officials and citizens speaking no English

might be prohibited. Yet such a prohibition would probably violate the First Amendment by precluding any communication at all. Reasoning along similar lines in 1990, a federal court invalidated Arizona's attempt to make English the language 'of all government functions and actions'. In any event, given the natural incentives to learn English for economic reasons, a legal sanction hardly seems necessary.

Large-scale immigration from both foreign and domestic sources has caused some states—notably California, which attracted six million new residents in the 1980s—to consider 'growth management' policies. But the right to travel freely from one state to another has been firmly established ever since the Supreme Court in *Edwards v. California* (1941) invalidated the Golden State's attempt to restrict migration of impoverished 'Okies', refugees from the Oklahoma Dust Bowl, in the 1930s. The constitutional framework, the court said, was based on the principle that 'in the long run prosperity and salvation are in union and not division'.

Despite their broad discretion and occasional inventiveness, the states have undergone a long, steady decline from vigorous independence towards dependence on the national government, whose functions and responsibilities have grown correspondingly. Although the constitution left the states substantial powers, they have not always chosen to use them very creatively or purposefully, and the vacuum caused by the failure of leadership at the state level has invited intervention by Washington—or by 'outside' forces. Some problems requiring government solutions, moreover, have grown too large, both physically and financially, for the states individually to cope with them.

A main cause of the states' failure is their political institutions. These differ from one state to another in many details, but all states resemble—indeed, set the model for—the national government in possessing a bicameral (except for Nebraska) legislature, an executive branch headed by a popularly elected governor, and a judicial branch. Unlike the national government, however, most state governments are thoroughly dominated by the legislature, which controls spending and taxation. Governors are relegated to a secondary role, possibly because they have no foreign affairs to conduct and no armed forces (except for a part-time militia) to command. There would be nothing unsound in this arrangement, were it not that the legislatures are often irresponsible, inefficient, corrupt, or all three.

Compared with Congress, the state legislatures attract few able and distinguished persons, their leadership is even less statesmanlike, and because of the relative inattentiveness of the mass media they function without the same glare of publicity. Often the long hegemony of a single party has left the state without an effective opposition. Many state legislators, moreover, conceive of themselves as agents of the localities they represent, rather than as trustees of the state's welfare, and make it their chief duty to exact from the treasury as much as they can for their home towns. Much of the legislative session is taken up by 'logrolling', in which the members support each others' efforts to pass bills bestowing largesse upon their constituencies. Until the reapportionment of the 1960s, moreover, cities were so underrepresented in the legislatures that rural and small-town representatives, those most immune to the spread of new ideas, tightly controlled the proceedings.

The venality of state legislatures is legendary. They may have reformed somewhat since the late nineteenth century, when Lord Bryce described proceedings in the New York and Pennsylvania legislatures as 'such a Witches' Sabbath of jobbing, bribing, thieving and prostitution of legislative power to private interest as the world has seldom seen'. But they are still hardly paragons of virtue. In Louisiana, a state rich in oil and roguish politicians, natives sometimes ruefully remark that the three co-equal branches of government are 'the governor, the mafia and Texaco'. The root of the evil is the difficulty of holding any particular member of the legislature responsible for awarding bonanzas to private interests—a member may sell his vote without remorse if the rest go along—combined with the fact that states are often dominated by a few great corporations that can offer legislators lavish temptations. The munificence of mining corporations may have something to do with the reluctance of some states to enact regulations to protect the health of miners and of the environment.

The legislatures are so little trusted that most state constitutions drastically restrict their activities in the apparent belief that the less done by the lawmakers the better. To tie their hands, the constitutions often contain hundreds of thousands of words, prescribing state policies in minute detail. They may specify the allowable uses for gasoline taxes, the restrictions on foreclosing mortgages, the formula for allocating school aid and other specifics that might have been left to the legislature. States must frequently amend their prolix constitutions to keep up with changing conditions. Although the US constitution has needed amendment only 26 times, the tiny state of New Hampshire has changed its fundamental document 140 times. Owing to planning restrictions embedded into its constitution, New York had to resort to the unwieldy process of statewide referendum in 1991 merely to allow a few acres of public land to be used in improving a minor airport. Most voters lacked a clear idea of where the airport was.

State constitutions, which were promulgated by conventions (some of them held in the last century), generally can be amended only by a referendum. In some states the legislature puts proposed amendments on the ballot at every election. In recent years, attempts have been made in most states to draft new constitutions or to substantially revise the old ones in order to give the legislature more discretion. But a number of new constitutions have been turned down by the voters, evincing the traditional suspicions.

Some state constitutions hobble the lawmakers by limiting the time they may spend in session. Although annual meetings are now usual, many legislatures formerly met only every other year. Each session may be restricted to a fixed period. (In some states it has been as little as thirty-six days.) Among the more important powers of the governor is the ability to convene special sessions, but even these may be constitutionally limited in duration. Infrequent and short legislative sessions often produce the opposite of the desired result, however. Many laws manage to get passed, but in the haste to meet the adjournment date few of them receive due consideration.

Various devices that might make legislatures more responsive to their constituents have attracted attention. As a perhaps natural extension of the traditional idea of limiting the length of a legislative session, it has been proposed that the length of time any person may occupy a legislative seat be limited—generally to two or three terms, depending on the length of each term. The rationale is that incumbency itself is the problem; proponents of term limits speak derisively of an 'Incumbent Party'—the fellowship of politicians united by a common self-interest in retaining office.

Term limits for state legislators and other office-holders were adopted by referendum in three states—California, Colorado and Oklahoma—in 1990. California limited members of the State Assembly, the lower house, to three two-year terms and State Senators to two four-year terms. Legislators who reach the limit are barred from ever returning to the office. The limit was upheld by the state's supreme court, which opined that 'restriction upon the succession of incumbents serves a rational public policy', even though the right of an individual citizen to seek and hold office may be curbed.

The term-limit concept raises traditional populist distrust of officialdom to a new level: it extends suspicion to the electorate itself, which is seen as succumbing to manipulation by well-heeled incumbents. Perpetually re-elected by gullible voters, the theory goes, politicians come to place their career interests above the interests of their constituents.

Is restricting state legislators to a finite number of elected terms likely to make politics more democratic? Regular elections are themselves tenure-limiting devices, forcing legislators to renew their mandate periodically; the voters have only to make good use of the ballot if they desire more frequent rotation in office. The actual result of a fixed limit may be to ensure that an elected representative serves without opposition until compulsorily retired, since potential challengers might shy away from the relatively difficult struggle to unseat an incumbent, preferring to wait for the expiration of his term limit. The net effect, thus, might be to decrease rather than increase competition on any given election day. By requiring wholesale turnover at frequent intervals, term limits could also result in a legislature composed mainly of novices and lame ducks, dominated by shrewd lobbyists and permanent staff. Considerable time might be spent just getting organized and sorting out the power relationships. No representative would be in office long enough to acquire seniority-derived clout or expertise in such technical matters as fiscal management or nuclear power regulation. Over-reliance on professional staff and civil service experts, which is more likely when career legislators are replaced by ephemeral amateurs, would further insulate the levers of power from the pressure of the electorate.

Term limits might, indeed, transform the legislature into a training camp for lobbyists; legislators would hold their seats just long enough to be schooled for a longer and more lucrative tenure as a paid agent of special interests. An army of out-of-work quondam legislators would augment the forces seeking to control the legislative process, further strengthening the grip of organized pressure groups. It must also be recalled that where state term limits have traditionally existed, politicians have often proven adept at manoeuvring around them. Barred from succeeding himself, for example, Governor George Wallace of Alabama managed to have his wife, Lurleen, elected in his stead; he remained the power behind the gubernatorial throne.

The legislature might be more dynamic and responsive if the executive branch were stronger, but most constitutions have ensured a weak, unco-ordinated executive by providing for the direct election of the principal officers who serve with the governor. The lieutenant governor, the attorney general, the comptroller (treasurer), the secretary of state, and other important figures in the administration are elected independently and may be of different parties. The governor is thus not fully master of his cabinet. Political bickering among members of the executive often makes it ineffective as a counterweight to the legislature.

There are indications that the traditional pattern of legislative ineffectualness and irresponsibility may be changing. The rural-urban imbalance has been righted, and the legislative chambers are increasingly peopled with more energetic young persons, women and members of ethnic minority groups. Many states have taken steps to streamline legislative procedures and introduce modern budgetary and fiscal management techniques. State governments have begun to show a greater interest in such pressing problems as conservation, consumer protection and urban redevelopment.

But while new blood and new methods may restore some of the importance of the states, they are unlikely to reverse entirely the trend of 200 years. Many problems are too large in geographical extent to be dealt with by a single state. For any one of them to remedy air pollution adequately, it would be necessary to make the clouds stand still. Crime increasingly requires national solutions. When bank robbers and kidnappers seventy years ago acquired cars that could quickly remove them from a state's jurisdiction, a federal law against these malefactors, enforceable by the Federal Bureau of Investigation, became necessary. Today, international organized crime syndicates, particularly of drug traffickers, defy effective state law enforcement, placing the burden on the federal government. Federal authority over the states grew, moreover, in response to the imperative of ending racial discrimination. Beginning in 1964, a series of civil rights laws, enforceable in federal courts, gave blacks equal access to the ballot box, to housing and to employment opportunities. Laws of national applicability were necessary because racial discrimination had been the official policy of some states.

More importantly still, economic life has simply outgrown state boundaries. It would make little sense for each state independently to attempt to deal with monopolistic practices, trade union organization, and fluctuations in the business cycle that are national in extent.

Besides suffering from relatively narrow jurisdictions, the states are hampered by a much more meagre revenue base than the federal government. The demand for social services, education, housing, roads, and law enforcement have simply overwhelmed the states' financial resources, which depend largely upon relatively static property and purchase taxes. The bulk of federal revenues, in contrast, derives from personal and corporate income taxes, which increase in proportion to economic growth. The discrepancy between the revenue-producing capacities of the two levels of government appears ironical in hindsight, since the constitution originally allowed the national authorities to levy, besides excises and customs, only uniform *per capita* taxes, thus precluding a graduated income tax. Had this provision not been abolished by the Sixteenth Amendment in 1913, because of fears of national insolvency, Washington might have needed subsidies from the states.

The states today naturally turn to the federal government for the solution of any problem that requires a great deal of money. The traditional method of channelling federal resources to the states has been grants-in-aid awarded for purposes specified by Congress. In the nineteenth century, the grants often were in the form of federal lands, which the states might sell for the proceeds. The 'land-grant colleges', fore-runners of the state universities, were funded in that way. There are now more than 1000 federal grant programmes for social services, health, education, law enforcement, highways and airports, conservation, and other purposes.

The grant system has spurred state governments into action while allowing them to operate their own programmes. Were the grants not available, it might have fallen to the federal government by default to undertake these programmes directly. In helping those who help themselves, grants also set a minimum national standard for public services, alleviating somewhat the inequalities between richer and poorer states. Mississippi still spends much less than New York on each schoolchild, but the disparity would be even greater without federal education funds.

The grant system can, however, be coercive and foster dependency. Induced by the promise of federal funds to undertake programmes which it does not really want or wants less than others, a state's priorities may be distorted to match those of Congress. Since most grants stringently limit the discretion of the recipients (they are accompanied by thick manuals of regulations), it is difficult not to sympathize with state administrators who complain that bureaucrats in far-off Washington, unfamiliar with local conditions, have denied them necessary flexibility.

To prevent the states from deteriorating into little more than disbursing agents for the national government, some funds have been provided in recent years in the form of 'block grants', which give state authorities more freedom to allocate the money according to their own estimates of local needs. A block grant system was used, for example, in the Omnibus Crime Control Act of 1968 to provide subsidies for state law enforcement.

The most radical approach to ending the client status of the states was embodied in the General Revenue Sharing Act of 1972, which authorized the transfer of $30 billion to state and local governments with virtually no strings attached. Washington established broad 'priority areas', such as public safety, transportation and environmental protection, but left the actual decisions about spending the money to the recipients. Only about one third of the money went to state governments; the remainder was allocated to more than 38,000 municipalities, counties, townships and Native American tribal governments. This 'pass through' system reflected the belief of many in Congress that the states, left to their own devices, would neglect the needs of the cities and the minority groups who live in them.

Congress thus demonstrated a strange ambivalence towards the states. While ostensibly trying to revitalize them, it did not trust them to distribute the money fairly. By transferring the bulk of the funds directly to local governments, in fact, Congress seemed to confirm the irrelevance of the states. Because they are the only sub-national units of government recognized by the constitution, the states have always been regarded as necessary intermediaries between the national and local levels. But since they now seem too small to be efficient and too large to assure popular participation, their position has been undermined. If the federal government affords local government a regular source of sustenance independent of the state legislatures, the state capitals will be displaced and local government brought into an immediate relationship with Washington.

This transformation would represent a long overdue recognition of the role of the great conurbations in the life of the nation. Since only 4 per cent of the population was non-rural at the time the constitution was written, it is hardly surprising that cities are not even mentioned in it. But today, when three quarters of all Americans live in cities of more than 50,000 persons, there is hardly any excuse for pretending that the states are the only entities that matter in the federal system and that states adequately represent and protect the interest of the cities within their jurisdictions. Cities have, in fact, suffered consistently from the neglect or outright hostility of state governments.

Continuing inattention to the needs of the cities has allowed their problems to reach crisis proportions. Most of America's larger cities exhibit decaying downtown business centres, inadequate housing, insufficient mass transportation, intense car congestion, and suffocating air pollution. They suffer from increasing rates of crime, violence and addiction to alcohol and other drugs. Vast tracts have become ghettos inhabited by poor blacks, Hispanics and Caribbeans. A large proportion of each city's population consists of persons, mainly children, who are more or less permanently dependent upon public welfare funds. (About one million of New York City's eight million inhabitants receive welfare benefits.) The cities, moreover, have been plagued by racial antipathies that have sometimes turned their streets into battlefields.

At the same time, the tax base on which the city depends has been shrinking as the white middle class and many business enterprises, fleeing the problems of urban life, move to the suburbs. A vicious circle is created: a shortage of revenue leads to poorer services, which drives out more taxpayers and makes revenue even scarcer. Borrowing heavily to meet their expenses, some cities have courted bankruptcy.

Not only are the financial resources of the city inadequate, but its political institutions are not equal to the responsibilities placed upon them. Legally, a city is a mere creature of the state government, which may amend the charter of incorporation at will. The city has no powers other than what the state legislature chooses to grant it. The degree of 'home rule' that the city enjoys, the form of government it has and the types and amounts of taxes that cities may levy are determined by the state. State governments, unfortunately, have been less than generous. When big-city mayors journey, cap in hand, to the state capital (usually located in a small town) in search of appropriations or taxing authority, as often as not they meet with indifference.

To rural Republicans, who long dominated and are still powerful in many state legislatures, the city is a hotbed of sin, corruption and Democrats. They care not to pave the devil's streets. Their distaste harks back to the late nineteenth century, when millions of immigrants from southern and eastern Europe arrived there. The earlier, assimilated immigrants from the British Isles and northern, Protestant Europe regarded the urban melting pot as a cauldron of strange tongues, alien religious practices and outlandish customs.

The most repugnant custom of all was the immigrants' tendency to acquire political power by building a 'machine'. The machine was a political organization, ruled by a 'boss', which dispensed patronage—mainly in the form of public jobs—in return for the voters' support of designated candidates in city council, mayoral and other elections. The boss and his lieutenants in the various neighbourhoods could also help their clients find their way through the bureaucratic maze of government; if there was trouble with the police, one knew where to turn. For the poor, non-English-speaking immigrant, machine politics was simply a means of survival in a strange land. Looking back from this era of distrusted politicians, it seems almost like a golden age when the political process was immediately relevant to people's lives.

But to the native sons who ran the state legislatures, machine politics reeked of corruption. Considering it a manifestation of ignorance and unfamiliarity with American ways, they attempted to reform the cities by educating the new citizens in the elements of 'good government'. In the meantime, however, the legislators thought it prudent to contain the evils of bossism by curtailing the power of city government while it was in the hands of the machine. Thus were produced charters which sharply limited the taxing and spending powers of cities, and typically divided authority between the mayor and numerous independent boards and commissions.

The circumstances which called forth those niggardly charters no longer exist in most cities. The immigrants have been assimilated, and few of the old-style bosses remain. The descendants of those immigrants, not needing the favours of bosses, have themselves joined in the reform movement in many places. Yet the cities still suffer from the heritage of enfeeblement.

The obvious remedy would have been for the cities to take control of the state legislature through their representatives and enact more favourable terms for urban government. However, rural Republicans often kept control, even though the population balance had shifted to the Democratically controlled cities, because of malapportionment. In a malapportioned legislature, the populous urban parts of the state would have disproportionally fewer seats than would the thinly populated rural areas. The disparities between constituencies could be enormous. In Connecticut, for example, some members of the lower legislative chamber represented 424 times as many constituents as other members; in theory, about 12 per cent of the state's population could elect a majority of the chamber's members. Urban dwellers in Connecticut and elsewhere complained that cows were better represented than people in the legislature.

Malapportionment was a sin of deliberate omission. Electoral district boundaries which, in some cases, dated from the nine-teenth century continued to be in use well past the middle of the twentieth. Often the apportionment of seats was mandated by the state's original constitution, assuming thereby an aura of immutability. A Democratic governor of New York in the 1920s remarked ruefully that the state was 'constitutionally Republican'. While the district lines remained frozen in time, enormous population movements from country to city and from overseas into the cities had occurred. But the rural Republicans—and in southern states rural Democrats--paid little heed to census returns whose implication was that power ought to be transferred to urban Democrats. Welded into place by old apportionments, they refused to vote changes in boundaries which could only diminish their numbers and influence.

Their power finally began to crumble in 1964, when urban dwellers successfully invoked the judicial power of the national government to force new apportionments. The Supreme Court held that grossly unequal legislative districts denied inhabitants of the more populous constituencies 'equal protection of the laws' as required by the Fourteenth Amendment. The court proclaimed the doctrine of 'one man, one vote', which necessitated distributing seats in both houses of a legislature in accordance with the principle of population equality. The argument that distinctive geographical and economic interests or traditional political units, like counties, deserved some weight in the formulae of representation was rejected.

During the late 1960s, under actual or threatened federal court orders, all of the state legislatures were reapportioned. But the result was bitterly ironic for the cities. For a good deal of the nominally 'urban' population had moved after the Second World War to the suburban fringes. These displaced urbanites were refugees from city life and, like most refugees, had rather unpleasant memories of their erstwhile place of persecution. The suburban residents also were richer, on the average, than those they left behind and, consequently, tended to convert to Republicanism. Thus, when the legislative districting was reformed, much of the non-rural gain in seats accrued to the suburbs, which were just as Republican and just as anti-urban as the rural areas. Finding common ground in their antipathy to the cities, the rural and suburban legislators coalesced to keep urban interests in subjection.

This development is all the more unfortunate in that the suburbs themselves are among the factors contributing to the urban dilemma. For the city and the suburbs together form a great metropolitan organism, an economic and social unit. People may dwell in one and work in the other; certainly the suburbs would not exist without the commercial heartland of the city to nurture them. Yet the authority of the city government terminates at the city limits. Beyond them, numerous expressions of suburban self-government, such as incorporated villages and townships, proliferate. Taken as a whole, the New York City metropolitan area sprawls across three states, twenty-two counties, and about 1400 units of local government. The government of New York City proper is but one of these units.

The obstacles to coherent administration presented by this patchwork quilt are readily apparent. The provision of housing, transportation networks, educational facilities or a water supply is complicated by the need to secure agreement among numerous village plenipotentiaries. Even more fatal to rational planning is what Professor Robert Wood has termed the 'segregation of resources and needs'. The cities become increasingly populated by the poor, the suburbs by the rich. Among the suburbs themselves, some are enclaves of the affluent few, others more densely populated but less wealthy. Since the public services of each village and town are supported by what can be raised from local property taxes, the rich communities enjoy such benefits as well-endowed public schools, while the city and the poorer suburbs must make do with more spartan facilities. Some state courts have accepted the argument that such disparities deny the children of poorer school districts an equal opportunity for an adequate education, as required by the state constitution. The Texas Supreme Court, for example, held that students in districts whose tax base lacked high-value commercial or residential property 'are trapped in a cycle of poverty'. If this reasoning ultimately finds favour throughout the country, the states may be forced to restructure fundamentally their mode of financing schools to give each student a fair share of the funds spent statewide. There is, however, considerable opposition to mandatory dollar equity from those who consider it a 'Robin Hood' strategy, based on the false premiss that educational performance invariably corresponds to investment of resources. The opponents argue that making equality of funding the overriding goal would discourage efforts by individual districts to strive for excellence and detract from the search for more effective techniques—which may not be more costly—of educating children.

Besides segregating resources from needs, the balkanized metropolis segregates whites from blacks. Some cities became predominantly black within the decade of the 1960s because of the white exodus to the suburbs. To help overcome the effects of residential apartheid within the city, federal courts have ordered white pupils bussed to all-black schools and vice versa. But the goal has not been achieved, because most of the white students in many metropolitan areas have taken shelter beyond the city limits. Too few remain to allow anything approaching racial balance in the schools. Hopes of exchanging students between the black city schools and the white suburban schools were dashed by the Supreme Court in 1974, when it ruled that suburban schools in most cases could not be compulsorily included in urban desegregation schemes.

The solution for many of these problems would be a single metropolitan government encompassing both needs and resources. In a few cities, notably Miami and Minneapolis-St Paul, metropolitan governments have been established. But elsewhere suburbanites, through their influence in the legislatures, have clung to that rugged independence which, like their lawns and trees, symbolizes the small-town American past that they left the city to recapture.

However, while urban interests are submerged in state politics, they are becoming increasingly salient in the deliberations of

Congress. Congressmen from large cities now constitute an important bloc, which has become more conscious of its power and more determined to use it to secure federal remedies for urban ills. One result of this new militancy has been federal capital improvement grants and operating subsidies for mass transit. Previously, national transportation outlays had gone almost exclusively for highways, a policy which benefited rural areas and made possible the very existence of commuter suburbs dependent upon cars. For the city, road building did virtually nothing except gorge its streets with cars and require the demolition of entire neighbourhoods to make high-speed corridors for passing vehicles.

There were proposals during the Reagan and Bush Administrations to create urban 'enterprise zones' that would harness the energy of the private sector to the task of regenerating city cores. Enterprise zones were typical of the new wave of non-bureaucratic 'empowerment' schemes designed to help the poor without increasing significantly the size of government. Businessmen receive tax credits and other concessions for establishing factories and warehouses in blighted urban areas. Modelled on the success of Hong Kong as a 'free port', the concept of the enterprise zone was adopted enthusiastically by about 30 states; more than 500 zones have been designated. But the federal government itself has not pursued the idea vigorously, apparently because there is evidence that tax concessions alone are not enough to attract business. Needed may be a comprehensive development policy, calling for infrastructure investment and social services: job training, better housing, effective crime-control and decent schools. Making federal enterprise zones work thus would require heavy outlays, which Washington abhors. In addition, some studies of functioning state enterprise zones suggest that their benefits do not accrue to the intended beneficiaries. Workers from elsewhere may be hired, and poor residents are often forced out through 'gentrification' once the economy of the neighbourhood improves. The history of the enterprise zone is, in a sense, emblematic of the national government's hesitancy to shoulder the urban burden, even though the states have proven unequal to the task. Until Washington is fully engaged, the cities are likely to remain the stepchildren of the federal system.

CHAPTER FOUR

The Protean Presidency

That the modern Presidency has grown from meagre constitutional beginnings testifies to the energy of the men who held the office and to the severity of the crises during which the country sought salvation in a strong executive. Among the most powerful persons the world has known, the President heads a bureaucracy of several million civil servants, commands an army with an awesome nuclear arsenal, and presides over a fiscal complex that is a keystone of the world economy. Yet he is subject to the rules of office laid down in a document written in the eighteenth century to govern a small, rural nation. The office has acquired power by usage while staying more or less within the spirit of the original document's system of checks and balances. If there is a 'genius of the constitution', the office of President is one of its outstanding products.

The President remains, as Woodrow Wilson observed, 'at liberty both in law and conscience to be as big a man as he can' because the constitution is characteristically laconic about his powers. Before devoting most of its text to stipulating how the President shall be elected, sworn in, paid, and if necessary impeached, Article II does mention that the 'executive power shall be vested in a President'. But what does 'executive power' consist of? Many seemingly executive functions have already been granted to Congress in Article I, including the authority to regulate commerce, declare war, and levy taxes.

The vagueness of the framers has left the Presidency to become whatever circumstances demanded, the merest hints in constitutional wording serving as justification. More details might have denied the flexibility which allowed the President to become today chief executive, legislative leader, head of state, leader of his party, supreme diplomat and chief warrior. Although presidential exploits in Southeast Asia, Libya, Panama and the Persian Gulf have made the military role controversial, these customary powers have won a grudging acceptance.

According to the organizational chart, the President manages the huge federal bureaucracy, yet his responsibilities as chief executive exceed his real powers. His supposed subordinates are frequently insubordinate, requiring political rather than managerial skills to keep them in line. This paradox prompted President Harry S. Truman's remark about his future successor, General Eisenhower: 'Poor Ike—it won't be a bit like the Army. He'll find it very frustrating.'

A large part of the bureaucracy, comprising the agencies under an independent commission or board, removes from the President's direct control a vast range of policy matters, including atomic energy (Nuclear Regulatory Commission), civil aviation (Federal Aviation Administration), telecommunications (Federal Communications Commission), industrial relations (National Labor Relations Board), banking (Federal Reserve Board), securities (Securities and Exchange Commission), scientific research (National Science Foundation), and maritime affairs (Federal Maritime Commission). The President could try to disclaim all responsibility for what happens in those fields, but another Truman epigram, 'The buck stops here', holds true. When the share index drops precipitously, the chief executive would have trouble diverting the public's rancour away from himself and towards the SEC. The difficulty is that the President possesses some, but not all, of the authority he needs. In dealing with inflation the President can administer a wage and price freeze, but the bank interest rate, a crucial economic determinant, is controlled by the Federal Reserve Board, whose members are notoriously autonomous.

The President influences the policy of the independent agencies by nominating the commissioners. But because of their lengthy terms, which exceed the President's, he may be unable to name more than a fraction of any commission. The concurrent power of the Senate to confirm the nominees, moreover, narrows the President's choice to those men who reflect his own view *and* could survive the confirmation hearings. Furthermore, the heady atmosphere of fixed tenure often makes a commissioner change the well-known policy views which led the President to name him. But a President is stuck with his appointees no matter how refractory they become. President Nixon quarrelled over the bank rate with his former trusted economic adviser, Arthur Burns, whom he had appointed chairman of the Federal Reserve Board.

The President is plagued by insubordination not only in the independent agencies, which are after all intended to be insulated from direct political influences, but in his own cabinet as well. Unlike the British cabinet which is invariably a collection of important party figures, the President's cabinet may be composed of men selected primarily for their help or loyalty to him personally or even for their obscurity (if the post is considered too politically sensitive for any person of known opinions). For reasons of party unity or prestige, the President may include a figure of importance in his own right: perhaps one of the presidential hopefuls who succumbed in the primary elections or the governor of an important state. Should the cabinet member prove uncooperative, the President can, by 'freezing' him out of the inner councils, force him to resign. But resignations in anger carry political costs for the President—no principle of collective responsibility restrains the ousted member—and the chief executive is likely to soldier on with an intransigent running the Department of Agriculture rather than risk an embarrassing departure.

At times of crisis, the resignation of a Cabinet member may signal serious dissension in an administration and give opponents of presidential policy a rallying point. Secretary of State Cyrus Vance resigned in protest over President Carter's decision to order the ill-fated commando mission to rescue American hostages in Iran. Coming as it did close to an election, the resignation probably contributed to Carter's defeat by lending support to critics who maintained that he had mishandled the hostage episode.

Lacking effective levers for manipulating the bureaucracy he nominally heads, the President relies on persuasion. His persuasiveness does not depend solely on his force of personality. He can trade his support for the pet projects of a cabinet secretary or agency commissioner. He can hold out enticing prospects of appointment to more desirable posts; the under-secretary of the Interior Department might fancy being ambassador to Venezuela.

And the President can, for those who have a political following at home, dole out patronage jobs to supporters. On the darker side of persuasion, the President can threaten to cut departmental budgets, kill favourite programmes, and withhold promotions. The way a President 'orders' his bureaucracy into action smacks more of Byzantine court intrigue than the principles taught in colleges of public administration.

The unwieldy bureaucracy stimulated the rapid rise in recent decades of the once tiny staff of the Executive Office of the President. In the privacy of the White House basement and the adjacent Executive Office Building, a staff of experts, speechwriters, lawyers, troubleshooters and liaison men provides the President with an inner council that can rival the cabinet. When he was nominally only a presidential adviser on foreign affairs, Henry Kissinger substituted for the State Department; a domestic affairs adviser may replace the secretaries of a whole group of departments in the President's confidence. Unlike the often unresponsive bureaucracy, the executive staff supplies advice and intelligence the President feels he can trust and carries out his orders unfailingly. No outside loyalties or departmental 'empire-building' intervene.

The increasing importance of the executive staff conjures the spectre of an elite cadre of officials outside the system of checks and balances. Most executive staff members are not subject to confirmation by the Senate, nor do they routinely appear before a congressional oversight committee, as a cabinet secretary. Presidents have often claimed that 'executive privilege', a supposed corollary of separation of powers, precludes prying into the workings of the executive office, but the existence of such a privilege has been hotly disputed. Of course, immunity from outside scrutiny is exactly what the President values in his staff.

A more serious objection is that the executive office can become a presidential Disneyland, peopled by devoted henchmen who assure their chief that his every dream is coming true. Such insularity may leave the President ignorant of outside opinion, the problems of the real world and even the activities of his staff. The moral of the Watergate scandal, which led to President Nixon's downfall, surely is that excessive reliance on a 'palace guard' can be a dangerous form of myopia. A somewhat similar scandal marred President Reagan's second term. A group of national security aides in the White House, conspiring with the Central Intelligence Agency, brokered a covert agreement to sell arms to Iran in exchange for hostages held in Lebanon. By means of creative international financing, the aides diverted the proceeds and supplementary funds to the Contras, opponents of the Sandinista government of Nicaragua, thereby defying a congressional enactment barring military assistance. The supplementary funds were raised from charitable donors—a remarkable example of privatization.

Since the President himself claimed to have been unaware of the Iran-Contra scheme, it amounted to a silent *coup d'état* of sorts. The culpable staff members formed a cabal, responsible to no political authority, which carried out its own foreign policy in the name of the United States. The plotters demonstrated that the system of checks and balances could be evaded by using secrecy and misinformation—traditional intelligence weapons—to deceive domestic political authority, rather than a foreign enemy. Although the culpable staff members were prosecuted for perjuring them-selves in testimony to Congress, most escaped serious retribution. The incident underscored the need for more effective means of containing a runaway White House staff.

Watergate and Iran-Contra also illustrated the great versatility of a presidential staff: it may include, along with mundane functionaries, specialists in breaking-and-entering, as well as international smuggling. Another advantage to Presidents is the malleability of the executive staff in comparison to the departments headed by cabinet secretaries and commissions, which are created and fixed by statute. The staff can be readily redeployed by the President without complex authorizing legislation. By promptly establishing White House councils on environmental quality, consumer protection, economic competitiveness and similar issues of sudden urgency, the President can satisfy a popular outcry for vigorous action. When delicate negotiations with Congress are underway, the President may employ a member of his staff as his emissary, in preference to the cabinet member most directly concerned. During the drafting of the Civil Rights Act of 1991, for example, it was the White House Counsel who represented the president's interests, although the subject of the legislation was within the purview of the Attorney General—formally the president's chief legal adviser. In such instances, the President clearly demonstrates more confidence in his personal assistants than in the leaders of the major departments, possibly because he considers the loyalties of the former undiluted by institutional influences.

Perhaps the most puissant of the executive entities clustered about the president is the Office of Management and Budget, which is charged with presenting to Congress a co-ordinated financial plan for the entire government. By concentrating in that office the power of allocating funds, the President has enormously increased his control over the departments. A massive, complex document, the budget is so difficult to amend after completion that a bureaucrat must come hat in hand to the office in advance, pleading his case. In exchange for his allocation the supplicant must promise *quid pro quo*. So effective is OMB in augmenting presidential power that Congress in 1975 voted to subject the appointment of the director and assistant-director to Senate confirmation. And when Ronald Reagan swept into office in 1980, vowing to halt the growth of federal expenditure, the most charismatic figure in Washington for a time was his OMB director, David Stockman. The director's aura of omnipotence was enhanced by reports that he knew the budget by heart.

The politics of the budget reveal how blurred are the lines that theoretically separate the legislative and executive powers. Although Congress, exercising the 'power of the purse', appropriates money, it is up to the chief executive to spend it. The President attempts to force the hand of Congress by preparing a budget request so detailed that even amendments in committee become difficult. Congress nevertheless manages to give the President less money than he asks for in some budget items and more than he asks for in others. (House and Senate committees now co-ordinate budget matters, presenting a united front.)

Cutting the President's funds is generally an effective means of congressional control, except that, as Vietnam proved, the President apparently can run a medium-sized war out of petty cash. Giving the President more than he wants is not a very satisfactory instrument of control. Even if the President were bound to dispose of the entire allocation—which would make the bureaucratic spending mentality compulsory—legislators could not depend on very enthusiastic implementation of the funded programme. The House Armed Services Committee in the 1960s failed to nudge the Defense Department into building a nuclear-powered aircraft carrier—the committee chairman's idea of the ultimate weapon—by voting unwanted millions for the project.

President Nixon thwarted congressional munificence by refusing, as an economy measure, to spend billions of the health, education and welfare appropriation. This so-called 'impounding' of money willingly voted made nonsense of the framers' intention to keep the purse strings tightly in the grip of the legislature. The impoundment controversy suggests that the framers, preoccupied with the sufferings of Parliament under free-spending monarchs, may have put the checks in the wrong place; they made no explicit provision (other than the veto) for checking free-spending legislatures. As the government's deficits have grown in recent years, proposals for controlling the budget have focused on capping public spending in a manner that neither branch of government can evade.

Although the constitution clearly vests the 'executive power' in the President it was much less specific about his legislative role. Article II stipulates that the President 'shall from time to time give to the Congress information of the state of the union and recommend to their consideration such measures as he shall judge necessary and expedient'. The annual event, more pomp than substance, that the State of the Union Message has become, celebrates the importance of transmitting presidential wisdom to Congress. Less well known than this televised ceremonial address to the joint assembly of House and Senate are the special messages on crime, education and foreign aid and the detailed bills that the President may regularly 'recommend to their consideration'. The outpouring of suggestions dominates the congressional agenda and makes the President by far the major source of proposed legislation. So dependent are they on presidential stimuli that, when the proposals are delayed, the legislators may complain that they simply cannot get organized.

The proportion of the President's programme enacted is regarded as an indicator of his overall success in office. *Congressional Quarterly*, which keeps score of roll-call votes for Capitol Hill connoisseurs, identifies every aye or no vote as a vote for or against the President. (Rarely does the White House take no position.) By this standard, any sober reassessment of the Kennedy Administration must conclude that he was not particularly effective; President Johnson, although seemingly less popular, was by comparison a smashing success in gaining congressional approval for his bills.

Although a President may have the initiative in firm grasp, he by no means has a legislative majority under his whip, as a British Prime Minister automatically does, to ensure passage of a bill. A President does not hold office by virtue of being the leader of a dominant parliamentary party. Many Presidents, particularly Republicans in recent decades, have faced a Senate and House solidly controlled by the opposition. Various theories have been put forward to explain this phenomenon of 'divided government'—election of liberal Democrat majorities in Congress to serve alongside conservative Republican Presidents. One theory is that voters are simply preserving the status quo in Congress—i.e., choosing incumbents (a choice which may simply reflect the campaign advantages accruing to those already in office)—even though they select a Republican President. Another theory is that the voters, heeding the advice of the nation's founders, are consciously opting for safe government by ensuring that party divisions reinforce the separation of powers. A third theory is that voters welcome the social benefits that liberal Democrat Senators and Representatives support but for the sake of balance wish a fiscally conservative Republican to be in charge of overall economic management at the White House.

Whatever the reason for perpetually divided government, some fear that it might be a formula for deadlock and paralysis. They therefore propose that in each Congressional district the voter be required to cast his ballot for a House candidate and Presidential candidate of the same party—the so-called 'unsplittable ticket'. In that manner, the winning Presidential candidate would be likely to enter office with a majority in the House. The concept could, indeed, be taken further—by permitting the House majority to unseat the President with whom it was elected—thereby creating the 'no confidence' mechanism that the framers of the constitution omitted. Since Americans seem to cherish their privilege of 'ticket-splitting', however, the appeal of such a dramatic change would probably be limited.

Divided government is a handicap, no doubt, to a President, but not a crippling infirmity, because neither party in Congress is sufficiently unified to create simple partisan confrontations. Virtually all bills are passed or rejected by a bi-partisan coalition; the President's identification with the minority party thus does not condemn him to perpetual defeat.

If the lack of an assured majority complicates his task, the President at least need not worry about a unified and well-led opposition. There is no official leader of the opposition, in the British sense, and usually not even a single figure of national prominence approaching the President's. A presidential hopeful may emerge from Congress to claim the right of reply to a televised presidential speech, but as often as not the networks are at a loss to know which politician qualifies as an opposition spokesman.

The dominant party in the House and Senate elect majority leaders, but they may have been chosen for their innocuous neutrality among party factions or for their effectiveness in day-to-day legislative routine. Few members of the public could recall the names of the majority leaders if asked. Although the legislative leaders cannot hope to compete with the President in mobilizing public opinion, they have at times formulated a co-ordinated programme as an alternative to the President's agenda. Lacking the prestige and focus of the Presidency, however, it is difficult for them to do more than react to White House initiatives.

The President's basic resource in promoting his legislative programme is his ability to bargain with key legislators. He may arrange a deal by promising support for their favourite bills and perhaps patronage appointments in return for approving his measures. The President's prestige alone, especially if he has just been elected by a margin sizeable enough to be called a mandate, may convince some legislators to go along. Flattery is also a powerful persuader; the chosen few congressmen relish being photographed on their way to presidential 'briefings' and White House breakfasts, where they are taken into the President's confidence over coffee and eggs. For the obdurate, the President's congressional relations advisers may recommend 'armtwisting', applying pressure by hinting at dire consequences for non-cooperation.

The President's most potent bargaining counter is his constitutional power to veto legislation. A bill becomes law when the President signs it, but, if he disapproves of it, the bill can be returned to Congress with his objections. (If a procrastinating President neither signs it nor returns it within ten days, it becomes law anyway.) The veto may be overcome by passing the bill again, this time by a two thirds vote of both houses instead of a simple majority. Given the difficulty of mustering even simple majorities, the veto is usually fatal. By the end of the third year of his presidency, George Bush had vetoed 24 pieces of legislation. Congress attempted to override a number of the vetoes but consistently failed, in some instances by as little as 12 votes in the House.

The implicit judgement of the framers that the President's view of legislation ought to prevail over that of 289 members of the House and 66 Senators—just under two thirds—betrays, perhaps, a certain pessimism about representative democracy. But there is reason to believe that routine use of the veto was not anticipated in the early days of the republic. The Provost of the Law Academy of Philadelphia wrote in 1834: 'It is but seldom that a president can have just cause to differ in opinion from the representatives of the people and those of the states.' Some of his contemporaries also had second thoughts about the veto, considering it, in the words of a Virginia judge, an 'incongruous . . . union of legislative and executive powers in the same man'. There was sentiment for repealing the two-thirds requirement for override, on the ground that simply sending a bill back to Congress for reconsideration was a sufficient safeguard against hasty lawmaking. In modern practice, the primary check on overuse of the veto is political: any president who resorts to the veto more than sparingly risks appearing to be an autocrat. Occasionally, though, the President has the opportunity to defeat a bill without a direct rebuff to Congress, by means of the 'pocket veto'. If he refrains from signing a bill and Congress adjourns before the 10-day time limit has elapsed, the measure becomes defunct.

The veto power would be more effective if it were a scalpel rather than an axe. Since a bill either must be signed or vetoed in its entirety, the President cannot surgically excise the paragraphs he dislikes, allowing the rest to become law. He must simply take it all or leave it all. Congressmen thus can append 'riders', provisions extraneous to the ostensible purpose of the bill. A President eager to set his seal on important tariff legislation may find himself reluctantly approving construction of a hydro-electric dam in Wyoming as well. Although these package deals hardly contribute to the coherence of legislation, the only alternative is to allow an 'item veto' of individual provisions. That would require a constitutional amendment.

Constitutional amendments are not subject to the veto power; in fact, the President plays no formal part in the amending process at all, a striking omission considering how much importance is attached to his judgement in the framing of legislation.

One source of 'legislative' power that the President has not been able to exploit is his constitutional authority 'on extraordinary occasions' to convene both houses and to adjourn them if they cannot agree on a closing date. Since the authority to convene and adjourn the legislature is one of the bases of executive power in parliamentary systems, it seems strange not to find it in the panoply of presidential powers. The reasons are not hard to discover. Congress meets continuously during about eight months of the year, recessing only for the summer, so there are hardly any 'extraordinary occasions' when the legislators are not already in town. And as the humid Washington heat approaches its August zenith, there is little disagreement about when to adjourn.

The President's authority as commander-in-chief of the armed forces is an explicit constitutional grant amplified by custom. The constitution appoints the President 'commander in chief' of the Army and Navy (the Air Force was understandably over-looked in the eighteenth century) and of the state militias when these reserves, normally commanded by the state governors, are summoned into federal service. A commendable effort to ensure civilian control of the military, this provision has had the paradoxical effect of making generals, from Washington to Eisenhower, seem particularly qualified to be President.

The framers proceeded to muddle the lines of authority, however, by granting overlapping military powers to Congress. Only Congress can declare war, authorize military expenditures, conscript soldiers and make rules for regulating the forces. There was an age when a President, learning of an approaching enemy armada, had time to draft a speech asking for a declaration of war. But in the Cold War era of push-button atomic brinkmanship, the response to military threats had to be instantaneous. Consequently, the President was granted the latitude to deploy forces in such a way that the country would be at war *de facto* if not *de jure*. Without a congressional declaration, President Truman sent an army to Korea, President Johnson used the troops to put down a revolution in the Dominican Republic, and both Presidents Johnson and Nixon commanded half a million ground troops and fleets of bombers and ships in Vietnam. Johnson argued that congressional appropriation of military funds for Vietnam was tantamount to a declaration of war, a disingenuous argument at best, since politically it was almost impossible for the legislators, presented with a *fait accompli*, to cut off supplies to 'our boys in the field'. The fact remained that no 'emergency' precluded asking Congress for a declaration at some point in a war which lasted almost a decade. In refusing to seek one, the President simply by-passed the mechanism of checks and balances, raising doubts about the maintenance of constitutional limitations. 'By the early 1970s,' Professor Arthur M. Schlesinger has observed, 'the American President had become on issues of war and peace the most absolute monarch (with the possible exception of Mao Tse-Tung of China) among the great powers of the world.'

'National security' became the universal justification for executive secrecy and the denial of information to Congress, further undermining the legislature's role. Finally, however, Congress roused itself to reassert its authority. Overcoming a Presidential veto, it enacted a War Powers Act in 1973 that limits the commander-in-chief's ability to deploy forces in combat without congressional sanction. The legislation requires the President to inform Congress within 48 hours of ordering US troops 'into hostilities or into situations where imminent involvement in hostilities is clearly indicated by the circumstances'. If Congress does not authorize a longer period, the troops must be withdrawn within 60 days—extendable upon Presidential request to 90 days.

Experience with the act demonstrates that it is less than perfect as an instrument for reclaiming legislative power in foreign affairs. For one thing, Presidents may evade the implications of the law by taking a narrow view of what is meant by 'hostilities'. President Reagan deployed Marines in strife-torn Lebanon for more than a year without explicit authorization; he disputed the contention of many in Congress that the Marines were engaged in hostilities—even after they sustained casualties. The dispute was resolved by a compromise in 1983 in which the President acknowledged at least some Congressional authority over the use of the armed forces in return for permission to keep the soldiers in Lebanon for up to 18 months more. This compact represented a dubious victory for the War Powers Act, since the President obtained a free hand over troop deployment for a longer period than many in Congress thought prudent.

Further doubt was cast upon the prospects for the War Powers Act by the Persian Gulf hostilities of 1990–91. President Bush extracted from Congress formal pre-authorization for military action in the Gulf. Both houses voted him discretionary authority to launch a military operation, accepting Bush's argument that the 'credible threat of force' was a necessary adjunct to diplomacy. As a member of the House put it, the President must be able to 'use the Marine Corps and the diplomatic corps with equal facility'. The war vote proved to be a satisfying substitute for a declaration of war and an alternative to the post-involvement procedures contemplated by the War Powers Act, even though forces were actively deployed for about two thirds of a year.

Congressional pre-authorization of war no doubt suits certain kinds of crises. Unlike the atmosphere of the Vietnam period, there was a high degree of consensus about the enemy in the Gulf, who was personified by a cruel and blustering dictator. The war was expected to be short, focused on a discrete objective, and waged with minimal US casualties by means of remote-control weaponry. (Indeed, development of such casualty-minimizing robotics may now be spurred as much for the domestic political benefits—making conflict more palatable to Congress—as for the impact in the field.) Should the Gulf become a model for future 'resource wars' in the Third World, pre-authorized conflict could well be the norm.

If so, the power of Congress to influence war-and-peace decisions will have atrophied substantially. Congress learned from Vietnam that as a practical matter it cannot exert control by withdrawing funding after Presidential commitment of troops, and it learned from the Gulf affair that it cannot withhold support in advance of hostilities either, if the commander-in-chief rouses the patriotic fervour of the constituents. The President can readily foment bellicosity and sustain it against a foreign enemy by controlling battlefield news—as he did during the desert fighting, even though 1,400 journalists were on hand. Those members of Congress who vote against a military option despite jingoistic appeals from the White House may suffer politically amid the euphoria of military triumph.

It is true that an exhaustive debate—virtually every member of Congress spoke—preceded the Gulf authorization vote; the airing of opinion contrasted sharply with the congressional failure to consider squarely the escalation of US involvement in Vietnam. Full discussion is a healthy precedent, and it may at least ensure that the possible consequences will be thoroughly explored before military action is undertaken in the future.

At the same time, the Gulf precedent may transform the congressional prerogative of declaring war into a vestigial function. The prerogative, after all, has been invoked only five times in the history of the republic, although Presidents have dispatched troops beyond the borders about 200 times. Too ponderous, perhaps, for the subtle interplay of diplomatic and military strategy, voting on a formal declaration of war has proven to be an impractical mechanism for deciding when use of force is appropriate. The mechanism certainly failed to fulfill James Madison's belief, as expressed in notes at the Constitutional Convention, that it would 'leave to the Executive [only] the power to repel sudden attacks'. Voting on a declaration is thus likely to be replaced in practice by the more flexible mechanism devised for the Gulf: licensing the President to take military action if he chooses. It ensures that some consensus for war exists but delegates an important act of legislative discretion—the actual decision to go to war—to the executive branch (and the United Nations).

On rare but significant occasions, the President deploys the forces domestically as well as internationally. The lavishly armed state and city police forces can handle most situations, but Presidents have ordered in troops to put down urban rioting, escort black children to newly desegregated schools, and to sort the mail when the postal workers went on strike. Presidents are loath to use the army inside the country lest they resemble a banana republic generalissimo and raise questions about the scope of their lawful powers. During the Second World War President Roosevelt, exercising what he assumed to be his domestic military powers, had all Japanese-Americans 'evacuated' from the West Coast to detention camps. The affair is remembered today as a grievous infringement of civil liberties for which reparations have been paid.

The American Presidency unites two roles that parliamentary systems keep separate: head of government and head of state. In British terms, the President is the Prime Minister and the sovereign. The chief of state function is not explicit in the constitution but has been inferred from the President's duty to receive ambassadors. Whatever its origin, the dual role creates precisely the kind of confusion other systems sought to avoid. Watching the President speak on television, the citizen cannot easily distinguish at the moment whether he is seeing the Olympian symbol of his nation or the leader of a partisan administration. That makes it difficult to evaluate the President's words.

The confusion tends to be exploited by a President in order to associate his policies with patriotism. When confronted by strident opposition to his Vietnam policy, President Johnson once reminded his critics: 'I'm the only President you've got.' Converting loyalty to the nation into loyalty for administration policy, known as wrapping oneself in the flag, is relatively easy in the realm of international relations. Americans feel guilty about carping behind the President's back while he is away representing the majesty of America at the Great Wall of China or the Kremlin. President Nixon was notably more successful when he asked Americans to support him as he negotiated with the Communist powers than when he invoked 'national security' to thwart the investigation of his re-election campaign activities.

Various proposals have been advanced to remove from the President's calendar the trivial chores of the chief of state, among them lighting the national Christmas tree, posing with a Thanksgiving turkey, and throwing out the first ball at the opening of the baseball season. But obviously a President needs to cultivate his ritual persona as chief of state, so that he may be higher and mightier in the thick of partisan battle. For every President is mindful that he represents all the power of the United States government but cannot exercise it fully. President Reagan actually seemed to prefer the ceremonial aspects of the job to the more cerebral duties. He shone as the affable presence who comforts the nation at state funerals and welcomes astronauts back from outer space. Much of the detailed policy-making was left to powerful aides. Reagan's comfortable relationship with the public was a source of political dynamism that undoubtedly helped propel those policies forward.

Since the nation needs to speak with a single voice in international affairs, a President who is chief of state and military commander seems eminently suited to be chief diplomat. The framers gave the President authority to conclude treaties, but added the qualifying phrase 'by and with the advice and consent of the Senate'. Two thirds of the senators must vote to approve any pact which the President negotiates. This incarnation of the checks and balances principle reflects the isolationism of the infant republic, epitomized by George Washington's Farewell Address warning against foreign alliances. Typically it has been the Senate which has registered periodic bursts of isolationist sentiment in America by rejecting treaties. Expressing the post-First World War disillusionment with European rivalries, the Senate refused to approve Woodrow Wilson's Versailles Treaty.

Even when there was no specific treaty to ratify, the Senate has, by extension, kept a watching brief over the President's diplomacy. The Senate Foreign Relations Committee, under Chairman J. William Fulbright, was an early opponent of the war in Vietnam and indeed all foreign commitments surreptitiously given by the President.

Because the Senate can veto them, a President may avoid formal treaties, preferring instead to arrive at an 'executive agreement'. The exchange of destroyers for bases with Britain in 1940 and the provision of military assistance to Vietnam and Thailand in the 1960s were accomplished by an executive agreement. Although it seems a case of treaty-by-another-name, Presidents have succeeded so far in keeping these agreements outside the Senate's jurisdiction. However, most require funding, which affords both the House and Senate some control. Funding the foreign aid programme every two years allows the legislators to express their opinion of particular aspects of presidential policy by well-aimed budget cuts. Until the Iran-Contra plotters went to work, budgetary powers also enabled legislators to thwart President Reagan's commitment to arm rebels fighting the Sandinista government of Nicaragua; millions of dollars needed to be appropriated to carry out the President's undertaking.

Overall, there can be little doubt that the President determines the nation's behaviour in international politics. The names of Presidents Monroe, Truman, Eisenhower and Nixon are linked to 'doctrines' that proclaimed significant policy decisions without the consultation or approval of any other branch of government. In times of crisis, the power of war or peace rests in the President's unfettered hands, as anyone who lived through the tense days of the Kennedy–Khrushchev encounter over Cuba in 1962 can attest; the man who holds the trigger inevitably gives the orders. When threatened with external dangers, the complex system of checks and balances reverts to a tribal dependence on the warrior chief.

Besides his duties as chief executive, chief of state, chief diplomat, chief warrior and chief legislator, the President must be chief of his party as well. In parliamentary systems, a politician becomes Prime Minister by being leader of a party. In America, the reverse occurs. By virtue of being elected, the President is thrust into the unofficial position of 'standard bearer' of the party which nominated him. As the most prominent party member, the President must keep his Gallup Poll popularity index high in order that candidates for lesser offices may bask in his reflected glory, and a disastrous party showing in the congressional elections or elections for state governorships may be construed as a symptom of public hostility to the President.

Although both the Republican and Democratic parties are merely loose confederations of state organizations, the President bears ultimate responsibility for maintaining his party's cohesion. He endorses candidates for mayor, Congress and governor, posing with his arm around the contender. Or he may be required to intervene in a dispute splitting a local party. President Kennedy helped the Reform Democrats prevail over their intra-party opponents in New York State by dispensing federal patronage jobs through the leaders of the favoured faction.

Despite his responsibility for keeping the fifty state organizations in fighting trim, the President exerts little influence over the nominations that mean most to him: representatives and senators. Were he able to prevent renomination of legislators, he would command a disciplined block of votes in Congress. But party organizations at the state and congressional district level are jealous of their independence and immune from presidential sanctions. Consequently, the President cannot rely on his own party alone for legislative support. That complicates his task enormously, since he must be both leader of his party *and* a statesman capable of organizing bi-partisan legislative coalitions.

With these several roles to be juggled, the effectiveness of the Presidency may seem to depend upon the personality of the man who fills the office. Certainly his skills, his strengths and weaknesses, his conception of the proper scope of the office are important determinants, but the office responds more to the pull of circumstances than to the force of personality. The office, and the demands put upon it, make the man. Franklin D. Roosevelt was an 'activist' President, but he served during depression and world war; Eisenhower was less energetic but his was an era of relative peace and domestic harmony. The steady expansion of presidential power under all incumbents has reflected the increasing world importance of the United States and the growing number of economic, social and technical problems, from inflation to air pollution, that demand national leadership. As the only official elected by the nation as a whole and the country's spokesman to the world, the President is looked to for leadership.

The Presidency has not usurped power; it has been offered up on a silver platter by Congress, which in parlous times is prone to delegate its responsibility to the executive. The reasoning is basically sound. Better able to respond to rapidly changing situations, the President can 'legislate' on behalf of Congress, which has laid down general guidelines. Given the vicissitudes of international economics, it makes sense to allow the President discretionary powers to raise and lower import duties on a range of items from teapots to transistors rather than to pass a new law for each fluctuation in the market. Moreover, even the most detailed regulatory acts require enforcement, and enforcement requires the exercise of executive discretion: Which firms are violating the anti-trust laws? When is it time to increase farm acreage allotments? The passage of much complex regulatory legislation inevitably means that executive authority is extended.

There are limits, however, to the amount of discretion Congress can delegate. Certainly, it could not, in a moment of generosity, grant *all* its powers to the President, thereby instituting a dictatorship. The Supreme Court has traditionally kept vigilant; in the 1930s excessive delegation of power was the ground upon which several New Deal regulatory laws—most notably the National Industrial Recovery Act—were held unconstitutional. The standards for economic regulation were relaxed in later years, but executive actions may still be challenged in court on the grounds that too much authority was ceded by Congress or that the President exceeded the authority granted. The challenge would be especially likely to succeed if the executive action impinged upon provisions of the Bill of Rights or the Fourteenth Amendment.

The general, almost imperceptible, slippage of power from legislative into executive hands is a feature of most twentieth-century democracies. In America the slide has not been as sharp as in other countries because the separation of powers has allowed the congressional committees and their staffs to remain as alternative centres of power. But in a way the potential for executive usurpation is much greater because the President, serving a fixed term, is not vulnerable even theoretically to a vote of no confidence.

The ultimate congressional check upon presidential power is to impeach the President. A bill of impeachment must be voted by a simple majority of the House of Representatives, acting as prosecutor. The Senate then sits as a jury to hear the case. A vote of two thirds of the members present is required for conviction, which removes the President from office. The former President is liable to be tried in the ordinary courts for any crimes he may be accused of committing.

What a President must do to warrant impeachment is a matter of dispute. One school argues that the 'high crimes and misdemeanours' spoken of in the constitution must be actual violations of law. Another school, patronized by many congressmen, contend that whatever misdeeds the House and Senate think sufficiently serious are grounds for impeachment. The danger in the latter theory is the natural tendency of Congress to interpret disagreement with the President as a sign of moral turpitude in the White House. In the only impeachment ever brought to trial, President Andrew Johnson was accused in 1867 of dismissing certain cabinet members against the wishes of Congress. He was acquitted by one vote, a narrow escape that left a strong distaste for the procedure and a presumption that it would never again be invoked.

The initial reluctance of Congress to take up impeachment during the Watergate scandal indicates how painful is the prospect of bringing proceedings against an official of such awesome responsibilities. Were the President in the dock of the Senate, the disruption of government business would be complete. (Even the international currency markets became fidgety when the prospect of President Nixon's impeachment was raised.) Moreover, acquittal might not totally vindicate the President, whose capacity to govern for the remainder of his term would be impaired.

Despite these objections, however, Congress did begin the task of impeaching Nixon when the available evidence left no doubt that he had committed criminal acts. Although the process was aborted by the President's resignation, the decision of the House Judiciary Committee to bring formal charges served notice that the impeachment provision is still a viable section of the constitution.

The resignation itself set a political precedent of some significance. Although parliamentary premiers resign as a matter of course when they lose the confidence of the legislature, fixed tenure of office has been a hallmark of the American Presidency. No President before Nixon had ever resigned the office, no matter how far his relations with Congress had deteriorated or how besmirched by scandal his name had become. The belief in a President's right to serve out his term is so strong that the main argument offered in support of pardoning Nixon was that by having to resign he had already suffered condign punishment.

The irony of impeachment is that the President's handpicked Vice President succeeds to the office, leaving essentially the same administration in power. But this is only one of several odd features of the Vice Presidency, an institution that can be called the missing link in the constitutional system. Dissatisfaction with the institution was evident as early as 1840. When President William Henry Harrison died a month after his inauguration in that year, critics mocked the Vice President who succeeded him as 'His Accidentcy'. They refused to acknowledge the successor formally under any title other than 'Acting President'. Often ridiculed, the Vice President is sometimes sardonically described as a deterrent to plots against the President's life.

A shadowy figure, the Vice President is part of both the executive and legislative branches, although he has no real duties in either. His only responsibility under the constitution is to preside over the Senate, a purely formal task, and to cast the deciding vote when ties occur, which is infrequently. Otherwise he merely waits in the wings in case the President dies, resigns or is removed from office.

Unlike the stand-in actor, however, the Vice President never has a chance to learn the part. Most Presidents have studiously avoided delegating any important administrative or policy making duties to their Vice Presidents. Often the vice presidential candidate is personally picked by the President at the nominating convention because he is thought able to deliver the votes of a section of the country, not because his service is valued. President Kennedy chose Lyndon Johnson as his running mate to attract the 'Southern vote'. After the election, Johnson, once the powerful majority leader of the Senate, went into eclipse until Kennedy was assassinated.

Vice Presidents are typically sent abroad to perform non-critical diplomatic functions. George Bush, preparing to take up the office of Vice President, remarked sardonically that if he did not quickly earn President Reagan's confidence he might be spending much of his time attending state funerals in South America.

When he became President, Bush bypassed leading party figures to select as his own running mate a callow Senator from Indiana: Dan Quayle. Not well known nationally, Quayle may have been chosen as a foil for his chief, heightening the President's lustre by invidious contrast. Plagued from the beginning by questions about his academic and military record, as well as doubts about his readiness for heavy responsibility, Quayle's selection seemed to deprive the No. 2 position even of its *raison d'être* as an asset to the ticket. Quayle was restricted to minor campaign appearances, owing to fear of a damaging miscue, and even after the election, he rarely emerged from deep cover without a fixed script. Quayle became a figure of fun. Night club comedians built standing routines around the Vice President, and a periodical devoted entirely to satirizing him (*The Quayle Quarterly*) reached a circulation of 15,000. The critics' implicit message was that a second-rate office had found a fitting occupant. Once again, it seemed, the vice presidency was diminishing the occupant's stature and hindering his attainment of higher office, rather than grooming him for promotion.

Recognizing that fecklessness is the bane of Vice Presidents, Quayle sought to carve out a leadership role for himself as head of the executive branch's Council on Competitiveness. Becoming the scourge of bureaucracy, he campaigned for a reduction in environmental and other regulations that impede business. Although it attracted the enmity of green groups and others, his staunch advocacy of right-wing views—perhaps further right than the President's—did counteract the impression that he was a mere satellite, an image that had burdened other vice presidents. A key question is whether an aggressively partisan persona can translate into the statesmanlike aura that enhances the prospects for succeeding to the presidency.

From a functional standpoint, Bush's primary lieutenant and confidant was Secretary of State James Baker. It was sometimes said that Baker held the informal position of First Friend, an extra-constitutional office that, unlike the vice presidency, exercised true influence. First Friend also seemed to be an excellent platform, perhaps better than the vice presidency, from which to launch a presidential campaign of one's own.

Another extra-constitutional rival to the Vice President is the White House chief of staff. At one time, the chief of staff was merely the President's doorkeeper, so to speak, inconspicuously coordinating the business of the Oval Office in the interest of efficiency. Under President Reagan, who remained aloof from detailed policy-making, the chief was delegated vast discretion in matters of strategy and the task of maintaining day-to-day liaison with the cabinet and the Congress. This practice was carried forward by Reagan's immediate successor, President Bush. The chief of staff, often a former senator, governor or cabinet member, became the grey eminence of the Reagan and Bush administrations, sometimes accused of insulating the President from unwelcome reality. One of the Reagan White House chiefs somewhat chillingly compared himself to 'a prime minister', as though the President had became a figurehead. The Vice President, in contrast, is hardly ever suspected of being the power behind the throne.

An important function of the chief of staff, offsetting his much augmented powers, is to spare his superior the consequences of policies that go awry. In a scandal such as Iran-Contra, the chief becomes the scapegoat—blamed for not keeping the President adequately informed. Aiming criticism at this surrogate has now become a polite convention, especially for members of the President's own party. When only the chief's removal will suffice to expiate the President's failings, Washington's code of political bushido dictates that the chief 'fall on his sword', like a dutiful samurai, by resigning. Chiefs of staff are, for that reason, less durable than Vice Presidents but more serviceable in a crisis.

Both Reagan and Bush were able to revive their flagging fortunes in mid-term by sacrificing unpopular chiefs of staff, even though the chiefs had been doing their bidding. After the Iran-Contra embarrassment, which was ascribed to Presidential obliviousness, the reassuring choice of former Tennessee Senator Howard Baker, a moderate Republican enjoying bipartisan respect, was crucial to restoring confidence in the competence of the Reagan White House.

A consequence of vice presidential obscurity is that when a President dies, precisely the moment when the country needs to be reassured about the succession, a virtually unknown and inexperienced figure takes the reins. One proposal for reform would have the President delegate some of his duties to the Vice President as an apprenticeship and keep him well informed about the business of the executive branch. Another suggestion is that the choice of a vice presidential candidate be thrown open to the nominating convention, thereby democratizing the selection process and ensuring that a person of independent stature in the party is chosen.

Still another proposal, favoured by former presidential candidate Gene McCarthy among others, is to repeal the Twelfth Amendment, enacted in 1804, which ensures that the President and Vice President are of the same party. Even if it resulted in officeholders of different parties, argue the proponents of repeal, separate election of President and Vice President would encourage voters to pay more attention to the latter office and ensure that it was filled only with a candidate who could find his own constituency.

A related but somewhat simpler solution—requiring no constitutional change—would be for candidates of the same party to put themselves forward in tandem, entering the season of primaries as a team of candidates for President and Vice President. By joining fortunes before the convention, the pair would combine their fiscal resources and offer the delegates an attractive opportunity to endorse a shadow government, ready to take charge. A pre-convention ticket would eliminate unseemly last-minute fumbling after the presidential nomination to cobble together a partnership for the sake of ethnic or regional balance. It might also leave the candidate who accepted the No. 2 slot—as a full partner from the outset—better positioned to succeed in his own right one day.

Some would go further and simply abolish the office of Vice President by constitutional amendment, substituting a special election whenever the Presidency becomes vacant. At the moment, no election follows the death, resignation or removal of a President, no matter how many years remain in his term. It is almost as if the Presidency were a popularly constituted monarchy whose succession crises had been institutionalized in a quadrennial election. When the 'monarch' departs unseasonably, the state is left without a satisfactory method of filling the void.

Even a satisfactory method of replacing Vice Presidents has been difficult to devise, as illustrated by the history of the Twenty-fifth Amendment. Adopted in 1967, it provides that when the Vice Presidency becomes vacant, the President may nominate someone to fill the office with the approval of both houses of Congress. Normally, that would occur when a Vice President succeeds to the Presidency. Few believed that the amendment would be invoked very often, but within the space of fifteen months in 1973–4 two Vice Presidents were chosen. One of these, Gerald R. Ford, eventually succeeded to the Presidency, becoming the first person ever to hold that office without running in a national election.

This series of events brought forth objections that the Twenty-fifth Amendment is fundamentally undemocratic, allowing a President—even one threatened with impeachment for misdeeds—to name his own successor. (The conflict of interest inherent in this arrangement was dramatized when Ford, shortly after succeeding to the White House, granted Nixon a Presidential pardon for any crimes that he may have committed while in office.) Since the House and Senate may spend months scrutinizing the credentials of persons nominated for the Vice Presidency, an election for the post could just as well be held, but it might result in a Vice President of a different party than the President's. That is the electoral outcome prohibited by the Twelfth Amendment.

Succession to the Presidency is such a sensitive issue that an amendment was required to resolve the question of how often a President may succeed himself. A fear of the autocratic potentiality of the Presidency prompted passage in 1951 of the Twenty-second

Amendment, limiting occupancy of the White House to two full terms. But to avoid the indignity of having to run for re-election, several Presidents have suggested it would preferable to create a single six-year term, long enough to achieve something yet avoiding the mixing of base electoral politics with pure statesmanship. Of course, forbidding re-election also eliminates fear of the electorate, probably the most effective restraint on presidential power. Even the present limitation brands the second-term President as a 'lame duck', the opprobrious epithet attached to any officeholder whose lack of political prospects renders him dangerously unaccountable.

Is the President, in fact, too powerful? An American's opinion of the proper scope of presidential authority depends on his political bias and his times. In the grip of the Great Depression, liberals seeking an agency for social reform were frustrated by the limitations of Roosevelt's office. In the early 1970s, facing a President with imperial inclinations, they decried the lack of constitutional restraints and urged Congress to reassert its authority. Conservatives have experienced a similar, though opposite, transformation in their attitude to the Presidency. These alterations have occurred cyclically throughout the history of the republic, and they are likely to continue. The various forms that the controversy takes demonstrates how readily constitutional philosophy subserves political expediency.

CHAPTER FIVE

Congress:
the Legislative Labyrinth

Looking back upon his twenty years in the House of Representatives, Nicholas Longworth, the speaker from 1925 to 1931, remarked ruefully that 'During the whole of that time we have been attacked, denounced, despised, hunted, harried, blamed, looked down upon, excoriated and flayed. I refused to take it personally.' In the ensuing half century not much has changed; Congress continues to be held in chronically low esteem by its constituents. Polls have sometimes shown that as little as one-fifth of the public believed that their legislators were performing even adequately. Yet most congressmen, following Longworth's example, are still not taking it personally, at least not enough to make them change fundamentally the behaviour which has made the name of Congress synonymous with ineffectuality.

One reason for its ill repute is that Congress does not seem to get very much accomplished of a positive nature. In an average session, lasting about a year, Congress may pass about fifteen major acts, but scores of other bills become mired at various stages of the legislative process for reasons unrelated to their inherent merit. Some proposals, such as national health insurance, languish for decades, unable to overcome the prodigious obstacles to enactment. Congress, in short, looms as a bastion of negation. Reinforcing that impression, Presidents have often chastised Congress for failing to deal with the agenda which they have set before it while neglecting to produce alternative measures. Congressional inertia is particularly noticeable in times of crisis. Despite energy shortages, economic slumps and environmental menaces, the sleeping giant slumbers on. When Congress does act in an emergency, frequently the only solution it can devise is to give the President virtual blanket authority to deal with the problem as he sees fit—a response which does nothing to evoke admiration for the legislators' creativity.

Collectively, congressmen seem to have a short attention span for important issues. As David S. Broder, a Washington political analyst, has remarked, 'The natural tendency of Congress is to fly off in dozens of directions at once. Every member—and particularly every Senator—wants to do his own thing, a tendency which would be funny were the consequences for the country not so great.' The distractions come with the office. Although Congress has two formal functions, legislating and monitoring the operations of government, congressmen individually have an informal duty, enforced by the desire for re-election, to serve their constituents. The great issues may have to wait while the legislators concentrate on securing a federal grant for improving a highway at home or having a local beauty spot declared a national monument.

Unfortunately, there is no one to check these centrifugal tendencies, because Congress lacks firm, centralized leadership. The President does not hold office by virtue of leading a legislative majority. Quite the contrary, the constitutional separation of executive and legislative powers ensures that the President and members of Congress will spring from different electoral bases, suffer different political risks and generally look at the world from different viewpoints. Very often the President is of the minority party in Congress. From 1945 to 1980, the Democrats controlled Congress in all but two years, but the White House was occupied by a Republican for fifteen years. Elected in 1980, President Reagan was the first Republican since the 1950s to enjoy a Republican-controlled Senate. The advantages of executive-legislative partnership were so impressive that proposals for an 'unsplittable ticket'—the balloting system in which each voter must choose candidates of the same party for President and Congress—were widely discussed.

If a President is not the natural leader of Congress, the leadership function might be expected to devolve upon the elected heads of the majority party: the speaker of the House and the Senate majority leader. But there can be no effective leadership without some means of coercion, which the party chiefs lack. Their whips have no sting. A member of the British parliament can be coerced, ultimately, by the threat of losing the party designation at election time for having rebelled against the party whip; the national party leadership can affect his chances of being selected by his local party organization. But nomination of candidates for the Senate and House of Representatives is in the hands of state and local party leaders. Even without their support, one can acquire the party label for a congressional campaign merely by running successfully in a primary election.

The party leadership in Congress, moreover, can hardly hope to commit its members to a common legislative programme when each party is a catch-all for a broad spectrum of political leanings. The system prevailing in Congress, in reality, is not two-party politics, but four-party politics among conservative Democrats, liberal Democrats, conservative Republicans, and liberal Republicans. On most issues, *ad hoc* coalitions are formed among these four groupings.

In the absence of centralized leadership, the houses of Congress are controlled by an infra-structure of autonomous standing committees, centres of decision-making which are often referred to as 'little legislatures'. Although not envisioned by the constitution, the committee system is by now a traditional institution, whose existence is usually rationalized by pointing to the need for legislative expertise. After long service in the House Committee on Agriculture, a representative learns enough about crops to scrutinize Agriculture Department officials and farm bills with a knowledgeable eye. The expertise of congressmen on specialized committees and their formidable array of staff resources has helped somewhat to balance the growth of executive power.

Deference to specialists is the strict rule by which committees support each other, and a committee's expert judgement is only rarely, and usually unsuccessfully, challenged from outside. When the Committee on Armed Services kills a defence bill, it is difficult for the other representatives to breathe life into it again. Moreover, since debate in the House is usually quite limited, the version of a bill which is reported to the floor by the committee tends to pass without much amendment. The committees are thus gatekeepers in the legislative process.

While every committee is lord of its domain, three committees of the House are pre-eminent. The Appropriations Committee is powerful for the simple reason that most bills call for expenditures, which it alone can authorize. If revenue is raised to meet those expenditures, taxes must be approved by the Ways and Means Committee, another crucial panel. But most powerful is the Rules Committee. Initially intended to serve merely as a legislative traffic director, the committee usually allows its political preferences to colour its scheduling decision. It has been compared, by Professor William H. Riker, to a 'toll bridge attendant who argues and bargains with each prospective customer; who lets his friends go free, who will not let his enemies pass at any price . . . '

Some bills, the committee decides, are of such perfection that they can be sent to the floor under a 'closed rule', a severe limitation on debate which makes it impossible for opponents to offer amendments. A bill that the committee does not favour is scheduled under an 'open rule', permitting opponents to amend it to death, or never scheduled at all. Sponsors of legislation often must make substantive concessions to the Rules Committee in order to have it released. Under a bylaw, a majority of the House can force the committee to schedule a bill by signing a 'discharge petition', but securing 218 signatures—each of them risking retaliation by the committee—is not an easy task. During the 1940s and 1950s, the Democratic majority of the committee was a pillar of southern conservative obstructionism, but in the 1960s, the committee was infiltrated by more liberal members, allies of the speaker. The committee, however, remains alertly posted at the toll bridge.

Although it may contribute to the expertise of the Congress, the committee system allows the majority will to be thwarted by a committee of thirty to forty members—or more precisely the committee's chairman. The chairman schedules meetings, controls the agenda, appoints subcommittees and their chairmen, hires the staff, and spends committee funds running into millions of dollars. Until recently some chairmen ran their committees like feudal baronies. The chairman is powerful because he owes his position not to the support of his committee members nor to the party leadership in the House, but to the automatic operation of the rule of seniority. The majority-party member with the longest tenure on the committee has always been acclaimed chairman by divine right. He has thus been, in the strictest sense of the word, irresponsible.

The seniority system has some virtues. In a legislature which values specialist experience, it elevates the member with the most time on the job. Moreover, it solves the problem of choosing a chairman without inciting bloody political struggles. Since the House must reorganize itself biennially, it could conceivably spend the entire two years in battle over the chairmanships if seniority were not the guiding principle.

However, although it does reduce conflict, the seniority system settles for 'peace at any price'. No effort can be made to choose the most worthy member, for the seniority rule precludes any sort of 'merit' selection. It is not the most dedicated or able member who is chosen, but simply the oldest in service and often in years. Age may confer wisdom, but it generally also breeds conservatism. The gerontocracy which presides over the committee structure is thus more conservative than the Congress as a whole.

The committee chairmen in previous decades had also tended to be more conservative because the seniority system ensured that they came from conservative districts. A congressman acquires seniority by being returned election after election, a consistency which is more probable in the districts where one party is dominant—the 'safe seats'. A large number of such districts were in conservative, rural areas, and many were in the south.

The influence of southern seniority was mathematically self-evident: more than half the chairmen in the House and Senate in the 1973–4 Congress were from the south, although only about a quarter of the population lived there. Arkansas alone, a thinly populated, rustic state, contributed to that Congress the chairmen of the Senate Foreign Relations Committee, the Senate Appropriations Committee and the House Ways and Means Committee. It is true, of course, that many urban House districts in the north were Democratic safe seats, but the cities had not capitalized on their advantage. Because of the relative poverty of the south and the insignificance of its local politics, talented southern politicians were more likely than their northern brethren to be attracted to Congress as a career. Occupants of northern safe seats abandoned them readily to become mayors and state judges. Those urban representatives who did remain in Congress for long periods often treated their positions as sinecures, devoting their real energies to managing political affairs at home and allowing the diligent southerners to become masters of the parliamentary process in Washington.

This pattern changed a good deal during the 1970s and 1980s because of demographic shifts in the nation as a whole. The industrial states of the northeast and midwest lost population, while the economically booming south and southwest, the 'Sunbelt', underwent dramatic urban growth. If current trends continue, the US Census Bureau has predicted, New York State (No. 2 in 1990) will drop to fourth in population, behind California, Texas and Florida, by the end of the century. In the south, this shift has been accompanied by the revival of highly competitive two-party politics and the demise of many formerly safe Democratic seats. The New South is making its presence felt in the House through its enlarged Republican and Democratic representation rather than by taking refuge behind the seniority system.

The seniority system and the committee satrapies trace their roots to a backbench revolt in 1910 against the autocratic rule of the House speaker, 'Czar' Joe Cannon. His powers were parcelled out among the committee chairmen, and he was stripped of his right to appoint them, the rule of seniority being substituted. In effect, a tyranny was replaced by an oligarchy. Efforts to reform the House since then have concentrated upon restoring the powers of the speaker, while making him formally responsible to the rank-and-file members of the majority party. Gathering strength during the 1960s, the reform movement effected a series of startling changes at the opening of the ninety-fourth Congress in 1975. Normally, only a small percentage of the representatives fail to return after an election, but the election of November 1974, the first after the Watergate scandal, registered a popular backlash against incumbent politicians. It brought to the House seventy-five new Democrats. Committed to institutional reform, this younger and more liberal generation of representatives was unwilling to accept the freshman's maxim that 'to get along, you've got to go along'. The newcomers immediately made their presence felt in the House Democratic Caucus, the party's plenary policy-making body. Three doyens of the southern old boy network, the chairmen of the Committees on Armed Services, Agriculture and Banking—two septuagenarians and an octogenarian—were deposed by a vote of the caucus and replaced by more liberal northerners. The success of the putsch signalled that, although still an important criterion for chairmanships, seniority had lost its status as the exclusive consideration.

The caucus also reformed the method of assigning Democrats to committees. Until 1975, that prerogative had been enjoyed by the Democratic members of the Ways and Means Committee, sitting as a committee on committees, who used it for their own political purposes: building support for their favourite tax bills. The caucus transferred the assignment function to the Democratic Steering and Policy Committee, composed of the House speaker, the Democratic majority leader and a cross-section of the party membership in the House. In the first demonstration of its new power, the Steering and Policy Committee appointed several liberals, some of them freshmen, to the Appropriations and Ways and Means Committees, hitherto strongholds of trustworthy conservatives with at least a decade of seniority. The Democrats thus seemed to be moving towards firmer leadership, under a policy committee responsive to the rank-and-file members, and away from the fragmentation of power among feudal chieftains. That, in turn, has opened up possibilities for a basic legislative programme to which all party members are committed.

Despite the problems inherent in allocating the chairmanships and seats, few doubt that the system of standing committees is necessary. In the House, especially, the size of the membership would not permit extensive deliberation as a whole upon every proposal. It is the committee's task to organize research, hold hearings, and thrash out compromises before a bill comes to the floor. Standing committees are also better able to maintain constant 'legislative oversight' of the executive departments in their special fields of policy. The House Committee on the Interior, for example, keeps watch on the Department of the Interior, examining its budget requests, criticizing administrative decisions and exposing mismanagement. Some bureaucrats spend most of their time preparing answers to congressional inquiries, and cabinet secretaries do not look forward to testifying at hearings, knowing that they may be in for a televised browbeating by a panel of legislators in a vengeful mood. The longevity of a committee chairman ensures that he will know the inner workings of 'his' agency the way he knows the politics of his home district. Many chairmen have far greater experience in their fields than the cabinet secretaries. Between 1947 and 1975 there were only three chairmen of the House Armed Services Committee while about a dozen Secretaries of Defense came and went.

It would be inaccurate, however, to describe the nexus between the committee and the departments as a wholly adversary relationship. Under normal circumstances, most business between congressional committees and executive offices is transacted in an atmosphere of cosy reciprocity. The committee approves the budgets and policies, making changes here and there, and the bureaucrats are properly deferential to each congressman's dignity and political interests.

Many executive decisions, in fact, are explicable only in terms of what they do for an important congressman's district. Military strategy and the constituency interests of Armed Services Committee chairmen, for example, show a remarkable coincidence. The model of the enterprising congressman was Mendel Rivers, who chaired the committee from 1965 to 1970. By the end of his tenure, his home district in South Carolina boasted eleven major naval installations, including shipyards, missile bases, hospitals and training camps. The Defense Department was spending almost $1000 there annually for every single inhabitant. His successor as chairman managed to have the Bureau of Naval Personnel and the Naval Reserve Headquarters transferred from the capital to his district and installed in a complex of buildings named after himself. During the Bush presidency, another influential member of Congress, Senator Richard Byrd of West Virginia, created his own administrative decentralization programme, persuading the government to relocate a number of its departments—including a headquarters of the CIA—from metropolitan Washington to his bucolic home state of West Virginia.

He overcame objections that a location so remote from the capital was unsuitable, especially since it required uprooting an urban workforce of thousands.

In essence, a three-way relationship exists among department, committee and lobby groups. Although not formally a part of the policy-making process, the lobby groups, representing economic or political interests, play a substantial role. Oil producers, soya bean growers, power-generating companies, car manufacturers, retired persons, veterans and racial minorities are among the groups which maintain lobbies in Washington. Trade unions make their influence felt through lobbying efforts. Even foreign nations, not content to rely on ambassadorial contacts, attempt to sway Congress directly, especially on foreign trade bills, by retaining lobbyists to stalk the halls of the Capitol. To represent their interests, Japanese business organizations retain former officials who had negotiated international trade agreements on behalf of the US, demonstrating that even foreign policy is open to sophisticated suasion by those whom it affects. Specialized lobbying firms, often headed by former legislators, provide a targeting service for their clients, using inside knowledge of the web of influence to advise them how to direct political contributions for maximum effect.

Members of Congress evidently do not resent seeing former colleagues become strategists-for-hire who live off their intimacy with the powerful. Indeed, successful lobbyists are widely admired. During the debate on President Bush's nomination of an ex-senator, John Tower, to the post of Secretary of Defense, the nominee's opponents called attention to his service as a highly-paid consultant/lobbyist for weapon merchants seeking to manipulate US arms-control policy. Dismissing that aspersion, a fellow Texan, Senator Phil Gramm, retorted: 'I don't want a Secretary of Defense whose advice isn't worth a lot of money.'

Exactly how much effect lobbying has is not clear, and it probably varies from one group to another. Lobbyists—or at least their clients—apparently believe they are effective for they officially report spending millions each year on their attempts to influence legislation. Many of the major lobbying organizations keep plush offices in the capital and employ large staffs, including former legislators and government officials with contacts in strategic places. Cultivated by lavish wining and dining on tax deductible expense accounts, these contacts are more important than such visible lobby activities as testifying at committee hearings. A friendly congressman can keep a lobbyist informed about the progress of pending bills. The lobbyist, in turn, can keep him supplied with data, such as industry statistics, to help the legislator champion the lobbyist's cause, or suggest ways to word legislation.

Most lobbyists probably spend their time working with legislators who are already sympathetic, but there is good reason to suspect they are not above making converts where necessary by offering tangible inducements. Lobbies representing large economic interests can afford to 'invest' some of the profits they expect to gain through legislation by contributing to the re-election campaign funds of congressmen. The dairy industry, for example, whose earnings depend on federal pricing policies, has funnelled money from its 'war chest' to the campaigns of more than eighty senators and representatives. While technically legal, such well-distributed philanthropy obviously buys support for the dairymen. Drinkers of milk, meanwhile, are hardly in a position to raise a counter-offer in order to avoid paying a few pennies more for each bottle.

Bringing legislators' influence to bear on the executive branch is another way in which contributors can extract benefits in return for the gifts. In 1991, the Senate reprimanded one of its members for intervening with federal regulators on behalf of a banker from whom he solicited $900,000 in campaign funds. The bank later failed in scandalous circumstances. Although the chastised senator claimed that the intervention was merely a routine service to a constituent, his colleagues discerned a link between the money and the senator's alacrity to render assistance. Certainly, the constituents who suffered from the bank failure did not get similar consideration.

Just how casually members of Congress accept money from special interests became clear during the 'Abscam' affair of the early 1980s. Abscam was the code name for an FBI operation in which agents posed as Arab businessmen offering to pay for legislative favours. Several members of the House and a Senator were convicted of criminal charges on the basis of videotapes, some of which showed congressmen stuffing wads of cash into their pockets during secret meetings with the 'Arabs'.

The Federal campaign law of 1974 reduced the influence of individual contributors by setting limits on their gifts to congressmen, but the law fostered the growth of indirect lobbying organizations called 'political action committees', which collect funds and distribute them to congressional and other candidates. PACs represent the concentrated power of money devoted to specific political ends. PACs have been formed by dentists, used-car dealers, realtors, trial lawyers, military contractors and similar groups whose interest in government is restricted to securing legislation favourable to their business or profession. PACs, moreover, are often deceptively packaged. The Committee for Responsible Government, for example, is none other than the Nevada Bankers' Association by another name. (One rule of thumb: conservative PACs have 'citizen' in their name, while liberal PACs tend to use 'people'.) 'Ideological PACs' support such general causes as environmentalism, child welfare or workers' rights.

By the 1988 election, there were more than 4,000 PACs, and they contributed $150 million to House and Senate candidates in that year. The recipients were mostly incumbents, even though some of them would seem to have little need for cash on the scale of the offerings they received. A Michigan Senator collected more than $1,350,000 from PACs to fight off an opponent who had only $7,000 in PAC aid. Five Representatives who amassed a total of more than $400,000 in PAC contributions ran against opponents who had no PAC money at all, and several Representatives who banked more than $300,000 were unopposed in their campaign for re-election. The giving is also highly targeted; a defence industry PAC is likely to concentrate its funds on members of a committee dealing with defence appropriations. In 1986, the chairman of the Senate Finance Committee received $170,000 from a PAC representing the life insurance industry.

Recipients of the PAC largesse deny that legislation is for sale, although their voting records often do seem to coincide with the interests of their contributors. Many legislators concede that donor groups gain 'access', which is precious coin in Washington. Telephone calls from contributors tend to be answered. It is undeniable that candidates craving cash for television commercials and campaign planes have become dependent on money sources with an interest in a particular policy outcome. The dependency has produced, in the words of Joseph A. Califano Jr., a cabinet official in the Carter Administration, 'the best government private money can buy'. At the very least, there is an appearance of possible impropriety and an erosion of confidence in the probity of the system.

In some instances, PAC money has been a means of priming the pump of Federal grants. The government's programme for providing housing to the poor was distorted by what came to be known sardonically as the 'cycle of poverty': PACs representing builders donated money to congressmen, who appropriated funds for the Department of Housing and Urban Development, which in turn distributed to the builders subsidies for low-income flats. Ensuring that the loop was closed, the 'poverticians' who benefited from the cycle hired a former cabinet secretary to lobby the department.

Adding to the potential for distortion of the political system is the fact that PACs contribute to a growing trend of financing elections from sources other than constituents. More than half the Senators seeking re-election in 1990 were receiving the bulk of their financing from outside their home states; some got more than 95 percent from outside sources, based in Washington and elsewhere. This 'nationalization' of Senate campaigns could undermine local self-determination: the selection of representatives to the capital would be heavily influenced by the capital itself and its constellation of lobbies. Some complain that funding from outside the state amounts to a violation of the one-man, one-vote principle: non-residents cast 'proxy ballots' in the form of contributions, diluting the impact of each vote cast by a resident.

Various reforms for PAC excess have been proposed. Generally, the proposals focus upon providing at least partial public funding for congressional campaigns, on the model of presidential campaigns. In return, limits would be imposed on spending and on contributions that may be received. There have also been proposals to limit the amounts of money that could be raised from outside the constituency. But there are strong partisan divisions, for both reasons of principle and self-interest. Republican opponents of public financing profess a principled objection to taxpayers' supporting candidates whose views they may abhor. The Republicans also have a practical reason to reject spending limits: their only hope of unseating the Democratic majority may be for the lesser-known Republican challengers to outspend incumbents. Democrats, on the other hand, tend to worry about curbing the 'free speech' of contributors. The Democrats also are quite content with unlimited PAC contributions because they flow mainly to the incumbent majority.

The sheer multiplicity and variety of PACs may cause them to balance each other's influence somewhat. In any event, the requirement that PACs report their outlays to the Federal government means that the money is at least given openly, so that a legislator's performance can be judged against his income sources.

The pervasiveness of big money undermines the argument that lobbying is nothing more than a healthy manifestation of interest group competition, an integral part of America's pluralist democracy. Even without the influence of money, though, it is doubtful whether all are equal in the clash of interests. Some lobbies have been lucky or crafty enough to become recognized as the mouthpieces through which *vox populi* speaks. The forestry subcommittee of the House Interior Committee for many years was wont to consult only the envoys of the lumber companies whenever it needed to discover what 'the public' thought about proposed dispositions for the national forests. By the 1970s, however, many of the unorganized and voiceless interests began to recognize the benefits of concerted lobbying. Today the forestry subcommittee's consciousness of the relevant public has been expanded to include the Sierra Club and other environmental conservation groups. A partial solution has also been found for the funding problem that had always hampered nonbusiness lobbies. The example was set by Common Cause, a 'public interest lobby' supported by thousands of small individual subscriptions.

For the lobbyists, blocking a bill is easier than getting one passed, because many bills die of sheer exhaustion along the tortuous route to enactment. A bill may begin life in either house, heralded by some public agitation and supported by a galaxy of lobbies and executive agencies. It may be introduced with the President's blessing or against his will. The bill is first referred to the appropriate committee. Since the jurisdictional boundaries of the committees tend to overlap, a dispute may erupt among several committees claiming the same bill. Sometimes these disputes are resolved by simply ignoring the bill. Several thousand bills go to committee in each session of Congress, but only a fraction of them ever return. Most are consigned to limbo, a procedure known as 'pigeon-holing'. The committee will select a few bills that it wishes to consider and hold public hearings. More often than not, the informative value of these hearings is slight; they are stage-managed to mould public support for the views already held by the committee.

The committee then meets in a 'mark-up' session to put the bill into final form. Here, in an atmosphere of intense bargaining, the members try to reach a compromise among themselves. If the bill can be reported out unanimously, its chances of passage are greatly improved. The version finally reported by the committee may bear little or no resemblance to the bill originally introduced.

The next hurdle is to move the bill onto the floor. Since the calendar is crowded, time for debate is at a premium. A bill which is 'called up' early stands a better chance than one scheduled later, because the chamber may fail to complete its agenda before the Congress expires. (The life span of a Congress is two years.) All unconsidered bills remaining must retrace their steps in the next Congress. Control of the House calendar is in the hands of the Rules Committee and, to some extent, the speaker. In the Senate, the majority leader determines the order of debate.

The floor debate is rarely a model of parliamentary give-and-take. The members' speeches often fall on empty seats, and few minds are ever changed by the outpouring of rhetoric. Most of the words printed in each day's *Congressional Record* were never even uttered on the floor. Since congressmen speak primarily 'for the folks back home', they considerately place their orations into the record without asking their colleagues to listen to them.

Probably the chief purpose served by the debate is establishing a legislative history so that the courts can better understand the intent underlying an enactment—a customary aid to interpreting statutes. On occasion a congressman may deliberately salt the historical record with his own highly-flavoured interpretation. During the debate on the Civil Rights Act of 1991, a member of the House, announcing that he 'would like to add some legislative history at the end of my remarks', appended a 9,000-word personal appreciation of the measure's evolution.

Debate is by no means all posturing. Significant amendments, either strengthening or weakening the bill, may be voted, perhaps as part of a 'horse-trading' strategy by sponsors seeking to assure passage. Many odd bargains are struck, involving seemingly unrelated items of legislative business. During the session that considered the civil rights bill, support for a crop pricing scheme was swapped for votes on censorship of publicly supported arts, a transaction that became known as the 'porn for corn' deal. Amid such a frenzy of bartering, the notion of legislative intent becomes somewhat abstruse.

The first question a congressman must ask himself about any bill is whether to vote at all. Absenteeism may be the better part of valour if the legislator is caught between his personal opinions and his constituents' demands. He can also escape the dilemma by means of a voice vote, in which ayes and nos are shouted in unison. But any member may demand a roll-call, in which individual votes are recorded.

Since a bill moves through the Senate and the House independently, it can fail in either place. If it is passed by both chambers, the two versions may be quite divergent. Although the constitution neglected to provide for such discrepancies, an institution known as the 'conference committee' has evolved for the purpose of reconciling bills. The speaker of the House and the Senate majority leader each appoint a team of 'managers' to the conference committee, which may meet in closed session. Often the only way for the committee to resolve the differences is to draft an entirely new bill. The bill reported back to both houses by the committee is normally accepted in a floor vote without further ado because of the pressure to get some kind of bill passed. The final version, approved by the House and Senate, is sent to the President, who has three options open to him. He can sign it into law, he can veto it, or he can allow it to go into law unsigned by merely leaving it on his desk for ten days. Although a veto may be overriden by a two-thirds vote of each house, that level of support is not easily obtained.

Given this complicated process, it may be hard to imagine how any laws are enacted. A bill may succumb at the committee stage, on the floor, in conference committee, or in the White House. Those that succeed may be so disfigured by compromise that their original sponsors oppose the final version. Yet compromise is the *modus operandi* of the Congress; most congressmen believe that some kind of bill, however deficient, is better than no bill at all. This half-a-loaf philosophy does not always produce legislation that is effective or coherent or even internally consistent. It sacrifices principle on the altar of consensus. But at least the framers of the constitution must be congratulated on having fashioned a system which avoided their chief bugaboo, the spectre of one faction taking control and running amok.

Although much elaborated by their heirs, the built-in negative bias of the legislative process was part of the framers' scheme for inhibiting legislative activism. The simple fact that Congress was divided into two chambers and assigned differing bases of representation laid the groundwork for stalemate. The House was to be the popularly elected chamber and presumably the most radical and headstrong. The Senate was to be almost an international council, each state's two ambassadors sitting on terms of sovereign equality with those of the others. Events have modified this grand design. Despite the Supreme Court's ruling in 1964 that each congressman must represent the same number of constituents, making the House even more egalitarian, it tends to be less likely than the Senate to disturb the *status quo*. The representatives are so intent on furthering the particularistic interests of their localities that they hardly have the time or inclination to forge broad national policy initiatives. Rather than acting the part of statesman, the representative is expected to 'do something' for the relatively small district (about 570,000 persons) that elected him. Often the district has a single, dominant economic interest, such as wheat farming or steel manufacturing. A representative may measure his success by the amount of government money in the form of defence contracts, public works and the like, that he can funnel home.

The Senate has not been affected by the reapportionment ruling because the constitution prohibits denying any state equal franchise in the Senate without its permission, a provision which is not subject to amendment. The only major alteration in the Senate has been the Seventeenth Amendment (1913), which provided for the election of Senators rather than appointment by the state legislatures. Wyoming's half a million citizens thus enjoy equal representation with California's 30 million. Of the 100 senators, 52 are elected by a mere 15 per cent of the nation's population. In spite of its undemocratic composition, however, the Senate tends to be rather more liberal than the House, partly because senators cannot help but be more sensitive to urban interests. Many members of the House represent totally rural districts, but every senator has at least one city in his state. The mixture of economic, social and ethnic interests in statewide constituencies spares the Senate from the particularism that pervades the House.

Reinforcing the senators' relatively broad outlook is the status of their chamber as the breeding ground of presidential hopefuls. Presidents Truman, Kennedy, Johnson and Nixon were all elevated from the Senate, and presidential candidates Humphrey, Jackson, Mondale, McGovern, McCarthy, Glenn, and Robert and Edward Kennedy, to name a few, ran while they were senators. At any given moment a number of senators harbour ambitions for the White House and seek a national constituency, carefully trying to avoid being stigmatized as a parochial 'corn belt' politician or a 'one-issue' candidate.

The senators have frequent opportunities, in fact, to act as a kind of presidential peer group, sharing with the chief executive several important constitutional responsibilities. Although he is the nation's spokesman in foreign affairs, the President can conclude treaties only with their advice and consent. This prerogative affords senators a strong voice in foreign policy decisions. Moreover, almost all presidential appointees, including cabinet officers and Supreme Court justices, must be confirmed by the Senate. A prudent President consults the senators in advance about their preferences. The custom of 'senatorial courtesy' encourages clearing the nomination of federal judges and prosecuting attorneys with the senators of the states where they are to serve, assuming that the President and the senators are of the same party. In practice, that often means that these senators are able to 'suggest' a nominee to the President.

Liberated by its heterogeneous constituencies and its quasi-presidential outlook, the Senate also tends to be less burdened by the weight of seniority and autocratic committee chairmen. Influence in the Senate is more personal, more a reflection of the respect earned from one's colleagues than the result of seniority. It could hardly be otherwise among such an elite band of seasoned politicians, many of whom have served for years as congressmen or governors of states. The system, prevailing in the House, whereby a representative accumulates power in proportion to his length of tenure, ill suits a legislative body whose 'freshmen' may already be political veterans or national celebrities such as astronauts. Even the relatively swift upward mobility of the Senate is too slow for some; a senator once remarked disgustedly that he would not seek a second term because 'by the time you get any power around here, you're ready to kick the bucket'.

The real power in the upper chamber, often referred to as the Gentlemen's Club, lies in an inner circle whose membership is informal and fluid; observers disagree on just who are the members of the circle at any moment. Generally speaking, the most influential senators will be those known as 'work horses' and 'inside men', as distinguished from the 'show horses' and 'outside men'. The former diligently tend the legislative vineyards, caring for mundane Senate business, while the latter are out campaigning for President. As in any organization, those who are present most of the time and devoting their full energies become more influential than part-time or absentee members.

Like any club, the Senate has certain rules of procedure but not enough to make life tedious. While the 435 members of the House must adhere closely to a bulky rule book and a strict time limit for speaking, the 100 senators can afford a relatively relaxed procedure and unlimited debate. That has given rise to a peculiar parliamentary tactic, the 'filibuster', in which a minority opposed to a bill refuses to stop talking until the measure is withdrawn. If the bill's sponsors cannot obtain a two-thirds majority on the motion for 'cloture', they often have to drop their bill in order to allow the rest of the agenda to be considered. A filibuster is particularly effective when the Senate is under pressure to deal with a backlog of bills.

A time-honoured senatorial custom, filibustering has produced some colourful moments. Senator Huey Long of Louisiana, a legendary figure in American politics, spoke for $15^{1}/2$ hours in 1935, punctuating his remarks with recipes for cooking chicken gumbo and other southern delicacies. In 1953, Senator Wayne Morse of Oregon set the record for a one-man filibuster: 22 hours and 26 minutes, part of which he spent reading names from a telephone directory. Stamina, rather than relevance, is the key to a successful filibuster.

Normally a group of senators will filibuster, yielding the floor to each other in turn. Opponents may try to stop them from 'talking a bill to death' by seizing upon some parliamentary misstep to take the floor away or by forcing the Senate into continuous session, both sides sleeping on cots in the hallways to be ready for a sudden vote. Usually, however, a cloture motion is necessary, and that has succeeded only about two dozen times since 1917.

Although it seems like a quaint ritual, the filibuster was a powerful tool in the hands of southern senators, who were able to obstruct civil rights legislation for many years. Two major civil rights bills, the 1964 act prohibiting racial discrimination in places of public accommodation and the 1968 act outlawing discrimination in housing sales, were passed only after southern filibusters were narrowly beaten. In earlier attempts, the southerners were able to muster more than one third of the Senate to vote against cloture because some senators, although unsympathetic to the southern cause, were nevertheless devoted to the principle of unrestricted debate.

Senators from small-population states argue that the right to filibuster makes their voice more important in the legislative process, helping to balance the influence of large states in the House. Even liberals at times have deigned to take advantage of unlimited debate to try to thwart legislation they opposed. The filibuster, in short, amounts to a *liberum veto*, a potential veto possessed by every member of the Senate, and none is eager to divest himself of it.

Nevertheless, the Senate did modify its rules in 1975 to reduce the required cloture majority from two thirds to three fifths, which makes it somewhat easier to halt a filibuster. The modification reflected growing appreciation of the wisdom of Senator Henry Cabot Lodge the Elder's remark that 'to vote without debating is perilous, but to debate and never vote is imbecile'.

Archaic and dilatory customs such as the filibuster contribute to the sluggish performance that has earned Congress its poor reputation. Also contributing is the perception that congressmen are pampered and venal. The perception is fostered by perks such as large staffs, reimbursed travel (often to exotic overseas locales) and franking privileges (the right to use the post without paying). The House was shamed into closing its members-only bank in 1991 after it was revealed that scores of representatives regularly wrote cheques that 'bounced'. With a nod to Watergate, an executive branch scandal, this legislative embarrassment was dubbed Rubbergate. A poll taken by the *New York Times* found that 83 per cent of the electorate viewed the escapade not as a series of errors but as a deliberate attempt to take advantage of privileged status.

Public support for Congress is further sapped by a trend toward non-competitive elections for seats. The trend is well illustrated by the 1990 Congressional election. Of the 405 members of the House who chose to stand again, a mere handful—15 Representatives—lost their seats. On the Senate side, too, incumbents were virtually impervious: only one was not returned. Defeat of an incumbent, in short, has become a freak occurrence.

Incumbency appears to be an intensely personal asset. Voters indulge their own representatives, even while disparaging the chamber in which they sit. Incumbent candidates are insulated from nationwide electoral swings away from their party—one reason why Democrats always outnumbered Republicans in the House of Representatives between 1964 and 1992 despite losing all but one Presidential election in that period. (When a representative retires voluntarily, his party's candidate for the open seat tends to attract about 10 per cent fewer votes than the incumbent did.) Incumbent invulnerability leads to what has been ruefully called the 'permanent Congress'.

The natural advantages of incumbency—high name-recognition and a record in office—are buttressed by a disparity in income from contributions and consequently in spending power. The congressional election results closely parallel the distribution of campaign wealth: incumbent Senators spent as a group $134 million on their 1990 re-election campaigns, while the challengers could afford only $38 million.

The disproportionate outlay by the incumbents amounts to massive overkill, for their unshakeable grip on office seems to be accepted fatalistically by the electorate. When there is no presidential election to stimulate interest, relatively few bother to vote. Only 36 per cent of the eligible population trekked to the polls in 1990. The assumption that the incumbent will win is plainly a powerful incentive to stay home on election day. Low turnover among office-holders thus goes hand in hand with low turnout by voters, producing a vicious cycle of cynicism and apathy.

The difficulty of unseating an incumbent by electoral means may explain the seeming preoccupation with sexual and financial peccadillos. Scandals have, to some extent, replaced elections as a means of securing rotation of legislators. Exposure of moral or ethical lapses, preferably leading to an incumbent's resignation or withdrawal from a re-election campaign, is often the challenger's main hope. Seizing upon personal foibles for partisan advantage has been called the 'politics of rectitude' and, in its most extreme form, 'ethical McCarthyism'. The 1980s were rife with accusations of dalliance and peculation, bringing down officials as powerful as a Speaker of the House.

'Character' has indeed become an important test of fitness for office. Officials and candidates may fall victim to a brand of moralizing that repudiates any distinction between private virtue and public performance. Politicians also may be held unfairly to a stricter code of sexual conduct than is widely heeded. On the other hand, exposure of personal indiscretions might be justified as a demonstration that a politician's private life is hypocritically at variance with his pious pronouncements. Here, the character trait at issue is sincerity.

In the 1980s, a revival of fundamentalist religion, rooted in traditional American Puritanism, melded with feminist militancy to heighten disdain for philandering, marital infidelity and flagrant insobriety, even when unconnected with official duties. Unfortunately for him, John Tower, the Bush nominee for Secretary of Defense, had developed a reputation for each of these faults when he was a senator from Texas; that reputation contributed to his being denied the cabinet post, despite taking an extraordinary pledge to remain abstinent (from alcohol) while in office. Ostentatious confession of sin nevertheless may bring forgiveness. Senator Edward Kennedy, scion of a dynasty dogged by sexual innuendo, sought to dispel a shadow over his 1992 re-election campaign by admitting publicly to unspecified 'shortcomings' in his personal life and promising to improve. Revealing an opponent's flaws may prove ineffective, moreover, if the revelation fails to result in criminal conviction or at least indictment. Members of Congress often manage to convince their constituents that lack of a criminal record is sufficient evidence of worthiness for office.

Another chink in Congress's public facade is the under-representation of women and minority groups. Although a Black Caucus and a Woman's Caucus have been formed in the House, their numbers remain comparatively small when measured against the national demographic profile. For long periods there have been no black senators, and there has never been more than two women in the Senate at the same time. That neither chamber is representative of the population at large becomes a particularly sensitive matter in an age of acute race and gender consciousness. When dealing with such issues, a bastion of white males often seems to be out of touch and lacking in credibility. The bastion may be falling, however; the number of women running for Senate and House seats has been on the rise.

Taken together, the absence of rigorous electoral competition, the palpable influence of money, the perception of ethical laxity and the lack of ethnic/gender diversity has provoked a congressional version of the anti-incumbency movement that has targeted state legislatures. Some of its goals are relatively minor reforms, such as the 'reverse frank'—free postage for letters to members of Congress, as well as from them. Other proposals are more sweeping. The most far-reaching is limiting the number of terms that can be served in Congress as means of ejecting entrenched legislators and promoting a regular turnover in office.

In the State of Washington, reformers sought by referendum in 1991 to limit their members in the US House of Representatives to three two-year terms and their Senators to two six-year terms. The measure, which would have applied retroactively to those already in office, was defeated, probably because it would have ousted yet another Speaker of the House, whose home state was Washington. But the term limit concept seems to have emerged as a durable political movement in a number of states. It is likely that an amendment to the US constitution, rather than a state referendum, would be essential to limit the number of congressional terms, unless the argument were accepted that the constitution merely establishes the length of the term while each state is free to 'instruct' its representatives to retire after a certain number of terms. It is always possible, of course, that candidates will voluntarily pledge to remain only for a few terms as an electoral strategy, and incumbents might be pressured into taking the same vow to meet the political competition.

President Bush and many other Republicans support a constitutional amendment on limits, which would help them undermine the Democratic hegemony in Congress by forcing many incumbents with safe seats to retire. (Oddly enough, some Republicans backed repeal of the constitutional limit on presidential terms—to permit Ronald Reagan to run for a third term.) The legislative term limit could well be an example of a supposedly timeless principle whose real attraction is short-term partisan advantage.

Many see congressional term limits as misguided effort—for the same reasons that term limits have been opposed for state-level officeholders. Replacing out-of-touch permanent congressmen with a steady stream of able amateurs is an inspiring vision, but the halcyon days when the citizen-farmer returned to the plough after a brief spell at the helm of state are long gone. Few talented people may be willing to interrupt a promising career in the private sector for a public office with no long-range prospects. Forcing members of Congress to retire just when they are beginning to learn the ways of Washington, in addition, may well increase the power of the executive branch, the fraternity of lobbyists, and the permanent congressional staff—about 19,000 persons who already play an influential role in drafting legislation.

Term limits could well bring about profound changes. They would doom the seniority system, under which power accumulates with longevity. More disciplined legislative parties might result from the absence of long-serving members of the House and Senate—those most likely to form independent power centres and personality cults. The propensity for divided government might decrease as well, because the party that carries the presidency would be more likely to sweep the congressional elections too if there were no veteran incumbents to stand, Gibraltar-like, against the national tide. Whether these changes would improve public confidence in the ability of Congress to cope with the issues of the day remains to be seen.

CHAPTER SIX

The Supreme Court:
Judicial Politics

Immediately after the 1970 congressional elections, *The Times* of London noted that proposals to lower the voting age were rejected by the voters in ten of the fifteen states where these proposals had been put to a referendum: 'The issue will be decided this term by the Supreme Court, which will almost certainly take the result of the state elections into account,' the report continued. To readers this may have appeared to be sociological jurisprudence carried to a ludicrous extreme or some primitive system of adjudication by popular acclamation. Of course, when the constitutionality of the federal statute fixing the voting age at eighteen was challenged in the court, the petitioners were not obliged to cite the election statistics in their brief, but the saying that the justices 'follow the election returns' is a maxim of American politics on which constitutional lawyers rely. What the maxim implies—something that foreign observers may misunderstand—is that the United States Supreme Court is not just a court, at least not in the usual sense of the word. To describe it merely as a court is to ignore the most important implications of its work, for it is very much a part of the political process.

The British jurist Lord Devlin has said that the English judicial mind 'hates politics'. But in the mind of the American Supreme Court justice, it is a daily consideration. The business of the court is often described as 'judicial politics', and political scientists pore over its opinions as intently as lawyers. By constitutional pronouncements the court resolves many important issues of policy and brings others into public prominence. In recent decades, for example, the court has engendered such political *causes célèbres* as racial integration of schools, reapportionment of the legislatures, abolition of capital punishment and legalization of abortion. The court, in fact, is expected to respond to broad changes in public opinion with new constitutional doctrines. That is why the justices are presumed to be analysing the voting results. That is also why the court, which was responsible for a reformation of the law, beginning in the early 1950s, is being watched for signs of retreat. From 1953 to 1969, when the court was led by Chief Justice Earl Warren, it used constitutional interpretation as a creative instrument for realizing American ideals of equality before the law. Although Americans of all races were theoretically equal, until the Warren Court blacks were excluded by law from schools attended by whites. Although rich and poor had a right to an attorney while in police custody, the right in practice was seldom exercised by the poor, often because they lacked knowledge of their rights. Urban and rural voters were theoretically equal, but a system of rotten boroughs ensured that the countryside enjoyed a disproportionate voice in the lawmaking bodies. In each of these spheres of life, the Warren Court saw to it that constitutional theory and reality became congruent.

The court's decisions evince a conviction that the constitution commands whatever concrete steps are necessary to give practical effect to abstract rights. Consider, for example, the court's ruling in *Miranda v. Arizona* (1966) that suspects had to be informed of their right to remain silent and to have a lawyer present during police interrogation. It sprang from a belief that routine reliance on confessions extracted from suspects in custody who were ignorant of their rights made a mockery of the Fifth Amendment's guarantee against involuntary self-incrimination. The chief justice warned sternly in *Miranda* against any attempt to have the 'accused threatened, tricked or cajoled into a waiver' of his rights.

As might be imagined, the Warren Court triggered a backlash, in part because many of the beneficiaries of its rulings were from a despised or disdained social underclass. The decisions often raised fears about crime or about racial minorities, and sometimes the two emotions were commingled. The court's opponents charged that it distorted the intentions of the framers of the constitution, depriving the police of valuable crime-fighting weapons and tipping the balance too far in favour of suspects. The justices were accused of being high-handed 'judicial legislators', rather than mere interpreters, who distorted the true meaning of the constitution to reach liberal goals and harboured an elitist disdain for the views of the majority. The backlash was in full flower as early as the 1968 presidential campaign. Richard Nixon, the Republican candidate, and George Wallace, then a segregationist third-party candidate, struck a responsive chord in the public by attacking the court's liberalism, purported disrespect for 'law and order', and undue solicitude for the rights of accused criminals.

The justices could take comfort, however, from the failure of Congress to exercise its constitutional authority to restrict the court's jurisdiction. Indeed, the Senate thought so highly of the court in the Nixon years that it incurred the extreme displeasure of the President by rejecting two of his nominees for the bench, one because he was thought to be 'mediocre'. Even the severest critics seemed ambivalent, anxious to withdraw power from the court with one hand and confer it with the other. Governor Wallace, a staunch opponent of what he considered judicial interference with state prerogatives, nevertheless did not hesitate to petition the court to override the officials of one state when they refused to list him on the 1968 presidential ballot.

Such ambivalence points to the court's fundamental weakness as an institution of government: the court suffers from a permanent crisis of identity that exposes it to periodic attacks on its authority by those who happen to disagree with its judgements. Popular disfavour has characterized much of the court's history. Accusing the Warren court of coddling criminals, atheists and abortionists, conservative critics resembled the liberals of the 1930s, criticizing the 'Nine Old Men' who, with dismaying regularity, held unconstitutional the economic reform legislation of President Franklin D. Roosevelt's New Deal. The ideology of the critics had changed but not their method of attack. They invariably accused the court of having overreached itself, of having exceeded its constitutional powers. There are many who disagree with the policies of the President or of Congress, but they do not nearly as often question the authority of those branches of government to act as they have. The accusation against the court is difficult to answer, because its Achilles' heel is that its constitutional authority is imperfectly defined and largely self-proclaimed.

One of America's distinctive contributions to the science of government was the addition of a third and co-equal branch, the judiciary, to the executive-legislative division of governmental powers. But it has never been entirely clear what role the framers of the constitution intended for their innovation. Article III of the constitution simply gives the court appellate jurisdiction to hear 'all cases in law and equity' arising under the constitution, laws and treaties of the United States—with such exceptions as Congress might wish to make. The article also provides for 'such inferior Courts as the Congress may from time to time ordain and establish'. The remainder of the federal court system was created by the Judiciary Act of 1789 and has been maintained ever since. However, Congress may, whenever it wishes, abolish every federal court except the Supreme Court, subject to the possible exception that it cannot use that power to deprive persons of their constitutional rights. Today there are about one hundred district courts, at least one in each state, and thirteen courts of appeal, each having jurisdiction over a group of states. The Supreme Court hears cases on appeal from these courts and from the highest courts of the fifty state judicial systems.

The Federalist, arguing for ratification of the proposed constitution, assured citizens in 1788 that the judiciary would be the 'least dangerous' branch of the government because it had neither 'force nor will' but could only decide cases at law that were brought before it. The authors of those predictions may or may not have been surprised by Chief Justice Marshall's declaration in 1803 that the court had the power to declare acts of Congress unconstitutional. Whether the constitutional convention intended or expected the court to assume the power of judicial review of legislation is still a matter of dispute, since the question was never discussed by the delegates. Because of the historical ambiguity of its mission, the court has been left to carve its own sphere of influence by proclamations such as Marshall's. While often acting as arbiter between Congress and the President, between the states and the federal government, the court has had no one but itself to prescribe its mission. The result, inevitably, has been an appearance of arbitrariness in the court's actions.

That appearance has heightened the natural suspicions aroused by a court of permanent appointees in a government otherwise composed of temporary officials in the upper echelons. Justices are nominated by the President, confirmed by a majority vote of the Senate and serve ' ... during good Behaviour', which means for life unless impeached by Congress. Often viewed as an anomalous institution in a democracy, the court is peculiarly vulnerable to recrimination for having thwarted the will of the majority. That was the accusation when the conservative court was laying waste the New Deal reform programme, and that was also the accusation in later decades, when the Warren court was decreeing change while the legislatures and executive officials, both state and federal, admonished it for going too far too fast.

A rigidly conservative court might have been anticipated originally, because lawyers are assumed by nature and training to be conservative. That usually prescient observer, de Tocqueville, predicted early in the nineteenth century that the legal profession and the judiciary would prove to be the only pillar of stability in the American democracy. The spectacle of a progressive judiciary, initiating change in the face of opposition by a conservative legislature, would not have escaped the sense of irony of the Frenchman nor of the founding fathers, whose fears of the unbridled popular will drove them to erect an elaborate system of 'checks and balances' primarily against legislative excesses.

Because unforeseen, the liberal activist court had not been explicitly limited by the constitution. A conservative court can be counter-balanced by a progressive legislature; statutes declared unconstitutional can be redrawn and may eventually survive through modest alteration. But when the court is initiating changes in the schools, in housing patterns and in legislatures themselves, there are remarkably few means of checking and balancing. The President cannot veto a court decision interpreting the constitution, and Congress cannot nullify it by statute. Apart from restricting the court's jurisdiction, a clumsy recourse, virtually the only method of reversing such a decision is the difficult process of formally amending the constitution. Winning the approval of a two-thirds majority of both Houses of Congress and then of the legislatures of three quarters of the states is a feat that is out of the question in all but the rarest moments of political consensus.

Thus it was possible for the Warren court as social and political reformer to range freely, rewriting the law of the land.

In the process, the court did much to bring about social and political equality. It proved eagerly responsive to what Justice Oliver Wendell Holmes termed 'the felt necessities of the time', promulgating by judicial fiat racial equality in schools and in housing, equality of representation in the legislatures, and equality of the poor before the law. But the court also drew attention to its precarious position: no branch of the government has less moral authority to be the prime mover of social change than a body of nine Platonic Guardians, insulated by lifetime tenure against the direct pressure of the electorate.

The consequences of emphasizing that contradiction eventually manifest themselves, for to declare the law is one thing, to enforce it quite another. Whether, for example, the court's prohibitions against discrimination do indeed transform the life of racial minorities in America largely depends on the willingness of citizens and the other organs of government to implement the judgements. Having no enforcement mechanism, the court's power is the power of public opinion. As Justice Felix Frankfurter observed: 'The Court's authority—possessed neither of the purse nor the sword—ultimately rests on sustained public confidence in its moral sanction.'

The obvious popular defence against an unpopular decision is simply to ignore it. The practical result of the famous 1954 school desegregation decision, *Brown v. Board of Education*, demonstrated that the reservoir of public deference to the court is not inexhaustible. More than twenty years after *Brown*, half of the black students in the south still attended schools that were predominantly black, because implementation was left to recalcitrant local school authorities supported by community sentiment. Securing compliance was difficult enough when the court was dealing only with segregation mandated by the laws of the southern states. A vestige of the south's 'peculiar institution' of slavery, segregation was wrought by state law and presumably could therefore be abolished by legal processes. But when the court began to require integration of northern schools, it was dealing with segregation sustained not by laws but by patterns of residential settlement. The product of bigotry among whites, these patterns amounted to demographic facts not easily erased by judicial decision. Ordering pupils bussed to schools outside their neighbourhoods has been the judiciary's primary method of forcing integration, but bussing has often provoked intense popular opposition and violent resistance.

Apart from creating practical problems of enforcement when it undertakes to satisfy what it believes are 'felt necessities', the court often appears to be disregarding the separation of powers doctrine, which confers equal status on the legislative, executive and judicial branches of the federal government. When, in 1968, the court banned discrimination in house sales (*Jones v. Mayer*), it ignored the delicate compromises in the housing section of the Civil Rights Act of 1968, which had been passed by Congress a few weeks earlier. Although the act exempted certain types of dwellings, the judicial decision applied to the sale or rental of every dwelling in the country. The opinion of the court, to be sure, was more satisfying logically than the act. Yet the passage of an 'open-housing' statute had been considered a monumental political achievement. The court might have recognized that, deferred to Congress and achieved almost the same result. One justification advanced for the court's 'legislating' expansively is that there frequently occurs what has been called a 'deadlock of democracy'. For example, southerners, by virtue of seniority, may have been occupying all the crucial congressional committee chairmanships and obstructing passage of civil rights legislation. But even assuming this to be a pathological political condition calling for judicial remedy, the emergence of the Civil Rights Act of 1968 indicated that the legislative processes were in fact working well.

Many critics, including dissenters on the court, have warned that the only barrier to the court's infringement of legislative prerogative is the justice's self-restraint. Whenever possible, they argue, an appointive court ought to defer to the judgement of a popularly elected legislature. But whether one is a proponent of 'judicial restraint' or 'judicial activism' usually turns upon whether one agrees with the court's current decisions. Formulating a rule of restraint that would satisfy both liberals and conservatives is difficult because the court often must choose among competing public policy preferences. The choice merely masquerades as a case in constitutional law. As de Tocqueville noted, Americans are quick to reduce to legal questions differences of opinion about what the government should do. The problem, for example, of how to draw constituency boundaries for state legislatures may be reduced to a Fourteenth Amendment question of 'equal protection of the laws', but it also is a matter of policy that traditionally has exercised the political parties of the states.

By invoking the doctrine of 'political questions', the court for a long time avoided proffered opportunities to try to settle disputes over policy. Certain issues were considered not amenable to judicial resolution and were relegated to the political process, on the ground that the court might make a decision, but could not easily provide a remedy. Justice Frankfurter, a political liberal, alluded to that difficulty when he cautioned his colleagues against holding that inequality of population among constituencies was a justiciable issue. Courts, he said, 'ought not to enter this political thicket'. The thicket he foresaw has become apparent to the many district court judges who have had to supervise the drawing of boundaries, or actually draw the lines themselves, ever since the court, in 1964, held that congressional (*Wesberry v. Sanders*) and state legislative (*Reynolds v. Sims*) constituencies must be equal in population. The judges have had to make the choices that had been so bitterly contested by the politicians.

The Supreme Court itself was soon visited with the consequences of its reapportionment rulings. In subsequent cases it was called upon to decide whether the difference of a few percentage points in the population of constituencies, not a gross disparity, was constitutionally permissible. The phrase 'equal protection of the laws' afforded little guidance, but the court did not hesitate to hold that constituencies must be as near to mathematical equality as is humanly possible. Despite the fundamentalist tone of the decision it was, after all, an exercise of discretion that was difficult to disguise as a clear constitutional constraint.

Whatever the difficulties involved in abandoning the 'political questions' doctrine, it must be said that only the court could have rectified an injustice like disproportional representation; left to the political process, it may never have been corrected. Here is a genuine 'deadlock of democracy'. Legislators from over-represented districts understandably resist voting themselves out of office by creating constituencies that are equal in population, and often those legislators have an unjustified stranglehold over the legislatures. If the rights of the under-represented—in this case, the majority of voters—were ever to be vindicated, they had to be vindicated at the bar of the court. It was left to the 'undemocratic' court to make America more democratic.

The reapportionment cases were only the latest example of the Supreme Court's historic role as a court of last resort for citizens shunned by the popularly elected institutions of government. Ignored by Congress and the state legislatures since the 1870s, blacks waged a campaign of litigation before the court in this century that succeeded in striking down numerous racial restrictions and culminated in the school and housing decisions of the modern era. Defendants in criminal cases, who are not likely to be regarded by an elected official as a significant pressure group, have had their chances of fair treatment vastly improved by the court while the legislators were denouncing rising crime rates.

That blacks were disenfranchised in many states and that defendants in criminal cases formed no discernible voting bloc did not deter critics from excoriating the court as a usurper of congressional and state legislative prerogatives. When criticism of its decisions, however unjustified, becomes as intense as it has been in these instances, a court must gauge carefully how much further it may go without endangering its ability to command public acceptance. A former United States solicitor general, Archibald Cox, has posed the court's dilemma in this way: 'The question is, how much and how fast can a court pursue what it sees as the goals of society without impairing the long run usefulness of judge-made law in contributing to their achievement?' Since the court's effectiveness depends on popular recognition of its words as authoritative, reformist justices may have to strike a balance between advancing social ideals and conserving judicial prestige. It is tempting, no doubt, for the court to opt for social justice; the gains are immediate and obvious. The losses to the court in the erosion of its authority are hidden until the accumulation of 'self-inflicted wounds' leaves the court critically weakened—and vulnerable to a counter-reformation.

Why the American people believe that 'the constitution is what the judges say it is', not what the legislators say it is, remains an enigma. But at least part of the answer is the obviously great popular reverence of the 'higher law' embodied in the written constitution, which is regarded as immutable, above mere politics, and revealed by judicial hierophants. The justices have been accorded the position of keepers of the constitutional mysteries because they too are believed to be above politics in the way that a legislature, subject to regular elections, never can be. It has been aptly remarked, however, that the court has been adopting a 'legislative mode' of conducting its business. Even that notorious legislative phenomenon, the preadjournment rush, has migrated to the court: judgement in many of the most sensitive cases is postponed until the approaching end of term in June increases the pressure for compromise. The numerous *amicus curiae* (friends of the court) briefs, which offer no novel legal arguments but do emphasize the large membership of the associations submitting them, have become a form of lobbying.

The most significant similarity, however, between the court and the legislature is that the justices often treat their previous decisions as cavalierly as the legislators do theirs. Depreciating *stare decisis*, the rule that legal precedents must be followed, can be especially dangerous for the court, making it seem politically expedient as well as confounding the popular notion of the immutability of the 'higher law'. Too sudden fluctuations of doctrine call into question the justices' subordination of mere personal preference to the supposedly timeless principles of the constitution, especially when doctrines only recently reaffirmed are overruled without decent mention by a 5-4 vote. Rather than seize the first opportunity to overrule a well-established precedent, the court might better bide its time until it had the authority of unanimity on the bench. However, that cannot be an inflexible rule. The *Brown* decision was unanimous but had there been only a 5-4 majority, it still would not have been preferable to let school segregation laws survive for another few decades in order to conserve the institutional authority of the court. The difficulty with *stare decisis*, as has been said of some religious doctrines, is that it has never been practised, and anyone who begins practising it will be at a distinct disadvantage. The court paid little heed to *stare decisis* when it first approved of the segregationist 'separate but equal' doctrine in 1896, and it would have been unfair to demand of the justices who were considering *Brown* more respect for precedent than shown by the predecessors. Moreover, circumstances had changed radically since the late nineteenth century.

Whatever the merits of *stare decisis* as a legal principle, its political implications for the Warren court were conservative. To that extent, it conflicted with the burden that the court was called upon to assume: representing the unrepresented or under-represented. These—ethnic minorities, women, aliens, the poor—all sought changes. Although new personnel may be giving the bench a more conservative complexion, it will be difficult for the court to refuse entirely the sympathetic response that these petitioners have been led to expect.

As the champion of the dispossessed, the court is doomed to unpopularity, because for the most part it finds itself opposing the majority. But the role is appropriate for at least two reasons. First, the unrepresented are those whom other branches of government have ignored, intentionally or unintentionally. Secondly, the essence of the entrenched rights in the constitution is the notion that some things may not be denied to an individual or minority group, no matter how despised, even by majority vote; hence, the court, as chief interpreter of 'due process of law' and 'equal protection of the laws', will be acting simply as referee of democracy's rules of the game.

The first consideration recognizes the prudence of avoiding bitter clashes over what other branches regard as their special preserves. For example, the court accomplished little, apart from conjuring the spectre of an internecine confrontation with Congress, when it ruled the exclusion of a member of the House of Representatives by his colleagues unconstitutional in 1969. The issue was probably moot, since the legislative session had expired, and unlikely to arise again, yet the court handed down an opinion that antagonized congressmen by presuming to review their own rules of organization.

The emphasis upon due process may seem to presage a revival of the now disgraced doctrine of 'substantive due process'. What made the Nine Old Men of the 1930s obsolete was their rigid application of this doctrine to government regulation of private economic activity. They would frequently construe the substance of an act as 'unreasonable', hence as a denial of due process, even though there were no irregularities of procedure. It is unfortunate that association with the *ancien regime* has stigmatized the idea that the substance of law, its effect as well as its ostensible procedural fairness, is worthy of consideration. Political scientists, after all, long ago abandoned the study of formal rules and procedures of organizations because they found themselves looking at the trees rather than the forest, and minority groups have realized from painful experience that procedural equality does not necessarily mean substantial equality of results.

The constitution, to be sure, is more than a charter of individual liberties, and it may be objected that the court has other tasks. Many of the classic and recurrent controversies that occupied the court, however, have been largely settled. The balance of power in the federal system has been thrown permanently to the national government; the power of Congress to regulate the economic life of the country has been firmly established. Beyond refinements of accepted doctrines, relatively little remains to be done. There is, however, a great clamouring for individual and group remedies by those who have not been heard from before. To this issue, the court has a great deal to contribute, because it can determine the scope and meaning of 'due process' and 'equal protection' in the modern age. Given the alternatives, most nations would consider themselves fortunate if their social tensions and dissensions could be settled in court.

Whether the court sustains the progressive spirit of the Warren era or humbly defers to the more 'democratic' branches of government hinges upon the justices whom the President nominates. The custom of referring to a 'Roosevelt Court' or a 'Nixon Court' reflects the enormous, if indirect, presidential influence on constitutional doctrine. Although tenured for life, justices die or voluntarily retire often enough to enable Presidents to choose successors about every two years. On the average, a President serving both four-year terms could thus expect to nominate almost a majority of the court.

By gracefully accommodating the immutable to the inevitable, fresh appointees have allowed the court to survive changes in the national consensus. Franklin D. Roosevelt's appointment of prominent New Dealers to the court ensured the judicial acceptance of his policies and saved the court from an ignominious last stand that could only have been fatal to its power as an institution. Many a justice, however, has surprised a President by changing his views dramatically after joining the bench. While a conservative governor of California, Earl Warren gave little hint of becoming a liberal chief justice, and President Eisenhower ruefully concluded that appointing him was 'the biggest damfool mistake I ever made'. Probably, what emerges in new justices are opinions suppressed during either a political career of lipservice to parochial orthodoxies or a legal career whose professional arguments have been mistaken for personal views. More would be known about the judicial outlook of appointees were it not that remarkably few of them have been nationally prominent judges before. Even chief justices have been drawn mainly from outsiders rather than sitting members of the Supreme Court.

Apart from being a lawyer-politician whose views are palatable to the President, an important advantage for an aspiring justice is to be a member of his party. All things being equal, Presidents prefer to award the most prestigious of patronage plums to loyal followers of the party he leads.

Although the Supreme Court was not intended to be a repre-sentative body, the concept of the court as mirror of the nation politically, ethnically and geographically is well accepted. To modify a rallying cry of the American Revolution, there can be 'No adjudication without representation'. When a vacancy occurs, it may be referred to as the 'Jewish seat' or the 'Catholic seat', or a President may pledge, as Nixon did, to give the southern states a 'voice' on the court. The importance of an emerging political group may be signalled by the appointment of a symbolic justice. President Johnson nominated the first black justice (Thurgood Marshall) at the height of the civil rights movement of the 1960s, and President Reagan made a gesture towards the feminist sentiment of the 1980s by appointing the first woman (Sandra Day O'Connor) to the court. The eventual nomination of a Spanish-speaking American and a Native American may be safely anticipated. (A Spanish-speaking Native American would be the ideal candidate.)

The representative principle does contradict the juristic ideal of impartial decision by the rules of logic, but, as Holmes observed, the life of the law is experience, not logic. Uniquely among jurists, the Supreme Court justice is free to decide according to a sense of justice that is a product of his life experience. In the American context, that is a strength rather than a defect. It is a chief reason why, in the hands of the Supreme Court, the constitution has stayed a flexible, useful basis for political life, rather than the remote codification of outmoded ideas, imposing the dead hand of the past.

The very process by which the justices arrive at their collective decision emphasizes independence of mind rather than devotion to a neat abstraction called 'the law'. For decisions of the court are made by negotiation and compromise, not merely ratiocination. In practice, after oral arguments are heard in a number of cases, the justices meet in private conference to embark upon the tortuous path of decision. Speaking in order of reverse seniority on the bench, each justice explains his position. They debate the issues for a time, trying not so much to convert each other as to search out common ground. Unanimity is considered desirable, of course, but no attempt is made to pressure dissenting justices into standing shoulder to shoulder in a monolithic front. Writing dissenting opinions is an old and honoured tradition. The dissent is considered an appeal to future generations, who in many cases have indeed found more wisdom in the dissenting opinions than in the majority's words. Some, like Holmes, have been as influential through their memorable dissents as through their opinions for the court.

After the discussion in conference, a vote is taken. The chief justice has only one vote, but as 'first among equals' enjoys the customary privilege of appointing the justice who will compose the majority opinion. If the chief is in the minority, the senior justice in the majority exercises that option. Sometimes a chief justice, realizing that he is of the minority view, votes against his own conviction in order to place himself among the majority, where he is in a position to minimize the damage, either by writing the opinion himself or choosing the majority justice most sympathetic to his outlook. In that manner, the force of the opinion may be blunted.

A draft opinion is then circulated, and dissenting opinions are composed. At this stage, too, justices may alter their views, or, in return for a concession by the opinion writer, change sides. Even when justices agree about the outcome, they frequently disagree about the reason for it, making it necessary to obscure or ignore some issues in the opinion in order to hold a majority together. That does not usually make for a very coherent or satisfying opinion. At times the court is riven with dissension, and the justices bring forth a number of overlapping opinions, selectively agreeing or disagreeing with various aspects of the result reached or the rationale adopted. The following juridical configuration accompanied the majority opinion in a case involving the First Amendment (*Allegheny County v. American Civil Liberties Union*):

> Justice O'Connor concurred in part, concurred in judge-ment, and filed opinion joined in part by Justices Brennan and Stevens.
> Justice Brennan concurred in part, dissented in part, and filed opinion joined by Justices Marshall and Stevens.
> Justice Stevens concurred in part, dissented in part, and filed opinion joined by Justices Brennan and Marshall.
> Justice Kennedy concurred in part, dissented in part, and filed opinion joined by Chief Justice Rehnquist and Justices White and Scalia.

Disentangling the significance of such a decision is often not an easy task for constitutional lawyers, much less the lay public. Long, discursive footnotes add to the clutter.

In most cases, however, the court is not quite so fragmented but rather exhibits a phenomenon known as bloc voting. Usually a conservative bloc and a liberal bloc exists, and sometimes one or two 'swing votes' who determine which of the blocs shall prevail in any given case. The solidarity of these blocs may vary from issue to issue but overall their cohesion can be statistically remarkable. In the 1973–4 term of the court, for example, the four justices appointed by President Nixon, forming the more conservative bloc, voted together in 75 per cent of the cases. With a single exception, they succeeded in attracting at least one other justice in each case so as to form a majority.

The hegemony of one block or the other at various periods in the court's history is what makes for 'eras'. During the Warren era a bloc of at least five justices, including the chief, regularly voted together to produce its characteristic liberal jurisprudence. By the early 1980s, under Chief Justice Warren Burger, the liberal bloc had been diminished by attrition, and dominance of the court passed to the bloc of justices appointed by three Republican Presidents: Nixon, Ford and Reagan. The transition was not marked by a sharp change of direction. While the Burger court was somewhat less eager to expand the rights of criminal defendants any further, it scaled some heights of judicial activism unattained even in the Warren era. It announced the constitutional right to an abortion (*Roe v. Wade*), and it struck down the 'legislative veto' by Congress of executive branch actions, thereby calling into question at a stroke perhaps 200 federal statutes. It even reached out to new groups of underprivileged, declaring that the millions of 'illegal' aliens in the United States were shielded by the equal protection clause of the Fourteenth Amendment against discriminatory state legislation. In general, the court slowed the pace of liberal activism but did not conduct a *coup d'état* against the principles of the Warren era. The court was more responsive to its own recent traditions than to the appointing authority.

By the end of President Bush's first three years in office, however, the changeover of personnel from the Warren era was virtually complete. No nominee of a Democratic president had joined the bench for about a quarter of a century. A conservative counter-reformation had begun in earnest, under William Rehnquist, who was elevated to the chief justiceship by President Reagan in 1986, and a bloc of five Reagan-Bush nominees. They, like hundreds of judges appointed to lower courts, had been selected from those who could pass an ideological 'litmus test' on key conservative issues. Each opposed expansion of the rights that individuals might assert against government—except those related to property.

Although they had pledged to 'get big government off your back', the Reaganites had tacitly excluded from the pledge their 'social agenda'—goals for state-assisted moral improvement. Bolstered by a resurgence of religious zeal, the social conservatives waged a cultural civil war against the forces of permissiveness, often associated with the 'liberation' movements of the 1960s and 1970s, which were held responsible for a general decline in traditional beliefs. Using the power of the state to enforce proper attitudes toward piety, chastity, fidelity and the like was quite legitimate, in their view, although requiring a businessman to maintain a safe workplace was an intolerable interference with personal autonomy. The theory underlying this authoritarian or statist strain of conservatism was that government regulation is somehow good for the soul but bad for the spirit of free enterprise.

The conservatives' objective was a return—through coercion, if necessary—to old-fashioned 'family values'. Implicit in this objective was a posture of 'judicial restraint' toward acts of the elected branches, on the assumption that those branches best reflected the sentiments of the majority and that the majority held family values dear. Deferring to the elected branches and their constituents meant relinquishing the justices' role as a court of last resort—a fair-minded grievance forum for ethnic and cultural minority groups and for individuals who had been shunned because of their unconventional beliefs or non-respectable lifestyles. There is little point in appealing against the tyranny of the majority in a court determined not to stand in the way of the majority.

In practice, exalting the will of majorities above the rights of individuals has been congenial to the Reagan-Bush judicial nominees because social conservatism had gained a foothold in some state legislatures by the 1980s. Legislators assaulted the symbolic fortress of permissiveness—the court's decision in the *Roe* case. That controversial 1973 ruling discerned, in the 'penumbra' and 'emanations' of several provisions of the Bill of Rights and the Fourteenth Amendment, a right of privacy and personal integrity that insulates a woman from government interference in her reproductive life. Privacy was perceived by supporters of *Roe* to be among the 'core values' that pervade the constitution. The ruling precluded enforcement of laws in dozens of states that barred abortion except to save the mother's life.

In the years since then, conservatives had pointed out that the Bill of Rights nowhere explicitly mentions a right to privacy, let alone abortion. They complained that the court had created the right out of whole cloth, suiting progressive ideas but lacking a basis in text, tradition or national consensus. Rejecting the concept of 'core values', which they regard as semi-mystical, these textual fundamentalists insist that the individual is entitled to no more than the 'original intent' that may be divined from the framers' words, even if a right to privacy is recognized in modern times as intrinsic to human dignity. The court had not only violated the canons of literalism, the critics contended, but also disregarded the state's proper interest in protecting 'the unborn', usurping the prerogatives of the 7,000 elected representatives, sitting in the 50 state legislatures, who are most closely attuned to popular sentiment.

In the 1989 case of *Webster v. Reproductive Health Services*, the court adopted much of the fundamentalist critique: it drastically narrowed the previously affirmed guarantee of intra-uterine privacy. All but abandoning *Roe*, a majority of the justices invited the states to closely regulate abortion. In the doctrinal contest to become the dominant rule of decision-making, *Webster* was a clear victory for 'original intent' over 'core values'.

Although ostensibly committed to judicial restraint, the triumphant conservative justices felt no inhibition about overturning a relatively recent precedent. Revisiting issues just settled merely because of personnel changes on the bench is hardly a sign of self-discipline. On the contrary, it leaves the court open to the same charge that had been levelled against the Warren Court: abandoning incrementalism and a decent respect for the opinions of their judicial forebears in favour of the free-wheeling *modus operandi* of a legislative body, which adopts and discards policies as it pleases. *Webster*, indeed, could be taken as heralding the replacement of liberal activism (barely restrained invalidation of legislation) by right-wing activism (barely restrained invalidation of precedent). Other doctrinal revisions appeared to be in the offing. The Rehnquist court has intimated that cases carried by the now defunct liberal bloc in a 5-to-4 vote may be reviewed systematically, suggesting the ironic possibility that judicial conservatism will bring wholesale instability to constitutional law.

The rise of conservative activism on the court during the Reagan and Bush Administrations illustrated how thoroughly constitutional doctrine could be transformed when the Presidency was held by the same party for a long period. The infusion of a number of justices, espousing a uniform creed, was a form of court-packing by attrition, requiring no expansion of the bench. With the White House in the hands of Republicans for three successive terms, it was incumbent upon the Senate, a bastion of the Democrats, to use its power of 'advice and consent' to ensure that at least a semblance of ideological balance was maintained on the court. Yet, as places on the bench became vacant, the Senate found that it had relatively little power to affect the composition of the court.

Three nominations, between 1987 and 1991, underscored the limitations of the confirmation process as a guarantor of balance. Even when riddled with misgivings, the senators are hampered by the conventional belief that the President, especially when riding the crest of a strong electoral mandate, ought to be accorded a relatively free hand in selection. In any event, the President can continue nominating candidates until the Senate relents. Reagan nominee Robert Bork, a former US Solicitor General, was rejected after 12 days of public hearings that resembled a combination of inquisition and grand disputation on constitutional theory. A second right-wing judge was nominated, only to withdraw after revelations of cannabis smoking in his past materialized. In the end, the jurist who took the seat had views quite similar to Bork's (albeit lesser known).

While the President might be faulted for naming a candidate lacking in lawyerly competence, probing the nominee's views on live constitutional issues has been considered unduly intrusive. The answer, after all, might be construed as a commitment to the Senate, compromising judicial objectivity and breaching the separation of powers. Even dead issues are sometimes regarded as taboo: Justice Antonin Scalia refused to comment on the classic case of *Marbury v. Madison* during his confirmation hearing, although it had been decided nearly two centuries earlier. Attempts to plumb the nominee's overall philosophical outlook have also proven unsuccessful, because the inquiry soon impinges on controversies that could come before the court.

Until well into the twentieth century, nominees did not testify in person at confirmation hearings. Today personal appearances are crucial, but often not very revealing. Faced with rambling, unsystematic questioning by more than a dozen Senators on the Judiciary Committee, nominees may profess an open mind and blithely disavow the positions they have espoused in the past (undergoing an epiphany known as 'confirmation conversion').

Solicitor General Bork, a leading proponent of 'original intent', was rejected because his voluminous scholarly writings—which he declined to renounce—attacked Warren court decisions expanding individual liberties. His belligerent testimony reinforced fears that he would overrule those precedents if given the chance. The nominee for the next seat that became vacant, Douglas Souter, clearly profited from Bork's experience. A reclusive New Hampshire state judge who had written little, Souter remained so inscrutable throughout the hearings that he was known as the 'stealth nominee'. Stealthiness won him confirmation by a vote of 90 to 9.

When a third seat was vacated, Clarence Thomas, a black conservative with slender judicial credentials was nominated. He sedulously evaded questions, striving to wring sympathy from the Senate with the inspirational story of his rise from humble beginnings in Pinpoint, Georgia. The Pinpoint Strategy, as it came to be known, was not entirely successful. A key member of the Judiciary Committee saw only 'inconsistencies, ambiguities, contradictions, lack of scholarship, lack of conviction and instability'. Accused of sexual harassment by a female former member of his staff, Thomas denounced the televised confirmation hearings as 'a high-tech lynching for uppity blacks'. The Thomas nomination ignited a divisive national debate about race and gender, leaving the nominee under a humiliating cloud of unresolved suspicion, and it caused a general collapse of civility in the Senate. Yet the Thomas nomination was confirmed, by a vote of 52 to 48. The victory margin was the narrowest in the twentieth century.

It was a victory nevertheless, and it was attributable in part to his leaving the impression that childhood privation would somehow transcend the right-wing predispositions he had acquired in adulthood; some Senators anticipated what might be called a 'post-confirmation conversion'. Nothing illustrates the flaws in the confirmation process more clearly than the spectacle of a nominee permitted to ascend to the highest bench upon the faint hope that he will turn out to be someone other than who he appears to be.

The fear that a lawyer of high public profile would be burdened with too many critics to survive the Senate hearings encourages presidents to search for ideologically sound nominees among the relatively obscure. Although justices in the past typically had played prominent roles in government—as senators, governors, or cabinet secretaries—or in political or intellectual circles, recent nominees have been colourless middle-level judges or bureaucrats. They left few footprints as leaders or thinkers. Justice Thomas, for example, held a succession of minor appointive posts as the protégé of Republican Senators and Presidents; a judge for a year, he was rated only minimally qualified by the Bar. In contrast, the 'black seat' he inherited had previously belonged to Thurgood Marshall, who had often laid his life on the line in the campaign to end segregation. The succession was construed as the replacement of a titan by a midget. Through the appointment of relatively anonymous justices, the court could become less a citadel of talent than a strong point garrisoned by unimaginative loyalists. To some, the nominations reflect a contemptuous strategy—also aimed at other institutions—of 'hollowing out', undermining the court's ability to threaten conservative goals by depriving it of justices with the stature of earlier members of the bench. If members of the court are viewed as fungible placemen, slavishly devoted to a narrow cause, the esteem which the court has enjoyed as a kind of council of distinguished elder statesmen may be dissipated. Rather than a broadly representative body drawn from various philosophical streams and the higher echelons of public life, the court could become a backwater for mediocrities whose chief recommendation is that they survived the litmus test.

Emblematic of disillusionment with the court are the doubts now expressed about the wisdom of lifetime tenure. The realization that Justice Thomas, a man in his early forties, could still be on the bench in year 2030, occasioned re-examination of the rationale for committing the nation to a choice that may be irrevocable for decades. Today the average life span is perhaps twice as long as it was in the eighteenth century. The framers may not have contemplated a justice serving long enough to decide issues that could not even have been imagined at the time he joined the court. When justices are vetted for the solidity of their views on a few flash-point issues of the day, they are likely to be particularly out of place in the distant future. A justice chosen for his views on Prohibition in the 1920s would certainly have seemed an anachronism by the 1960s. The litmus test of the 1990s may not be at all relevant to the political agenda of 2030.

A fixed term of 15 years, perhaps, would be sufficient to guarantee judicial independence without imposing the dead hand of the past. It would remove some of the symbolic tension that surrounds the decision, preclude justices from holding on to the bitter end, despite ill health, and ensure a steady turnover of justices, keeping the court attuned to contemporary values. And the normal pattern of retirement would ensure that each President most likely would name at least one justice. Under lifetime tenure, some presidents (Jimmy Carter, for example) never get the chance to influence the composition of the court. History shows, moreover, that a talented justice can make an impact in only a few years; Benjamin Cardozo, a luminary of the law, left his mark in the brief space of six years in the 1930s.

Limiting a justice's time on the court would require a constitutional amendment. The amendment could take the forms of a fixed term of years or a minimum age requirement similar to those already embedded in the constitutional scheme for elected officials (25 years for the House, 30 for the Senate and 35 for President). Fifty years has been suggested as a suitable age, securing mature judgement and the probability of retirement within about two decades.

Others would leave lifetime tenure intact but ensure that the Senate's consent was wholehearted. Drawing upon the analogy of treaty ratification, a minimum of two-thirds of the Senators could be required constitutionally to confirm nominations to the court. That would eliminate approval by a bare majority, as in the

Thomas episode, along with the bitterness and doubt engendered by such sharp divisions of opinion.

The Senate might also take seriously its constitutional power to give advice as well as consent. The Senate could seize the initiative by proposing names to the President, as it did when the Senate persuaded President Herbert Hoover to nominate Cardozo in 1932. The President might on his own initiative consult the Senate about possible choices or suggest several names for consideration. By exerting influence in the pre-selection phase, the Senate might avert internecine struggles in the post-selection phase. A more consultative process of picking justices would, of course, require the executive branch to drop the litmus test and put forward candidates who are closer to the consensus or 'mainstream' constitutional view.

A consultative approach would apply pressure to the President before a nomination is sent to the Senate, and it would obviate the unsatisfactory business of trying to predict the future rulings of a nominee on the basis of sketchy knowledge. In addition, the Senate Judiciary Committee would act in a more informed fashion if it insisted that the nominees explain their method of interpreting the constitution. The President is well acquainted with a nominee's views on the major issues at the time of selection—indeed, probably bases the selection upon those views—and the senators are entitled to equal familiarity in carrying out their constitutional duty to confirm. A nomination for lifetime tenure on the bench is not, after all, due the same deference that might be shown to a Presidential nomination for an executive branch post, where solidarity with the Chief Executive's outlook might be considered a prerequisite. No doubt more light would be generated during hearings if the often confused mixture of questioning and posturing by all committee members were replaced with systematic interrogation by a committee staff member, the format used in many Senate fact-finding hearings. The object would be to amass a comprehensive factual record, containing the candidate's declared views.

The Senate could also give 'advice' in a more general sense by making constitutional issues part of the give-and-take of politics in between nominations, educating the public about the practical consequences of changes in the direction of the court.

A constituency that favoured a bench with balance and depth and that opposed extreme departures from mainstream adjudication might be created. Greater airing of constitutional issues would also acknowledge the fact that the nominating process now resembles a plebiscite, down to the approval polls and speculation about the candidate's 'momentum'. The nominee's standing with the public at large has become an important influence on the voting patterns of the Senate during confirmation.

Regardless of how the nominating process is changed, the justices already on the court ensure that the trend towards conservatism will continue for the foreseeable future. One consequence is that state courts have begun to take the lead in assuring their citizens' fundamental rights—based on the state constitutions, which often have provisions similar to the Bill of Rights. The Supreme Court generally acquiesces in such rulings, recognizing the highest court in each state as the final arbiter of the meaning of its own state's constitution. Another consequence of the Supreme Court's conservative trend has been to wean liberal reformers and civil rights advocates away from litigation and force them back into classical politics. Many of those who sought redress from the court in the past must now rely on electoral and lobbying strategies. Indeed, the ready availability of a judicial remedy may have displaced normal politics, cutting off legislative strategies, both at the state level and in Congress, for achieving the same goals. When *Roe* was decided, for example, 18 states had already responded to shifts in public opinion by legalizing abortion. Now that the old obstacles to democratic reform, such as malapportionment, have vanished, withdrawal of *Roe*'s constitutional guarantee should not prevent states from continuing the legalization trend spontaneously.

Where the court's rulings turn upon statutory interpretation, Congress may correct the justices by enacting clarifying provisions, although it may need to override a presidential veto. The Civil Rights Act of 1991, for example, negated at least six significant decisions since 1989 that created obstacles—never intended by Congress—to obtaining remedies for employment discrimination under previous versions of the law. If its treatment of civil rights is any guide, the court may be less willing to defer to Congress when the latter pursues a liberal agenda. The court could subtly flout the

legislative will through restrictive interpretation of laws intended
to expand individual rights. The conservative bench's dedication
to judicial restraint could be sorely tested.

Besides personnel changes, the Supreme Court faces the possibility of a reorganization of the structure of the appellate judicial
system, a step which could have far-reaching consequences.
Proposals for the reorganization have arisen, in judicial circles
and elsewhere, because of the enormous increase in recent decades
of the court's caseload. In 1951, only about 200 cases were filed
annually; by 1983 the number had exceeded 4000. Since the
Supreme Court need accept only the cases it wishes to review—in
those not reviewed the lower court ruling is left standing—the
overwhelming majority of the cases filed are denied a hearing. The
justices hear and decide only about 150 cases a year. However, the
effort required merely to screen out the remainder imposes a crushing burden on the nine justices, who must at least cursorily read the
preliminary papers. Unlike the other branches of government, the
court is in no position to rely upon expanded staff to cope with its
burgeoning workload; each justice has but a few law clerks to assist
him. Many cases are denied review simply because the justices must
ration their time, not because the suits lack intrinsic importance.
In some instances, the failure to review a case leaves standing
troublesome conflicts among decisions of the courts of appeals.
    Three main proposals have been put forward for dealing with
the caseload, all of them suggesting the interposition of another
court between the Supreme Court and the existing lower courts.
One proposal is to create a court that would perform the screening,
handing up to the Supreme Court only those it deemed most
important. This proposal has met with the objection, that it would
abridge litigants' right of access to the Supreme Court. A second
proposal would assign whole categories of cases, such as tax law, to
the new court; agreement has been lacking, however, about which
categories to treat in this manner. A third plan would have the
Supreme Court accept its usual 150 cases but assign another
group, composed of cases in which circuit courts disagreed, to
an 'intercircuit tribunal'. The principal defect of this plan is that
the Supreme Court might ultimately need to review the decisions

of the new court as well. Thus, another layer would have been added to the judicial hierarchy without decreasing the burden on the Supreme Court. Whatever alternative is adopted, the difficulty of finding an acceptable substitute for the personal attention of the Supreme Court is a touching indication of popular reverence for that institution.

CHAPTER SEVEN

The Bureaucracy:
Administrative Politics

Most bureaucratic tables of organization appear simple on paper and complex in reality; the American bureaucracy is complex even on paper. For although the executive branch is divided along functional lines into a few main departments, the equivalent of British ministries, alongside them exist more than eighty independent commissions, boards, agencies, councils, administrations, corporations, foundations, institutions, authorities, systems and services. Another two dozen agencies form a kind of super-cabinet level within the Executive Office of the President, the apex of the bureaucratic pyramid. In so ponderous an apparatus, it is hardly surprising that functions tend to overlap and that lines of authority are often blurred. The bureaucracy departs from the rational model because the executive branch was not created according to plan but grew, like a coral reef, by accretion. Each agency represents an attempted solution to a problem that was acute at some time in the nation's history. The confusion and overlap betokens the ease with which new agencies are founded and the difficulty with which old ones are abolished.

The framers ignored the subject of administrative organization. The constitution mentions the 'executive departments' only in passing, by stipulating that the President 'may require the opinion, in writing, of the principal officer in each'. It was left to Congress to create the departments by statute as it saw fit. Today there are, in order of seniority, Departments of State (foreign relations); Treasury; Defense; Justice; Interior; Agriculture; Commerce; Labor; Health and Human Services; Housing and Urban Development; Transportation; Energy; Education; and Veterans' Affairs. The first two departments were established in the late eighteenth century, the last three during the 1970s and 1980s.

The secretaries who head each of these departments are appointed by the President, with the consent of the Senate, and constitute his cabinet. Secretaries are not sitting members of the legislature nor are they responsible to it. The extent to which the cabinet exists at all as a decision-making body varies with the preferences of the President. Eisenhower frequently called upon the cabinet to make decisions collectively; Johnson sought the 'consensus' of cabinet thinking while reserving decisions for himself; Nixon convened his cabinet infrequently and favoured the advice of the White House staff.

Except for the secretary of state, whose chief duties are diplomatic, the cabinet members are primarily administrators. Their authority is exercised not collectively, in council, but severally as the overseers of the executive departments. Relying upon these departments to implement legislation, Congress has delegated to them considerable discretion. About 100 agencies are empowered to issue rules, regulations and orders which, when printed in the *Federal Register*, the official gazette, have the force of statute. Administrators' faithfulness to their legislative mandate is kept under constant review by Congress, which approves departmental budget requests, and they may be called to account by the courts. But the departments are surrounded by an aura of expertise to which the other branches defer, and between the poles of legislative and judicial scrutiny administrators enjoy wide latitude.

The degree to which Presidents supervise the mundane work of administration varies greatly. President Carter normally displayed a thorough grasp of the details of administrative policy, in contrast to his successor, Ronald Reagan, who usually assumed an air of detachment and contented himself with setting a 'tone' for his administration. One benefit of the Reagan approach was that unpopular policies or embarrassing *faux pas* were generally blamed on incompetent or malevolent underlings rather than on the President personally.

Perhaps the most severe restriction upon administrators is the structure of the bureaucracy, which does not necessarily correspond with the dimensions of its tasks. The urban crisis, for example, is a combination of unemployment, crime, welfare dependency, inadequate housing, and paralysing traffic congestion.

Yet each of these aspects of the same problem falls under the jurisdiction of a different department, and coordination is often lacking. Even a relatively small objective, such as preserving a forest, can fall foul of bureaucratic divisions. One grove of the trees in the forest may be classified as 'National Park', the province of the Interior Department, while another is listed as 'National Forest', the province of the Agriculture Department. National parks are primarily for conservation and recreation but one purpose of a national forest is to assure a supply of trees for lumbering. Securing agreement between the two departments, each with its own sets of rules and organizational interests, may prove difficult.

There is also a deep conflict of missions between the Department of Agriculture and the Department of Health and Human Services. The former is charged with promoting the interests of tobacco growers, including administering a crop allotment system, while the latter strives mightily to prevent consumers from buying and using the crop because of the health hazards of smoking. Even within the same department, there may be intense rivalries between subordinate bureaux whose missions are in conflict. The Interior Department harnesses together two such agencies: the Bureau of Land Management and the Fish and Wildlife Service. Both are concerned with administration of the vast government lands, which lie mainly in the west, but their objectives are radically different. The Wildlife Service is concerned with preserving the game on public lands, but the BLM has been traditionally inclined to protect the rights of those who wish to graze livestock there or extract mineral deposits. Locked in perpetual warfare with each other, the two agencies compete for dominance, each finding support in different 'constituencies'. The BLM expects the grazers' and miners' lobbies to do their bit on Capitol Hill, and the Wildlife Service relies upon the support of the conservationist groups. The shape of public lands policy will thus be determined by the outcome of an intra-mural struggle waged with the support of extra-mural political allies.

At times the departments appear to be mere holding companies for a collection of self-motivated bureaux, each with its own interest-group constituency and champions in Congress. Such units as the Federal Bureau of Investigation in the Justice

Department and the Forest Service in the Agriculture Department have so much political support that the departmental secretaries may find it difficult to order them to do anything they are unwilling to do. Bureaux, moreover, like the FBI, have managed to establish their own 'closed-career' cadres which are removed from the regular civil service channels. New members are recruited directly after university graduation and spend their entire working lives within a single bureau, dependent upon the senior ranks for their promotions. The bureau does not exchange personnel with other government offices. All members of the bureau may share a common professional background, such as lawyer, engineer, or geologist. As Herbert Kaufman has said of the Forest Service Officers, 'They are absorbed into the organization by a kind of gradual social osmosis, during which they, in turn, absorb many of the prevailing values, assumptions, and customary modes of operation.'

The autonomy of the bureaux leaves power in the executive branch diffused among many centres of decision-making. But while the independence of these bureaux is only informal, the class of 'independent agencies' is formally separated from the departments. The independent agencies have but one common characteristic: they are outside the control of the cabinet secretaries. Otherwise, they fall into two categories: those run by administrators directly responsible to the President and those that are headed by autonomous boards of commissioners serving fixed terms. The two categories have diametrically opposed purposes. The former allow the President to supervise certain government activities closely, while the latter take supervision of other activities entirely out of his hands.

The autonomous commissions were created to administer a variety of matters which, for one reason or another, Congress was reluctant to entrust to the regular departments or the President. Usually, the motive was to take politics out of the administrative process by employing bi-partisan boards one step removed from the chief executive's direct authority and patronage powers. Although the President, with the consent of the Senate, appoints the commissioners, they serve fixed terms and, unlike ordinary administrators, cannot be removed by him, except in clear cases of neglect of duty or malfeasance. Since the commissioners' terms may exceed a presidential term (some are as long as fourteen years), any one President is unlikely to alter the composition of the board dramatically. Security of tenure assures the commissioners considerable discretion and permits statutory mandates to be implemented dispassionately. It is an appealing mechanism to those who view administration as an objective science. There are some, however, who argue that independent agencies seriously weaken the executive branch because they are not responsive to the President. Among the critics are free-market conservatives who view such agencies as uncapped wellsprings of business-stifling regulation. The creation of administrative entities not responsible to the White House, say the critics, infringes upon the integrity of the executive branch and thus violates the separation of powers principle.

The Board of Governors of the Federal Reserve System is an agency that has come under particular scrutiny because it enjoys autonomy in setting interest rates. The independence of 'the Fed', according to its champions, insulates it against political pressure for 'easy money' (lower interest rates), which might be popular in the short term but cause damaging inflation in the long run. Yet the fact remains that monetary policy, a critical element of the national economy, has been entrusted to a non-accountable institution. In most democratic nations, both monetary and fiscal policy are in the hands of officials responsible to the electorate.

To establish a degree of accountability, some have suggested, the Secretary of the Treasury should sit on the Federal Reserve Board. Others have proposed that both the Secretary of the Treasury and the Federal Reserve Chairman be made subordinate to a new cabinet position—Secretary of Economic Affairs (similar to a Chancellor of the Exchequer)—charged with co-ordinating fiscal and monetary policy. At the very least, argue the proponents of change, the Federal Reserve Chairman's term should expire when a newly elected president takes office. A vacant chair would give the incoming administration, armed with a fresh mandate, an opportunity to nudge monetary policy in another direction if that were deemed necessary.

Some commissions, such as the United States Postal Service

and the Tennessee Valley Authority (which operates hydroelectric generating plants), are really public corporations, functioning in a manner similar to private enterprises. Others, like the National Science Foundation and the National Foundation on the Arts and Humanities, operate as private charitable institutions, bestowing grants to support scientific, educational and cultural activities. The most important group of commissions are those that regulate commerce. Beginning in the late nineteenth century, Congress created a number of agencies to control abuses in what had been until then essentially a *laissez-faire* economy. The first of these was the Interstate Commerce Commission, established in 1887 to set maximum rates for rail freight. In 1914, the Federal Trade Commission was created to control the monopolistic practices of the giant corporations, the 'trusts'. As part of President Roosevelt's New Deal of the 1930s, a number of other 'alphabet agencies' came into being, including the National Labor Relations Board, the Securities and Exchange Commission, and the Federal Communications Commission.

From the beginning, the regulatory commissions encountered the objection that Congress had unconstitutionally delegated its legislative powers to administrators, in violation of the principle of separation of powers. For, while the statutes creating the commissions set out the basic policies to be followed, administrators were to fashion the rules. The Federal Trade Commission, for example, was charged with controlling 'unfair', that is, restrictive trade practices, but it had to decide which practices were 'unfair'. By the early twentieth century the Supreme Court had accepted the necessity of at least some delegation of rule-making authority in order to give practical effect to the will of Congress. In distinguishing between constitutional and unconstitutional delegations of authority, the court has insisted that sufficiently clear and specific standards be prescribed to guide the administrators' discretion. The court has even upheld the delegation to administrators of the power to make rules whose violation is a criminal offence.

Besides possessing these quasi-legislative powers, the commissions exercise quasi-judicial functions. They decide when their rules have been broken, and they may enforce their judgements by issuing 'cease and desist' orders or by assessing fines. This practice, too, has brought complaints that functions properly committed to another branch of government have been usurped. In response, Congress has made administrative proceedings respect individual rights. It passed the Administrative Procedures Act in 1946, laying down uniform rules to preclude arbitrary decisions by administrators. Beyond that, however, the Supreme Court has held the commissions accountable to the Fifth Amendment's command that no person be deprived of life, liberty or property without due process of law. The most basic element of due process is the right to adequate notice and a hearing, at which an individual affected by a proposed administrative action may enter his objections. As the Supreme Court declared in 1937, 'Those who are brought into contest with the government in a quasi-judicial proceeding aimed at the control of their activities are entitled to be fairly advised of what the government proposes and to be heard upon its proposals before it issues its final command.'

In the second category of independent agencies, those whose chiefs report directly to the President, are about a dozen units, including the Farm Credit Administration, and the Environmental Protection Agency. No imperative of logic requires them to be separated from the regular departments; the Farm Credit Administration, certainly, would be suitably sheltered under the umbrella of the Department of Agriculture. The creation of the environmental agency in the early 1970s suggests that the main motivation is to establish highly 'visible' offices to deal with controversial issues. Merely creating a division within an existing department might give the impression that the problem was being buried, which is one indication of the degree of popular confidence in the regular bureaucracy.

Similar reasons explain the enormous proliferation, beginning in the 1960s and 1970s, of agencies within the executive office of the President. Although the executive office once comprised only the closest staff advisers of the President, it has been filled out with agencies having direct administrative responsibilities. Some of these agencies, like the National Security Council, co-ordinate at a 'super-cabinet' level matters falling within the jurisdiction of two or more departments, assuring co-ordination and suppressing inter-departmental feuds. In some instances, an agency can thoroughly dominate the departments it is supposedly 'co-ordinating'. Before officially assuming the title of Secretary of State, Henry Kissinger effectively supplanted the State Department while serving as director of the National Security Council. Other agencies, such as President Johnson's Office of Economic Opportunity, created to wage the war on poverty, were intended to administer new, high-priority programmes that the President feared to entrust to the more fossilized sections of the bureaucracy.

From festering crisis often arises a frustrated cry for a 'czar', a powerful inter-departmental chieftain who, it is hoped, can squelch bureaucratic quibbling and focus the government's attention on the emergency at hand. Drug addiction, airline safety and defence procurement are three matters of urgency that have prompted demands for a czar. When President Bush seemed unduly distracted by foreign affairs, a 'domestic czar' was proposed by his fellow Republicans in Congress to devise measures to combat an economic recession. In any administration, the Vice President, appearing to be unoccupied, may be considered a candidate for such assignments.

In the case of drugs, a vigorous former Secretary of Education— William Bennett—was in fact appointed czar by President Reagan. He was charged with fashioning a national drug control plan and co-ordinating the activities of approximately 40 agencies, ranging from the Coast Guard to the health authorities. But Bennett's czardom soon came to be regarded as a Potemkin village. The President declined to accord him cabinet-level rank, a loss of prestige that deprived him of leverage with the agencies he had to shepherd, and refused to accept some of the czar's key recommendations because they conflicted with the President's long-standing opposition to gun control. In less than two years, Bennett had declared victory in the 'war on drugs' and resigned, although it was clear that the operational objective had not been attained. Many suspected that the war was being waged more for appearance than effect. Bennett's less dynamic successor, a governor of Florida who was given the post as a consolation prize after losing an election for the Senate, was virtually invisible.

The drug campaign suggests that appointing a czar may be initially useful in catapulting an issue to the top of the agenda but that the device offers no panacea when the real difficulty is lack of political will to do what is necessary rather than lack of co-ordination. It is incongruous, in any event, that a nation congenitally concerned about limiting power should seek salvation in the mystique of an all-powerful administrator. Turning to a czar signifies that the ingrained fear of excessive government has given way to the fear that lack of strong leadership may be even worse.

Probably the most powerful of the executive office agencies is the Office of Management and Budget. A descendant of the old Bureau of the Budget in the Treasury Department, the OMB was moved into the White House during the 1960s to enhance the President's control over his subordinates by applying the budget sanction systematically. The OMB has evolved into a general planning agency, reviewing departmental budget requests in light of the President's overall strategy. By controlling the funds that each department gets, the OMB sets policy guidelines, determining which programmes shall be expanded and which run on thin rations. Most recent Presidents have relied heavily upon the budget agency to make the bureaucracy more responsive to them.

In its bulk, if not in its efficiency, the bureaucracy is an awe-inspiring sight. The federal government employs about three million civilians, and their occupations are almost as varied as those in the private sector. There are about 15,000 job categories, ranging from astronauts to specialists in chicken diseases. Half of the employees are engaged in defence-related activities, one quarter are in the postal service and the remaining one quarter are left to cope with all the rest: social services, housing, education, agriculture, conservation, law enforcement, commerce, labour and regulatory activities.

Those in the career civil service are expected to take vows of abstinence from politics. The Hatch Acts of 1939 and 1940 prohibit federal civil servants from taking 'any active part in political management or in political campaigns'. The acts were intended to prevent civil servants from being pressed into political service by their appointive bosses, but there are grounds to question the wisdom—or the constitutionality—of depriving so many of the citizen's right to participate in politics.

Civil servants have also been deprived of normal rights to

unionize and bargain collectively over salaries and conditions of employment. By executive order, presidents have granted federal employees a limited right to bargain, but striking is still a felony. In most places in the United States, a strike by employees of any level of government—local, state, or federal—is regarded as a form of mutiny against lawfully constituted authority. President Reagan set a firm example for dealing with such strikes when he discharged about 15,000 professional air traffic controllers who had gone on strike illegally, protesting against unsafe conditions. He replaced them permanently in the control towers and had the union disbanded.

When paranoia over communist subversion was at its height in the 1940s and early 1950s, civil servants became particularly suspect. 'Loyalty boards' were created in most federal agencies to examine the political beliefs of thousands of civil servants, many of whom had been denounced by anonymous informers. A number of civil servants were discharged or resigned because their careers had been ruined by these witch hunts. The courts eventually blunted the sharper edges of the loyalty programmes by requiring procedural due process at the hearings and by limiting inquiries to civil servants in 'sensitive' positions.

From the way in which government employees are restricted and sometimes hounded, one may detect that the notion of a permanent civil service is still suspect. During the republic's first century, recruitment to government posts was conducted according to the principle that to the victor in politics belong the spoils of office. When a new President, especially of a party different from his predecessor's, entered the White House, there was virtually a complete turnover of officeholders. All but the clerical staff were replaced by political supporters of the new administration, and in some offices even the clerks were not spared.

There were, of course, arguments for the spoils system other than avarice. Among them was that 'sweeping Washington clean' every few years administered a strong antidote to corruption and entrenched power. Replacing officeholders frequently, it was contended, preserved democracy by preventing a mandarin class from forming and by affording a great number of citizens the opportunity to perform public duties. These duties were held to be simple enough for the average, reasonably intelligent person, regardless of his formal education. In the late nineteenth century, Professor Richard Hofstadter points out, 'The professional politicians succeeded in persuading themselves that civil-service reform ... would restrict job-holding to a hereditary, college-educated aristocracy; and that all kinds of unreasonable and esoteric questions would be asked on civil service examinations.' Probably the most compelling reason for the spoil system, however, was that it provided a huge bonanza of patronage jobs, the promise of which candidates could use to induce party members to work for their election.

By 1883 Congress had tired of the excesses of amateurism and passed the Pendleton Act, which replaced the spoils system with the merit system for about three quarters of all federal posts. A civil service commission began to administer competitive examinations. The merit system gradually expanded until it covered about 90 per cent of all posts, but the large number of policy-making positions immediately under the cabinet secretaries are still filled mainly on partisan political grounds. Few career civil servants ever rise to positions equivalent to Permanent, Deputy or Under Secretary in Britain.

A change of administration still occasions a boom in the real estate market around Washington as incumbents prepare to leave for their home states and new appointees arrive. The period of uncertainty lasts for half a year or more, from election day in early November until several months after the new President takes office on 20 January. During this prolonged 'lame duck' period, the executive branch is not notably productive, since most of its important officials are either nervously contemplating the future or actively looking for another job. It is an exciting time for the Washington press corps, however, which avidly reports the names of those 'mentioned' for various posts.

The transition is particularly thorough if one party has been in power for a long time. When Eisenhower assumed office in 1953, Republicans, who had been shut out of the sweepstakes for twenty years, were not only hungering for the usual appointive posts but demanding removal of many career civil servants who had risen through the ranks during the Democratic reign. The merit system by that time was well enough established to prevent the Republicans from completely satisfying their appetite for office, but many high-ranking civil servants who had become identified with Democratic policies were displaced.

Because of this system of recruitment, the upper echelons of the executive branch lack the continuity and professionalism of the British higher civil service. Most of the executive officials are businessmen, lawyers, academics or state politicians who have taken two or three years off from their regular occupations. While some bring experience in private life that specifically equips them for their official tasks—a banker may become a Treasury Department official—many do not. According to the rules of campaign patronage, the talented and untalented alike must receive their just rewards. One reason why the bureaucracy tends to expand is the necessity to create non-critical posts that can be safely entrusted to the President's eager but less able political supporters. The diplomatic service offers a particularly good example of the patronage system in action; small African countries sometimes have been parcelled out *pro rata* to aspiring ambassadors, according to the size of their campaign contributions.

Even when they are not incompetent, those who obtain positions through politics are likely to go on placing politics above official duty. At any given time, a number of federal bureaucrats may be planning to use their posts as stepping stones to elective offices, perhaps in their home states, so that political considerations weigh heavily with them. That is not unethical or illegal, but when the Under Secretary of Agriculture for International Affairs has his eye on the governorship of Iowa, it may be unclear whether his policy decisions are based on international conditions or conditions in Iowa.

A similar doubt surrounds the official whose public service is merely an interlude in a business career. However honestly he endeavours to carry out his responsibilities, he can hardly keep from being influenced by his past and more especially his future. Can a person who has been an executive of a mining company, and intends to be one again, really take a detached view while serving as an official of the Bureau of Mines? Although interchange of personnel between government and industry is often considered an excellent way of bringing the hard-headed experience of businessmen into public life, the business world does not seem to do badly by the arrangement either.

In the field of defence, the ready exchange of personnel between government agencies and military contractors causes a certain blurring of distinctions which prompted President Eisenhower to warn against the growing influence of a 'military-industrial complex'. The Defense Department buys vast quantities of goods and services from contractors. A congressional inquiry in the 1960s discovered that the 100 largest of these firms retained in their executive ranks 1400 former military officers, including 261 retired generals and admirals. The firm awarded the most contracts employed 187 former officers *and* a former Secretary of the Army. All of these ex-warriors obviously knew their way through the labyrinth of power in the Pentagon, where many of the civilian officials, too, are once-and-future employees of the contractors. To combat incestuous relationships between private business and government, a number of 'conflict of interest' measures have been adopted in recent years. Government officials must wait a decent interval, usually about two years, before accepting a position in a firm with which they have done business.

To further slow the revolving door between private business and government, the Ethics in Government Act, a post-Watergate measure passed by Congress in 1978, prohibits former senior members of the executive branch from lobbying their old colleagues on behalf of private clients for one year after leaving office. But Whitney North Seymour Jr., who prosecuted an ex-aide to President Reagan, has described the law as 'riddled with exceptions and loopholes', making it 'extremely difficult to enforce except for the most flagrant violators'. For example, the act allows a lobbyist who is still within the prohibited period to send an emissary to his old agency, even though he cannot come in person, and to approach policy-makers at social gatherings. The executive branch, in addition, is compartmentalized by the act's provisions: the White House alone is divided into nine separate agencies. The target of Seymour's prosecution, who was formally attached to one of them, thus was legally permitted to lobby the eight other agencies as soon as he resigned, even though his influence as a Presidential confidant obviously extended throughout the White House complex.

Practitioners of the art of influence peddling thus still have free rein. One of the most unabashed practitioners is James Watt, who had been President Reagan's Interior Secretary. To ensure the granting of a subsidy to his client, the builder of a housing project, he made one visit to the Secretary of Housing, who was his friend, and eight telephone calls. Watt received a fee of $300,000 for his pains. Defending his brokerage service before a congressional investigating committee in 1989, Watt insisted that he had merely 'used his credibility to accomplish an objective', a use that he described proudly as 'legal, moral, ethical, and effective'.

Some government departments, of course, exist primarily to promote the interests of private industry. The Departments of Agriculture, Commerce and Labor try to discover what their 'clientele' want done, so that government may do it for them. A famous case in point was the attempt by the Kennedy Administration to impose more stringent controls on farmers to reduce over-production of wheat; before it could legally do so, it was necessary for the Agriculture Department to put the question to a referendum of wheat farmers, who naturally voted against being regulated more strictly. The devolution of public power to officially recognized private interests is not always so glaring. But at all times, the representatives of interest groups are quietly making their wishes known to receptive administrators in the appropriate departments as well as to congressional committees.

In the business-oriented departments, the client relationship is quite open and recognized. But, unfortunately, even in those agencies whose ostensible mission is to regulate industry, not promote it, a covert client relationship often develops. The regulators become the captives of the regulated. The Interstate Commerce Commission, the first of the regulatory agencies, set the pattern. Created in response to the nineteenth-century railroads' exploitation of farmers who shipped grain, the commission was supposed to be a watchdog, curbing abusive practices by the rail companies. But the commission eventually became the railroads' chief protector. Until it was abolished, it allocated routes and set rates in a manner that guaranteed them a generous profit in a safe, non-competitive environment. Ironically, the regulatory agencies that were supposed to eliminate restrictive business practices have sometimes elevated them to the status of government policy.

The capture of the regulatory agencies began with the practice of appointing commissioners with 'expertise', that is, in the case of the ICC, former railroad executives. Although the practice is natural in the client-centred departments, choosing regulators from among the regulated has proved self-defeating. Industry well understands this. When the Federal Energy Administration, predecessor of the Department of Energy, was being created in 1973, one large oil company paid a huge bonus to an executive who left to take a post in the new agency. Although a controversy erupted when the farewell gift was discovered, the assumption that oil executives without dowries are suitable for regulatory posts went unchallenged.

Sensitivity to improper corporate connections seems to have grown, however. Under President Reagan the integrity of the Environmental Protection Agency was called into question, partly because it had been staffed with officials who had formerly worked for known industrial polluters. The head of the agency and a number of others ultimately resigned when Congress challenged its apparently sluggish antipollution enforcement policy.

Even officials who were never business executives tend to develop undue sympathy for industry, owing to what has been delicately termed 'excessive interaction' with the businessmen they are supposed to regulate. A Federal Aviation Administration staff member spends his working days—and sometimes his weekends—listening to the complaints of airline executives, but he hardly ever has an official conversation with a passenger. At formal hearings, moreover, all too often the voice of industry dominates. To right the balance, a Consumer Advocacy Agency has been proposed that would have no administrative authority of its own but would represent consumer interests in regulatory proceedings. A bill to establish the consumer agency has failed in Congress several times, partly because of heavy lobbying by industry—an indication of how deeply it cherishes its exclusive 'interaction' with the regulators.

The regulatory agencies, however, are beginning to feel pressure from the 'public interest' organizations that represent non-industry views. By pressing their arguments at hearings and in the news media, these groups have started to force policy-making out into the open. Some notable victories have been won.

In 1974, the Federal Communications Commission decided for the first time not to renew the licence of a television station because of a complaint by a group of viewers about the station's performance. In previous years, broadcasters' applications had usually gone uncontested and were granted perfunctorily. Such counter-pressure may not be able to abolish entirely the cosy relationship between business and regulatory agencies, but it should at least dispel the myth of dispassionate administration and foster a frank recognition that the agencies are as much an arena of politics as is Congress.

Despite the relatively benign attitude of the regulators, a movement to 'de-regulate' the economy has gained considerable support. Its premise is that ham-handed bureaucrats have dampened the spirit of free enterprise, burdening American industry with unproductive paperwork at a time when it must perform as well as less regulated economies in other parts of the world. As a result, the detailed route and fare controls which had applied to the airline industry for decades were relaxed in favour of more competition during the 1980s, as were many restrictions on the banking industry. Ironically, the de-regulation was followed by the collapse of many airlines and banks. The most fervid de-regulation sentiment has been directed at the apparatus created in the 1970s to protect the workplace from health and safety hazards. Under President Reagan, occupational health regulations and inspections were curtailed, and new controls against dangerous industrial chemicals were approved only if it could be shown that they would secure an increase in employee health proportional to the cost of complying with them.

At the same time, Congress was abruptly deprived of a weapon it had used to restrain the administrative apparatus. During the 1970s, it had adopted much legislation that delegated rule-making authority to agencies—with the frequent proviso that Congress could kill any rule it disliked by a simple majority of either house. This proviso, known as the 'legislative veto', was incorporated in about two hundred enactments. When the Federal Trade Commission, in a typical instance, proposed regulations against deceptive practices in the sale of used cars, Congress, responding to pressure from trade associations, exercised the legislative veto to overrule the regulation. For that reason, public interest advocacy groups often opposed the legislative veto, which they considered an escape hatch for business interests seeking to avoid complying with a regulation. Although Presidents often denounced the device, the executive branch sometimes used it as bargaining chip: the President might agree to such a provision to improve a bill's chances of passage.

The practice of granting conditional authority to administrators ceased in 1983, when the Supreme Court held that the legislative veto violated the principle of separation of powers (*Immigration and Naturalization Service v. Chadha*). Each veto amounted, in effect, to a new piece of legislation, the court reasoned, yet legislation requires approval by the President as well as Congress to take effect. The solo role that Congress created for itself thus infringed upon a presidential prerogative.

Although it removes a potential check on the bureaucracy, the demise of the legislative veto could produce salutary results by discouraging Congress from approving overly vague legislation— often the unhappy result of irreconcilable differences among the lawmakers. (The Environmental Protection Agency was assigned the nebulous mission of maintaining 'conditions under which man and nature can exist in productive harmony'.) Unable to erase agency rules it abhors, Congress is more likely to guide administrators carefully in advance. The abolition of the legislative veto thus may confer upon the agencies more authority in the short run but cause them to be held to stricter standards in the long run.

Another question of boundary definition between the executive and the other branches arose in the matter of 'special prosecutors' like Mr Seymour. An outgrowth of the Watergate scandal, the special prosecutor (also known as an 'independent counsel') is a lawyer from outside government who is appointed on a temporary basis to investigate a specific allegation of misconduct by a member of the executive branch. The post of special prosecutor was intended to relieve the crisis of confidence that typically erupts when institutions investigate themselves. How can vigorous law enforcement be assured if the prosecutor's responsibilities are in potential conflict with his own political interests (or those of his allies), or if the President can remove a prosecutor whose investigation threatens to embarrass the White House? Watergate provided the *locus classicus*: President Nixon dismissed prosecutor Archibald Cox when his inquiries came uncomfortably close to the Oval Office itself.

Under the Ethics in Government Act, a special prosecutor is selected by the Circuit of Court of Appeal. Unlike typical officers of the executive branch, who serve 'at will', the prosecutor may be dismissed by the President only for 'good cause'. President Reagan, whose administration was probed by several special prosecutors, challenged the act, claiming that Congress had ceded to a free agent discretionary authority that properly belonged under his control. Although it acknowledged that considerable discretion had been vested in the special prosecutor, the Supreme Court wrote in 1988 that 'we simply do not see how the President's need to control the exercise of that discretion is so central to the functioning of the executive branch as to require . . . that the counsel be terminable at will by the President.' The court rejected the argument that the only constitutional remedies for executive misconduct are political: impeachment or electoral defeat. In concluding that the wall of separation between the branches remained intact, the court was influenced by its finding that 'Congress retained for itself no powers of control or supervision over the special prosecutors' (*Morrison v. Olson*).

In contrast, the court had ruled two years earlier that Congress had breached the wall of separation when it enacted the Balanced Budget Act of 1985. The act required automatic, across-the-board cuts in spending if the government's deficit grew beyond a predetermined limit. The Comptroller General of the United States was empowered to detail the necessary cuts. The court found that the comptroller was an officer of the legislative branch because Congress, not the President, had the power to remove him from office. Yet, the court said, the act had assigned him functions calling for 'independent judgement and evaluation' and 'plainly entailing execution of the law' (*Bowsher v. Synar*).

Policing the boundaries between the branches, as these examples suggest, often entails carefully assessing the employment status of an official who seems to exist in a disputed no-man's-land. When usurpation of executive authority is alleged, the issue may be resolvable by determining which branch of government wields the ultimate sanction: the threat of the sack.

CHAPTER EIGHT

Mass Media:
the Fourth Branch

Two theories have been put forward to explain the role that the press plays in the American democratic system, each of them tied to widely divergent notions of how that system works. The traditional, and probably still most accepted, theory is that the press informs the sovereign electorate of what their officials are doing or planning to do, enabling 'public opinion' to crystallize. The press then takes soundings of public opinion and reports on the 'mood of the people' so that officials may make an appropriate response to the wishes of their constituents. This two-way theory assumes that citizens are rational beings, who gather facts and develop opinions about public affairs, and that officials pay attention to those opinions, as articulated by the press. It evokes a populist image of democracy, a town meeting writ large, in which the dialogue between officials and the electorate is carried on through the medium of the press. As Walter Lippmann, one of the most eminent American journalists, observed, 'Acting upon everybody for thirty minutes in twenty-four hours, the press is asked to create a mystical force called Public Opinion that will take up the slack in public institutions.'

The populist theory has enjoyed long currency. Although the early-nineteenth-century American press was coarse, abusive and violent in tone, de Tocqueville found 'it makes political life circulate in every corner of that vast land. Its eyes are never shut, and it lays bare the secret shifts of politics, forcing public figures in turn to appear before the tribunal of opinion.' Later in the century, Lord Bryce noted that 'in America public opinion is a power not satisfied with choosing executive and legislative agents at certain intervals, but [is] continuously watching and guiding those agents ... The efficiency of the organs of opinion is therefore more essential to the government of the United States than even to England and France.'

Wholeheartedly embracing this view of its role, the press considers itself the adversary of the government. Its job is to serve, as one modern American journalist has put it, as 'surrogate sovereign', a watchdog on behalf of the absent electorate. The newsman's mission is to ferret out corruption, malfeasance and misuse of the taxpayer's dollar. Without him, the newsman believes, the government would soon degenerate into an irresponsible cabal, perpetrating its schemes in secret.

There is, of course, a great deal of truth to that belief. Many government policies and plans die when exposed to the cruel light of day, which may prove that they were not fit to live in the first place. There are also deficiencies in the performance of government that would not be remedied were they not publicized. During the war in Vietnam, correspondents on the battlefields consistently deflated the false optimism of the Pentagon by sending home accounts that contradicted official assessments of the fighting. The press eventually moulded a popular consensus against continuing the conflict.

The second and more *avant-garde* theory of the press postulates an elitist form of democracy, in which officials pay lip service to the electorate while acting according to their own values and perceptions. Officials consult with each other rather than with the populace. The press reports information provided by officials mainly for the edification of other officials, thereby serving as a forum for those who make decisions.

The elitist theory portrays journalists as carrier pigeons rather than watchdogs. Their mission is not maintaining vigilance for the electorate but dispensing facts useful to officialdom. Proponents of the elitist theory point out that the American press has always had a peculiarly close working relationship with officials. Compared with those in many other countries, American officials go out of their way to feed the press information. They maintain 'press rooms' and retain public relations officers to deliver briefings as often as several times a day. Care is taken to meet the various deadlines of morning and afternoon newspapers. The press releases that are churned out diligently in Washington assure that reporters will always have a story. Informally, officials provide newsmen with juicy titbits at 'background briefings' or in the form of 'leaks', which the reporters cryptically attribute to 'usually reliable sources' and 'high government officials' so as to protect the informant's identity. (Reporters who have worked in Washington and London testify to the relative openness of American officials.) That the press observes these conventions is one measure of its dependence on the government information machine for satisfying its appetite for news.

The willingness of officials to supply information is not entirely altruistic. Officials use the press to promote their own goals and discomfit their enemies. Journalists may try to avoid being manipulated, but they do not really care about the motives behind a 'leak' so long as the information is accurate, which it usually is. Manipulation occurs in a variety of ways. Let us say that the President is planning to nominate a justice of the Supreme Court but is uncertain how the nomination will be received in the Senate, which must confirm the selection. He may try sending up a trial balloon by leaking to reporters the name of the person 'under serious consideration'. If a group of senators wished to discredit the nominee, it might then leak word that he was a bigamist or favoured vivisection. Embarrassed, the President might turn to another nominee. Thus, the entire confirmation debate would have been carried out in the press through leaks and counter-leaks.

One of the most famous examples of leak-driven nomination politics occurred when the Senate was considering Clarence Thomas for the post of justice of the US Supreme Court in 1991. As the nomination was about to be put to a vote by the entire chamber, a source, presumably in the Senate Judiciary Committee, leaked to reporters a witness statement in which a former employee accused Thomas of sexual harassment about 10 years earlier. A firestorm of feminist outrage swept over Washington, symbolized by a march on the Senate by a group of women members of the House of Representatives, who demanded a full investigation of the charges. The result was a sensational series of televised special hearings that nearly derailed a nomination that had been a virtual certainty a few days before.

In such cases, the elitist theory of the press seems quite accurate, for the newspapers merely serve as passive conduits for information voluntarily supplied by one set of officials to another set of officials. It is difficult to discern what role the electorate might play other than that of a Greek chorus. The elitist model is also supported by the fact, readily admitted by journalists, that the *Washington Post* has more influence upon the course of national events than does, for example, the *Los Angeles Times*. While that superior influence may be attributed to the quality of the former's staff, it is surely helped immeasurably by the newspaper's appearance upon the breakfast tables of all decision-makers in the capital. As a veteran of the Washington press corps has observed, 'Even if an official doesn't read it, his wife does and he hears all about it from her.' The *Los Angeles Times*, in contrast, may be read by the representatives and senators from California as part of their office routine, but that would be the extent of its impact in Washington.

It may also be argued, in favour of the elitist model, that members of the press are themselves closer in opinions, attitudes, values and backgrounds to government officials than they are to the masses. How then can they pretend to serve as tribunes of the common people? The press, it is often claimed, is dominated by an 'Eastern Establishment' which reflects the concerns of politically liberal, educated persons living in big cities on the Atlantic seaboard but not those of the 'middle Americans' (i.e. middle class, midwestern and middle of the road) whose guardians they have appointed themselves. Thus, the policies that the press is likely to treat harshly and try to 'expose' may, in fact, be policies which most of the electorate endorses or is blissfully unconcerned about. When the press, at its hard-nosed best, tries to extort the truth from an official it suspects of malfeasance, most people may feel that the poor fellow is being unjustly persecuted. (Some persons, apparently, will forever believe that President Nixon was hounded out of office by the newspapers.) Consider the example of the FBI. The agency is often discussed in ominous tones by the press because it is secretive and believed by many journalists to contain the germ of a Gestapo. Yet since most citizens are terrified by high crime rates, they no doubt look gratefully upon the FBI as a protective bulwark. Such discrepancies between popular sentiments and the professional biases of journalists produce a credibility gap between writer and reader. Survey evidence indicates that a vast number of people do not credit much of what they read in the papers.

Ironically for the watchdog theory, the press seems to be relied upon more by the officials it is supposed to be watching than by the populace whose interests it is supposed to protect. For while the public may be sceptical about what appears in the papers, policymakers depend on the media to bring problems to their attention. Officials were not blind to poverty, hunger, discrimination or opposition to the Vietnam War, but somehow they did not respond to them until the press made them real by documenting their existence. Minor social and economic dysfunctions, especially those confined to one state or region, often would not be noticed by Washington were they not discovered by the news media. The press thus helps set the agenda for government. A cruel prison system in Arkansas, discontent among the Native Americans in South Dakota, severe unemployment in Alaska—situations like these suddenly become important in the capital because the press makes them immediate. One merely has to count the number of references to newspaper articles in congressional debates to realize how heavily the legislators rely on the press as an intelligence network. Groups of the discontented have learned that lesson so well that the real purpose of most demonstrations and picket lines is to be a 'media event', that is to attract decision-makers' attention by appearing in the papers or on television, thereby legitimizing their grievances. (Even dissidents overseas recognize the importance of carrying picket signs intelligible to an English-speaking television audience.)

In recent years, the press has gained a better understanding of how its presence stimulates its subjects to perform. Television crews have sought to be less provocative at rallies and demonstrations, and after the excesses of the 1988 election, which deteriorated into a patriotism contest, media outlets vowed to prevent the obscuring of political issues by visual and aural hoopla. A test of substance and accuracy began to be imposed. Some outlets pointedly abstain from covering mere 'photo opportunities' (also known as 'video press releases') as if they were genuinely newsworthy events. When a photogenic, on-location bill-signing ceremony was meticulously arranged for President Bush in 1991—he put his pen to transport legislation amid a sea of hard hats at a Texas highway construction site—some television reportage omitted the video, drew attention to the deliberate staging, or recalled that Bush had only recently opposed the bill. Presidents are now likely to feel less sure of the media response when they strike out across the country for the sole purpose of ostentation—cavorting in a Sioux war bonnet or devouring Polish sausages at an ethnic barbecue.

In a similarly self-critical mood, the media have begun to focus on the phenomenon of the shrinking 'sound bite'—the exiguous excerpt from a candidate's remarks that actually gets on the air—as an index of shallowness. The average modern sound bite has been clocked at nine seconds—considerably less than the television industry standard of forty-five seconds some years ago. Recognizing that such evanescent snippets rule out substantive political discourse (and hoping to save travel expenses), many television reporters have abandoned the ritual of riding the press bus along the campaign trail in pursuit of a candidate who is dashing frenetically from one scenic backdrop to another. Rather than swelling the candidate's retinue, the journalists are devoting blocks of time to systematic analysis and relying for their basic day-to-day newsgathering on 'pool' arrangements, patterned after war-zone reporting. A major source of generic footage is C-SPAN, an organization that supplies without narration a 'video verité' record of political happenings. Efforts are also underway to widen the restricted circle of pundits who are routinely called upon for commentary.

At the same time, the media have seized the initiative by commissioning more or less continual polling. Funded by consortiums of electronic and print outlets, polls monitor voter perceptions of the President's performance. Although satisfaction is difficult to quantify, the overall approval rating has nevertheless become a crucial barometer of the political climate, followed with acute interest by the President and his party in Congress. Steep decline in the rating figure can lead to the downfall of the White House Chief of Staff or a cabinet reshuffle; a high rating, on the other hand, may dissuade potential opponents from contesting the President's re-election or resisting his legislative proposals.

Polls do have flaws, of course: they over-emphasize the 'horse race' aspects of campaigns, fixing attention on relative standing rather than on evaluation of the competing policy positions. Polls are also notoriously prone to vicissitudes—Bush went from a 90 per cent approval to less than 50 per cent within the space of a year—that lend an air of instability to politics, particularly since the sibyls who interpret the oracular results are often unable to produce a convincing explanation for the quirky alternation of peaks and valleys.

Polls illustrate a media axiom that may be compared to Heisenberg's Uncertainty Principle in physics: observing politics affects the phenomenon being observed. Considered in this light, the true function of the press probably lies somewhere between the elitist and populist models. In any given day's outpouring of news, some of the stories reveal information hidden in the darker recesses of government. Other stories present data, such as crime statistics and balance of trade figures, that are generated by government specifically for dissemination. Occupying the middle ground is news that the press itself generates directly (polling data, for example) or indirectly by its presence (the atmospherics of campaigning). The role of the press in recent years as creator of facts that affect politics has been grafted onto its inquisitorial and disseminative functions.

The balance between the inquisitorial and disseminative roles of journalists has shifted somewhat towards the former since the Watergate affair of 1972–4, which was a crisis for the press as well as for the constitutional system. In many respects, Watergate represented American newsmen's finest hour. Displaying exemplary courage and initiative in reporting malefaction at the highest levels of government, the press stirred a lethargic Congress and judiciary to question seriously the probity of a President. Of all institutions, the press emerged from the scandal with the most enhanced reputation.

But Watergate also necessitated a sober re-evaluation of the customary ways of purveying information provided by government. Newsmen had suffered a betrayal and a loss of innocence. Throughout Watergate, many of those 'reliable sources' had proven amazingly unreliable, leaking erroneous tips, and many an official had looked reporters in the eye and blatantly dissembled. Gone was the traditional assumption that officials, though prone to embellish and self-serve, did not deliberately lie. As Katharine Graham, publisher of the *Washington Post*, commented: 'the process of deception has always been at least a theoretical possibility to working journalists throughout history. But in our time it became a major hazard.' The process of deception had first been detected during the Vietnam war in wildly exaggerated enemy 'body counts' and annual predictions of victory by Christmas. Yet those untruths were never so patent as in Watergate and did not involve moral turpitude or conspiracies to obstruct justice.

Concluding from Watergate that government was rife with corruption, many reporters embarked upon crusades to uncover it. 'Investigative reporting', blending the skills of the journalist and the private detective, became the watchword. Any official who had ever taken a shady political contribution or perpetrated a 'dirty trick' against an election opponent was liable to be exposed by hard-digging newsmen. Little Watergates were cropping up in the remotest villages. President Nixon, after all, had proclaimed 'I am not a crook,' and it turned out that he had been lying. Why believe lesser officials when they said the same thing?

In its zeal, however, the press began to establish a single criterion by which to test an official's qualification for public office—honesty. It acted as if there were no germane questions to be asked about the suitability of a public official other than whether he was a criminal or a liar. In the rush to test the candour of those in public life, the press often neglected their opinions about public issues and their performance in previous offices. An example of this occurred during the congressional hearings in 1974 on the nomination of Nelson Rockefeller to be Vice President. Although he had been governor of New York for about fifteen years, the press hardly discussed his record in that office, preferring to concentrate on the ethics of his having made personal loans to other public officials.

The tone of hostility towards officialdom that some reporters have adopted may strain the adversary relationship to the breaking point. By acting upon the premise, as one reporter put it, that 'there is only one way for a newsman to look at politicians, and that is down', the press could jeopardize its traditional close ties to government. What is gained by subjecting officials to trial by ordeal may be lost by making them less open with the press and less willing to provide those copious daily helpings of information. The press might become more argumentative and moralizing, but less generally informative, jettisoning all pretence to objectivity. Investigative reporting has already produced a strike force of self-proclaimed 'advocacy journalists', who use the press to espouse such causes as consumerism.

The search for crimes, conspiracies, foibles and cover-ups does not promise to be a fruitful way of explicating the broader issues of public policy. Yet, because investigative reporting has become the glamour assignment in the journalistic fraternity, the press gives the impression that all would be well were public officials not corrupt or immoral. It is a simple and satisfying view of the world, but it can be grossly misleading.

There are, however, some signs of retrenchment by the press. Within a decade after Watergate, many editors began to recognize that reporters had fallen into questionable habits in pursuit of their stories. The reporters too often relied on unnamed sources for accusatory material or engaged in deceptive tactics, such as impersonation. In a few sensational instances, exposés were found to have been totally invented by over-eager reporters. (A series in the *Washington Post* about a child drug addict was awarded a Pulitzer Prize—until its author confessed that she had fabricated the entire story.) Press harassment also became an issue. Colorado Senator Gary Hart was driven from the 1988 presidential primaries by stories about his dalliance with a model—stories that were obtained by a reportorial stakeout of his private residence. Hart was asked highly intrusive questions at press conferences about the status of his marriage and his history of adultery. The relevance of the inquiry to his fitness for the presidency was dubious, as was the propriety of the reporters' tactics. Similarly, the press expended considerable effort investigating the real estate business of the husband of Geraldine Ferraro, the Democratic Vice Presidential candidate in 1984. The *New York Times*, the *Wall Street Journal* and the *Washington Post* assigned a combined total of 16 full-time reporters to comb the Ferraro records. In the end, no 'smoking gun' was found that might impugn her fitness to be Vice President.

There are signs, however, that the standards of proof in ethics matters may well be relaxed in order to simplify the reporters' task. In the case of another politician accused of adultery, as well as conflict of interest, the subject of its investigation, a nominee for the post of Secretary of Defense in the Bush administration, was said to have an 'appearance problem'. The evidence did not amount to a smoking gun, one reporter explained, 'but there sure was a lot of smoke'. The nominee, former Senator John Tower, did not get the post.

The Hart, Ferraro and Tower episodes are examples of what has been described as a 'media feeding frenzy', a metaphor that brings to mind schools of piranha fish savaging their hapless prey. The comparison is a bit harsh on the press, however, because the media have at other times lavished unduly flattering coverage on the same politicians. At those times, the more apt animal kingdom comparison would be to sheep. A fairer critique would be that, whether obsequious or abrasive, the press often behaves like a herd. The news outlets rarely exercise independent judgement but follow each other mindlessly, either in flattery or savagery.

The press also may seem unnecessarily insistent because the exposé is less crucial, in the post-Watergate era. 'Special prosecutors', appointed under the Ethics in Government Act, diligently investigate whenever serious charges are levelled at important members of an administration. Congress, too, has played a more aggressive investigative role. The press has been left with the relatively passive task of reporting investigations. The press, indeed, arrived late for two major scandals of the Reagan Administration. The sale of arms to Iran and the illegal diversion of the profits to the 'contra' rebels in Nicaragua was exposed by Congress, as was influence-peddling in the awarding of subsidies by the Department of Housing and Urban Development. The Iran-Contra affair was pursued by a special prosecutor for more than five years, at a cost of $28 million—far greater resources than the press could have devoted to the task. Although the investigation resulted in few serious penalties, the public did learn a good deal about the inner workings of the White House and intelligence agencies.

The tendency of the press to focus on crime and corruption is not entirely new. Watergate exacerbated a tendency; it did not create one. American newspapers have always preferred a juicy scandal to the mundane details of budgets, taxation and legislation. Uncovering corruption has been the quick route to a Pulitzer Prize and other awards for journalistic excellence. No doubt this preoccupation reflected the sad fact that government officials, especially those in local government, have not always shown a scrupulous regard for the distinction between the public purse and their private bank accounts. And since officials are not eager to prosecute themselves, it has been left to the press to bring public censure to bear. The archetypical case was the *New York World*'s expose in the 1870s of the 'Tweed Ring', operated by Boss Tweed of the New York City Democratic Party. But while corruption is an enduring feature of municipalities, it gets more attention from the press than do subtler but at least equally important dysfunctions of urban government, including the ways in which it plans development, decides zoning patterns, builds highways, runs schools, and raises taxes.

Why do these issues not receive adequate attention from reporters? Part of the answer is the journalist's belief that readers would find such stories boring—certainly less interesting than a good scandal—and probably would not even understand them. The newspaperman's mental image of the average reader is a picture of a barely literate boor. Rowland Evans, a leading journalist, has described him thus: 'The average newspaper reader works in a Chicago steel mill, and his big occasion is Friday night at the local tavern with his wife and friends. Mostly he reads the comics and the sports.' Attempting to interest such a reader, newspapers emphasize those themes which might appeal to his supposedly limited comprehension: blood, sex and money.

Another part of the answer, although most journalists would be reluctant to admit it, is that newspapermen themselves have difficulty understanding the more complex processes that underlie the day-to-day operations of government. American journalists have never been intellectuals; until the last few decades higher education was not a prerequisite for the job. Aspiring reporters worked their way up from copy boy by displaying industriousness and perseverance, not esoteric knowledge.

But the demands of the job are changing. The modern reader craves an understanding of the dynamics of inflation, balance of payments and credit squeezes. He is curious about why there is a food shortage in parts of the world and what can be done about it. If he is asked to conserve fuel, he wants to know the reason. To explain these complex phenomena, journalists need expertise in economics, agriculture, geology and other technical subjects. Some newspapermen are, in fact, arming themselves with graduate training. 'Speciality reporting' could challenge investigative reporting as the journalism of the future.

But it remains doubtful whether the journalists, however good their intentions, can overcome the inherent contradiction between the complexity of the real world and the format of news presentation. Traditionally, a news story is supposed to simplify events for the reader, not merely serve them up with all their ambiguities showing. As journalist Douglas Cater has observed, 'A reporter is a simplifier ... he tends to ignore complexity when he can't understand it.' He does the same when he can understand it but despairs of being able to make the reader understand it. Yet the process of policy-making in government is full of subtleties: costs and benefits, alternatives and counter-alternatives. Since it is difficult to deal with such shades of grey without feeling that he has confused readers even further, he prefers whenever plausible to attribute the ills of society to corruption in high places, a clash of personalities, in-fighting among political cliques, and similarly dramatic causes.

Even the layout of the newspaper militates against sophisticated discussion of issues. Events must be graded by order of magnitude to determine the placement of stories on the page, the size of the headline and the length of the text. But the standard of measurement is not the history of mankind, the last century or even the last decade: it is merely a single day. The consequent distortions become obvious if one imagines a day on which an important tax reform bill passes and an airliner crashes, killing scores of people. The crash is interesting because it is sudden and dramatic and evokes sympathy for the victims. But its significance in the grand scheme of things is fleeting. It will be forgotten the next day. The tax bill, on the other hand, will have consequences for every citizen for a long time to come. But having dragged through Congress for many months, the tax bill is not really 'new' or dramatic. So the plane crash merits a grand display and lengthy coverage as the important story of the day, while the tax bill is relegated to the status of minor story.

The failings of the press are all the more disappointing when one considers what enviable freedom to enlighten and criticize it enjoys. The news media in America have been accorded a constitutional position of immunity that surely must be the envy of journalists labouring under more restrictive conditions elsewhere in the world. The First Amendment stipulates that 'Congress shall make no law abridging freedom of speech or of the press'. Because of it, nothing even remotely similar to the British Official Secrets Act or the system of D-notices hinders American newspapers. No suppression of news, no licensing of publishers nor taxation of newspapers (other than normal business taxes) may be imposed. Not even criminal trials are sheltered—although there have been attempts to do so—from the press's virtually absolute right to 'publish and be damned'.

The First Amendment was intended primarily to preclude prosecution of the common law crime of seditious libel. But, recognizing the crucial role of the press in the democratic order, the Supreme Court has read the amendment as a broad charter of editorial freedom. In a 1931 decision, *Near v. Minnesota*, the justices declared in ringing terms that preventing publication by court order was the 'essence of censorship' and was prohibited by the First Amendment. Forty years later the court reaffirmed its stand against prior restraint of the press in the Pentagon Papers Case. A secret report recounting the political and military stratagems employed by the United States in Vietnam was stolen from the Defense Department by a former employee, Daniel Ellsberg, and given to the press. Although the official documents in question were purloined and although the attorney general asserted that their disclosure threatened 'national security', the court judged the government powerless to prevent their publication by the *New York Times* and the *Washington Post*. Justice Hugo Black, in one of the opinions in that case, observed that 'The Government's power to censor the press was abolished [by the First Amendment] so that the press would remain forever free to censure the Government. The press was protected so that it could bare the secrets of government and inform the people.'

Although protected against prior government censorship, the press might have been forced to censor itself if it could be held legally responsible for words already printed. But the Supreme Court has prevented public officials or even 'public figures' from recovering damages for a false and defamatory statement unless made 'with knowledge that it was false or with reckless disregard of whether it was false or not'. A similar test applies to reports published about private individuals incidentally connected with 'matters of public interest', such as victims of crimes. Few plaintiffs can meet that heavy burden of proof, which is precisely what the court intended, since it considered libel damages contrary to 'the principle that debate on public issues should be uninhibited, robust and wide-open'. The court has deemed it better to tolerate falsehoods than to deter free expression.

While it has not extended protection to the subjects of press investigations, the court has acted to make publishers honour obligations to their own sources. In 1991, the justices held that a newspaper is bound by an implicit contract to keep a promise of anonymity given in return for information. That same year the court found that an identified source who is misquoted could recover damages if he could prove that the quotation was 'materially' inaccurate as well as damaging to his reputation. The standard of accuracy is, however, something less than absolutely faithful reproduction of the spoken words.

If there is a serious legal threat to freedom of the press today, it lies in the confrontation between journalists and the criminal courts. One source of conflict is the grand jury. Courts empanel grand juries to investigate suspected criminal activities and hand up indictments. The juries may subpoena witnesses, and those who refuse to testify after being granted immunity from prosecution can be convicted of contempt of court. Some grand juries have attempted to secure information about crimes by compelling journalists to testify, but the reporters have refused for fear of compromising their confidential sources and deterring others from talking to the press. Journalists contend that drying up confidential sources would defeat the public's 'right to know', a right which newsmen claim as a corollary of freedom of the press. Although at other times it has seemed convinced that the purpose of the First Amendment was a well-informed public, the Supreme Court in 1972 denied that there is a 'right to know' or that newsmen possess any special occupational privilege to refuse to testify before grand juries. Several states, however, have attempted to create that privilege by statute, enacting 'shield laws' to protect journalists from grand-jury questioning.

The reporting of criminal trials also brings journalists and the judiciary into conflict. There is no law that routinely restricts disclosure of the facts of a criminal case or the proceedings in the courtroom. It is generally agreed that such restrictions would violate the First Amendment. However, on a few occasions, judges who were concerned that newspaper accounts might prejudice the defendant's right to a fair trial have ordered journalists not to report certain crucial facts on pain of contempt. The Supreme Court has frowned upon these 'gag orders', but the Court has ruled that judges possess the power to exclude the press from pre-trial hearings in some circumstances. Several states have sought to shield victims of crime, particularly rape, from publicity by requiring the press to withhold their names, even though the trial itself may draw nationwide attention. The constitutionality of these laws remains doubtful, and they have not always proven to be enforceable as a practical matter in sensational cases. The press has generally maintained a policy of voluntary restraint, dubbing the victim as 'the Central Park jogger' or using a similar oblique reference, and even where cameras are allowed in the courtroom, the accuser's face may be blanked out. Some editors now believe that the stigma of rape will be overcome only if the victims choose to identify themselves, thereby educating the public about the nature of the crime. In any event, voluntarism on the part of the victim and the media appears to be a more feasible solution than legal regulation.

There is a much more serious, if more subtle, threat to the

free flow of news than judicial orders or grand jury investigations: the tendency of officials to 'classify' too many documents on the flimsy ground that their publication would not be in the public interest. All too often, as Justice Potter Stewart once observed, the classification system may be 'manipulated by those intent on self-protection or self-promotion'. To counteract the bureaucratic mania for stamping 'Classified', 'Secret', and 'Top Secret' on papers without valid criteria for doing so, Congress passed the Freedom of Information Act in 1966. The act declared all federal documents open public records, except those dealing with personnel, private financial dealings, national security and criminal investigation. It requires officials to establish standards for deciding which documents are in the exempt categories and allows citizens to challenge these classifications in court. Congress, which often has trouble itself extracting information from bureaucrats, amended the act in 1974 to further broaden public access by disciplining officials who capriciously refuse to disclose information and allowing judges to examine all challenged documents *in camera* to determine if they are properly classified. The law may one day cover Congress itself, assuring access to legislative documents.

President Reagan, however, tightened the information tap considerably by promulgating classification standards which tend to err on the side of over-protectiveness. The standards reflect a conservative view that the act facilitated espionage against the US. The Reagan administration also required former officials to clear their writings with the government censor before publication if they had access to classified information. In addition, the Intelligence Identities Protection Act, signed by Reagan, makes it a crime for anyone to reveal the names of US intelligence agents. Taken together, these measures chill the legal climate for discussion of national security matters.

A favourable legal climate has been one important factor in the development of the American press. Another, perhaps equally important factor, is the structure of the newspaper industry. The striking feature of newspaper publication is that it is extremely localized. In Europe, the newspapers published in the capital or the larger cities are read throughout the country, but in America a person reads only the newspapers published in his own city. The circulation of the two most highly regarded newspapers in the country, the *New York Times* and the *Washington Post*, are confined almost exclusively to those two metropolises. A few persons outside New York do receive the *Times* by various means, but that accounts for only a small percentage of the readership. If an American reads a newspaper at all, it is almost invariably a local product, one of the approximately 1800 published daily across the country. Their circulation ranges from a few thousand to about one million; tied to a single city, the typical American newspaper cannot approach the multimillion readership of British and other European papers.

One consequence of localization is that most newspapers are not very good, since they lack resources. There is, however, a great diversity of editorial judgements, both in the 'play' that news events are given and in the opinion columns. At one time there was even more diversity; numerous newspapers competed vigorously in the large cities. But since the Second World War, the economics of newspaper publishing has taken a heavy toll. Scores of newspapers merged with competitors or simply disappeared. New York City, which boasted nine dailies in the 1950s, has now been reduced to two morning and two afternoon papers. Cities as large as Dallas, with a population of more than one million, have but a single newspaper. Dailies compete in fewer than 40 of the nation's 6000 cites and towns. In a desperate effort to promote editorial competition, the federal government has acceded to economic monopoly. The Newspaper Preservation Act of 1970 permits newspapers 'in probable danger of financial failure' to form a 'joint operating agreement', under which they publish separately and maintain editorial independence but share advertising, circulation and printing functions to reduce costs. The joint agreements have been attacked, however, as a form of official licensing of newspapers, since the federal government retains the discretion to approve or disapprove the necessary exemptions from anti-monopoly regulations.

Concentration of ownership has also taken the form of newspaper proprietors buying the local television stations. A number of 'chains', each controlling newspapers in several cities, have become influential. Even more damaging to diversity than concentrated ownership is the dependence of most newspapers on the sole major wire service, the Associated Press. Still, the very large number of newspapers assures that none dominates the national reading public.

A second consequence of localization is the tendency to emphasize local news. Journalists follow the Newtonian principle that the gravity of events varies inversely with the distance from the readers. Sometimes the principle produces ludicrous results. An earthquake killing hundreds in Asia is likely to get about as much attention from Chicago newspapers as a single pedestrian knocked down by a bus in that city. For that reason, news of foreign affairs tends to be woefully ignored by all but a few papers whose readers are presumed to rise above purely provincial concerns. Attention to local events, however, is consonant with the decentralized politics of a federal system. Readers are well served by a press that reports local politics as conscientiously—and usually more knowledgeably—as it does national politics.

The local emphasis, combined with the large number of newspapers, tends to dilute the impact of editorials. As de Tocqueville noted: ' . . . [W]ith so many combatants, neither discipline nor unity is possible . . . Therefore American papers cannot raise those powerful currents of opinion which sweep away or sweep over the most powerful dykes.' Unlike European journals, American newspapers are not sharply divided along ideological lines nor do most of them maintain firm links with a political party. There is no 'party press' to speak of. The newspapers' neutral position has been achieved at least partly by having journalists who are largely liberal and Democratic work for proprietors who are mostly conservative and Republican. Newspapers do customarily endorse candidates in elections, and since the editorials are generally the voice of the proprietors, newspapers have tended to support Republicans at the presidential level. But the editorials strike readers with the force of a feather. That 75 per cent of all newspapers took a stand in favour of his opponent did not prevent John Kennedy from winning the Presidency. Newspaper support may carry somewhat more weight in minor elections, in which neither opponent is likely to be a celebrated figure, but generally what is said about a candidate in the news columns is far more persuasive than the imperial 'we' of the editorial pages.

If there is a 'national' press, in the sense of exerting significant influence, it consists primarily of the *New York Times* (which is considered the general newspaper of record despite its geographically limited core readership), the *Wall Street Journal*, the *Washington Post*, the three mass-circulation news magazines—*Time*, *Newsweek* and *US News*—and the Associated Press. *USA Today*, a daily that circulates throughout the country, is read widely by travellers, but it is a popular rather than 'quality' paper. (Because of its lavish use of colour graphics, it has been called the 'Hawaiian shirt of American journalism'.) On the electronic side, the news divisions of the three major private broadcasting networks have been joined by the Cable News Network, which has become a kind of video wire service, and by a non-commercial television and radio broadcasting network that is supported by a public funds and contributions from viewers. That many of these media outlets maintain headquarters or important offices within a few blocks of each other in New York City is partially responsible for the often expressed belief that an elite, eastern liberal bias pervades the news. The hundreds of local newspapers in circulation make it difficult, however, for an elite, liberal or otherwise, to monopolize any given reader's intake of news.

Television is particularly open to the charge of elitism, because, although there are almost 700 independently owned television stations in the country, most are affiliated with one of the main commercial networks. While the local 'outlets' are responsible for local news programming, each broadcasts national news that is packaged in New York by the networks. In former days, when announcers merely read the headlines, network control of the news drew little attention. However, the networks have begun to do their own investigative reporting, and whenever a trenchant documentary appears, the subjects are likely to complain of unfairness.

Newspapers, which answer to no authority or appeal body, freely ignore such complaints, and they are quite inured to them. But television lacks immunity from sanctions. Newspapers were fortunate enough to have been invented by the late eighteenth century, when the First Amendment was written, but television was not. Therefore, Congress, with the acquiescence of the courts, has made 'electronic journalism' a thing apart from the branch of the trade which uses printing presses. The difference in technologies, perhaps, made governmental regulation of television inevitable. While myriad newspapers may compete for readers, television stations operate on exclusively assigned frequencies. Acting upon the theory that the airwaves were in the national domain, Congress, in the Federal Communications Act of 1934, parcelled them out to private enterprise—commercial broadcasting stations—much as it parcelled out the rights to exploit mineral deposits. (Non-commercial broadcasting appeared much later.)

Naturally, a great many strings are attached to broadcasting licences. The Federal Communications Commission may deny or revoke a licence if it believes a broadcaster is not serving the public interest, convenience or necessity. For, as the Supreme Court said in 1969, 'it is the right of the viewers and listeners, not the right of broadcasters, which is paramount'. FCC guidelines determine whether the broadcaster is, in fact, serving the public interest. The commission has, for example, required a certain minimum proportion of time to be devoted to news, and it has prescribed that the coverage be 'fair'. In some instances the commission has required persons mentioned unfavourably in news or commentary to be given free air time to reply. Thus, whenever complaints of 'unfairness' are lodged against television stations by viewers, the station has cause to fear for its very existence. In the past, licences have almost never been denied because of such complaints, but 'viewer power' could gain influence in licensing.

The fair coverage expectation that applies to television has no counterpart in the print media. In 1974, the Supreme Court struck down a state law that obliged newspapers to print replies to its editorial commentaries. Many newspapers have, however, voluntarily appointed ombudsmen, usually former editors, who enjoy authority to investigate reader complaints and write columns criticizing editorial decisions. The child addict fabrication, for example, was carefully analyzed in print by the *Washington Post* ombudsman.

Government regulation is one reason why television is a less probing news medium than print. Another is that newscasting is imbued with the values of the entertainment industry, of which the small screen is a part. Television newsmen prefer 'infotainment'—simple and diverting to the eye. As a television executive has observed, 'If it didn't happen on film, it almost didn't happen.' Events like inflation, which are difficult to capture on film and more difficult to explain in thirty seconds, tend to be dismissed in brief bulletins. Moreover, television newsmen do not share the cynical, adversary tradition that print journalists have had 200 years to develop. Television reporters—sometimes called talking hairdos—are chosen for their comely looks and soothing voices rather than for their enterprising spirit, and few have had the rugged training that newspapermen undergo with demanding editors. As a result, television newsmen are not noted for spontaneously asking penetrating questions.

That is all the more unfortunate since television has now replaced newspapers as the main news source for most persons. People tend to read newspapers for further details of stories that interest them, but their first, and often only, impression of events comes from the picture tube. Opinion research, moreover, indicates that Americans believe what they see on television more readily than what they read in the papers. Despite Walter Lippmann's conviction that the newspaper is the 'bible of democracy', it has never had quite the authority of holy writ; the accuracy of the news columns has always been doubted. The advent of television merely confirmed these doubts by persuading audiences that seeing is indeed believing.

Politicians have been quick to recognize the superior credibility of the electronic medium. Although they may ignore critical newspaper stories and hostile editorials, secure in the knowledge that few read or believe them, politicians are extremely anxious about their television image. President Johnson kept three televisions in his office so that he could monitor all network news broadcasts simultaneously, and President Nixon often resorted to television, speaking to 'each and every one of you', in his effort to mobilize popular support. At the same time, he launched a vigorous campaign to discredit network newsmen for their allegedly prejudicial coverage of him. Among the practices which particularly irked Nixon was 'instant commentary' by newscasters following his television appeals. He felt, for good reason, that they negated the effect of what he had just said.

Nixon was aided by his Vice-President, Spiro Agnew, whose alliterative denunciation of 'nattering nabobs of negativism' was directed at a press that was perceived as dominated by liberals. The Nixon-Agnew critique succeeded in making television (and indeed the rest of the media) self-conscious about 'fairness', and it probably caused newsmen thereafter to bend over backwards to avoid any hint of disdain in their reporting of conservative candidates and administrations. This attitude redounded to the benefit of Ronald Reagan, whose press conferences were treated very gingerly by television, even when, as a few newsmen pointed out, he often showed a surprising unfamiliarity with the details of public issues. At a press conference during the Falkland Islands conflict, for example, the commander in chief seemed confused about whether the military air base on Ascension Island belonged to the US or Britain. And he sometimes failed to recognize members of his own cabinet. He once greeted the US Secretary of Housing and Urban Development on camera as 'Mr Mayor'.

Reagan was, in fact, dubbed the 'great communicator' for his uncanny rapport with television audiences, even though his most successful appearances were thoroughly scripted and scenically elaborate. His successor, George Bush, was also skilled in manipulating television coverage by exploiting 'visuals'. During his successful bid for the presidency in 1988, Bush visited a firm that manufactures American flags—for no evident purpose other than to appear before a backdrop of patriotic regalia. This pseudo-event was covered as campaign 'news'. Such incidents suggest that the networks have found in the Nixon-Agnew critique an excuse to indulge their natural attraction to showmanship. It remains to be seen whether the excesses of some recent campaigns will persuade the electronic media to eschew entertainment values and discriminate between real news and picturesque fluff.

CHAPTER NINE

Elections:
Throwing the Rascals Out

Americans enjoy elections. They may feign boredom when election time comes, but only because the campaign has not lived up to their expectations of a grand show. The best proof of how deeply elections are valued—or how much entertainment they afford—is the number of official posts which are filled by popular vote, rather than appointment. There are approximately 78,000 units of local government in the country, and even the most exiguous of these will have several elected officials. There are also state officials to be chosen, US representatives and senators to be selected and, capping it all, the Presidency to be filled. Even though a President is elected only once in four years, an election of some import to the voters occurs on the first Tuesday in every November.

The various levels of government are but one reason for the multitude of elective offices; another is that Americans are loath to fill any office without hearing the voice of the people. To an American, democracy means elections: balloting is a mechanism which, whatever its flaws, is the closest approximation to obtaining the consent of the governed. Thus, a great many officials are elected whom it might make more sense to appoint.

In most counties the sheriff, who is the chief law enforcement officer, is elected; so are the public prosecutor and the judges. Indeed, virtually the only participant in a criminal case who is not elected may be the defendant. Making a political issue of law enforcement has several undesirable consequences. Aspiring sheriffs make campaign promises to lock up more criminals, candidates for prosecutor pledge to prosecute unflinchingly, prospective judges vow on television to hand down severe sentences. Even if these candidates avoid making other private promises to their supporters (the normal currency of electoral politics), the maintenance of civil liberties and the impartiality of the judicial process are endangered by such campaigning.

In about half the states, the most senior judicial posts—justices of the supreme court—are filled by election, and in many other states, where the justices are initially appointed by the governor or legislature, they must be confirmed in office by the voters after the initial appointive term. In these states, the lawyers who practice before the courts are often the leading contributors to the justices' election campaigns, a practice that verges upon barrister baksheesh.

Besides electing important officials who ought to be appointed, Americans spend a great deal of time and effort voting for persons to fill quite minor positions, especially at the state and local levels. Commissioners of water supply and commissioners of sewers are selected by the ballot box in many places; a community in the New York City suburbs duly elects commissioners to administer an escalator in a train station. Most members of school boards (education committees) are elected and their annual budget subjected to a referendum. State commissioners of parks and administrators of forests are sometimes elected officials. When one considers the variety of elective posts, the Old American aphorism, 'he couldn't get elected dog catcher', does not really seem so far-fetched.

The combination of local self-government and elections for all offices does take its toll of the average citizen's powers of concentration. Where voting machines are not used, for example, the voter is given a single paper ballot, listing the candidates from President down to hamlet councillor; the paper is so huge that it is called a 'bedsheet ballot'. Under these conditions the theory of the informed voter choosing rationally among candidates whose position he knows is hardly accurate. The United States may have reached democratic overkill, the point at which so many elections are being held that no voter can possibly pay attention to them all.

The sheer volume of electoral politics helps explain the fragmentation of the two main parties. At the national level, the Republicans and the Democrats exist in name only. Each is a coalition of state and local organizations which carry the

Republican or Democratic banners in their own bailiwicks. The parties may convene nationally every four years to nominate a presidential candidate, but in the years between, the local party organizations have their eyes fixed upon electing governors, mayors, county commissioners, state legislators and dozens of officials who mean more to their supporters in bread-and-butter terms than the President.

A monolithic, centrally controlled party with a well-defined manifesto could hardly cope with so many electoral contests. Such a plethora of local issues need to be addressed that a rigid party line would limit a candidate's freedom of movement intolerably. In a British general election, every seat helps decide which party shall rule the country; even by-elections are taken as a sign of party strength nationally. But in America the local party organizations and candidates are engaged in campaigns whose national significance is usually minimal. They have little incentive for co-ordinating efforts with the party organization in the next county, let alone the next state.

Party politics is thus carried on primarily at the state and local level and only secondarily at the national level. The total number of representatives and senators elected for each party in these state contests does of course alter the balance of power in Congress, but the constituents vote mainly according to local political considerations. The closest equivalent to a British general election, the presidential election, is the only contest where the issue is clearly national rather than local.

If the parties have no programme, then why bother with parties? For one thing, having no ideological commitment is not the same as having no goal. Parties have a very definite goal: seizing as many offices as possible. They also provide a vehicle for involving people in politics, even if only at the level of factotum in campaign headquarters. For those who care about such things, participation yields a sense of having some influence on public affairs. For those who don't care, the parties perform the task of nominating candidates, removing the burden of having to decide for whom to vote. Because there is not much ideological content in American parties, the process of choosing one's party need not be a matter of rational choice at all. The very considerable effort which has been expended by American political scientists studying the voting behaviour of their compatriots indicates that party affiliation is generally inherited, along with social characteristics, like religion, race and income level, from one's parents and maintained because of one's friends and relatives. Thus, the social bases of the two parties differ, if not their theoretical underpinnings.

Despite the striking correlation between income level and party affiliation, however, Republicans and Democrats are not nearly as close to being class parties as are Labourites and Tories, primarily because ethnic as well as economic characteristics determine voting patterns. In general, the Republican party tends to be the party of the more affluent. The party draws its strength from small towns, suburbs of big cities and rural areas. Ethnically, the party is the stronghold of the WASP (White Anglo-Saxon Protestant), a term for Americans who trace their ancestry to early British, Germanic and Scandinavian settlers. The Democrats, on the other hand, are the party of the lower-income groups. Democratic strength is concentrated in the large cities, and the party has generally held the allegiance of the descendants of the post-Civil War immigrants who congregated there: Jews from Eastern Europe and Catholics from Ireland, Poland and Italy. The party has also enjoyed the disproportionate support of urban blacks. Until the late 1960s, the Democrats maintained a geographical bastion in the south. The region was dubbed the 'Solid South' by grateful Democrats, who reaped the benefits of the traditional resentment of the Republicans for their role in Reconstruction.

Welded together by the Great Depression of the 1930s, the Democratic coalition of ethnic groups and trade unions has undergone great strains in recent decades. The civil rights movement of the 1960s and the advent of black militancy made blacks and many Southern whites reluctant coalition partners, a tension which Nixon's 'Southern Strategy' of campaigning was intended to exploit. In the north, blacks and 'ethnics' crowded together in many cities have been at odds over such issues as crime and racial balance in the urban school systems. In both 1968 and 1972, when Vietnam was an issue, the anti-war activist wing split the party by backing respectively the candidacy of Eugene McCarthy (who was not nominated) and George McGovern (who was nominated and disastrously defeated by Richard Nixon). The trade unions, meanwhile, had grown increasingly independent of the party, perhaps reflecting conservative stirrings among their members. In the 1972 presidential election, the AFL-CIO conspicuously refrained from endorsing the Democratic candidate, and the Teamsters Union actually entered into a tacit alliance with President Nixon. By the 1980 election, the labour defection was so broad that the blue-collar vote played a sizeable part in electing Ronald Reagan.

Under Reagan, the Republican party hammered a wedge into the Democratic coalition of middle- and lower-income Americans. Marrying middle-class Democrats to higher echelons, Republicans forged a 'top-down' alliance hostile to society's most disadvantaged elements. Social support programmes were portrayed as aiding the poor at the expense of the middle class, and organizations promoting civil liberties, workers' rights, and fair treatment of ethnic minorities were deprecated as selfish 'special interests'.

The Reagan approach tapped a deep vein of hostility, especially toward blacks, who were seen as undeserving beneficiaries of 'affirmative action'—hiring preferences designed to compensate for past discrimination. Reagan passed the baton to George Bush in the election of 1988, after a campaign which will principally be remembered for Republican television commercials featuring Willie Horton, a black convict who kidnapped and raped while on a weekend pass from prison in Massachusetts—the home of Bush's opponent, Governor Michael Dukakis. The personification of white middle-class fears, Horton's menacing visage became emblematic of 'soft on crime' liberalism.

By the 1992 election, the Republican alliance was showing signs of strain between economic conservatives—primarily eager to reduce taxation, public spending and regulatory restraints on the free market—and social conservatives. The latter, often motivated by spiritual concerns, were dedicated to combating 'secularism' (a form of immorality), prayer-less school, legal abortion and tolerance of homosexuality. At the same time, the Southern/Willie Horton Strategy had invited competition from bigotry-driven ideologies further to the right, as evidenced by the emergence of

David Duke, a former Nazi sympathizer, and 'America First' advocate Pat Buchanan, as national Republican figures.

A Democratic coalition has begun to reassemble, although the amalgam contains new elements. The Hispanic population, which grew by half during the 1980s, has become a major political force, and the traditionally diverse Democratic Party is a natural home for many citizens of Latin American descent. Women's organizations are now also a formidable presence in the party, as are ginger groups seeking major changes in environmental, health and social service policies. Blacks, who were charter members of the old coalition, are claiming a greater voice in party councils. Douglas Wilder was elected the first black governor of Virginia, a former slave state, in 1989, and Jesse Jackson ran widely admired, albeit ultimately unsuccessful, campaigns for the Democratic presidential nomination in 1984 and 1988. The Jackson candidacies stimulated an exponential increase in black registration and voting—a phenomenon that, if durable, could prove to be a reservoir of strength for Democrats generally.

Reacting to anti-labour policies of the Reagan Administration, the union movement has returned to the Democratic fold. The AFL-CIO went so far as to endorse a Democrat (Walter Mondale) before the primaries leading up to the 1984 election, seeking to gain an early foothold in the formulation of campaign strategy. The crushing failure of the Mondale and Dukakis candidacies highlighted, however, the decline in union leaders' influence on the voting habits of their members. Many unionists had become 'blue collar Republicans' who flowed with the tide of 'Reagan Democrats'.

Although still convinced that some essential social goals can be achieved only through active government, the Democrats have taken sober account of the widespread perception that liberalism relied too heavily on programmes geared to oppressive and ineffective bureaucracies. 'Post-liberal' Democrats are keen to expand individual choice and opportunity rather than the administrative apparatus—for example, by granting tuition funds directly to parents so that they can select the school they prefer for their children. Some Democrats also back character-building schemes to combat welfare-state dependency syndrome, foster a sense of personal accountability and civic responsibility, and restore the balance between individual rights and community obligations. There is support for a volunteer service corps, for instance, in which youngsters could earn funding for university education through community or military service, and for 'work-fare' and 'learn-fare' plans, requiring benefit recipients to acquire job skills or educational credentials. The new Democrat is typically pro-business in the sense that he favours a national industrial policy based not on 'picking winners' but creating a sound physical infrastructure and qualified workforce, thereby allowing private enterprise to compete more effectively in world markets. Many Democratic planners now accentuate tax credits and market incentives, instead of regulation, as a means of achieving their objectives.

Various third parties have cropped up throughout American history whenever large numbers of voters have deemed themselves unrepresented by either of the two main parties. (Any party other than the Republicans and Democrats is termed a 'third' party; even a fourth party is generically a 'third' party.) They have proven ephemeral, however, because usually either the Republicans or the Democrats move towards the position of the third party just enough to capture most of its supporters. When they do emerge, however, third parties can pose a serious threat to the major candidates. In 1968, Governor George C. Wallace amassed about 13 per cent of the votes cast, running as a candidate of the American Independent Party, enough to deny either main candidate a popular majority. In 1980, however, the presence of a third-party candidate, liberal Republican John Anderson, did not prevent Ronald Reagan from winning a resounding electoral vote victory. A potential successor to Wallace appeared in 1991 in the person of David Duke, the telegenic ex-Nazi (dubbed the 'Robert Redford of hatred'), who formerly paraded in a swastika armband. Engaging in the 'politics of resentment', Duke became nationally prominent as the result of a racially polarized gubernatorial election that year in Louisiana. Although he lost, Duke secured a clear majority of the white vote by denouncing the 'welfare class'—a code term for blacks. His strong showing was interpreted as a distress signal from a state whose main industry, oil, had been in a prolonged depression; support for him was most pronounced among voters with low-to-middle income and education levels. Ethnic animosity had erupted once again from economic ruin—a Deep South reprise of the Weimar Republic. Duke's movement also could be viewed as a reiteration of a characteristic southern paradox: economic populism wearing the uniform (in this instance, the Brown Shirt) of intolerance. In bad times, loathing for the racial underclass frequently had been a rallying point for white discontent. The key variable was whether the Duke message could be refashioned, by him or another candidate, to rouse pockets of economically disaffected whites located further north.

In the early 1990s, feminists, too, talked of founding their own party. A Women's Party would be devoted to matters ignored by male politicians, particularly women's rights, child care and family health. Half the population, obviously, would have a natural affinity for such a party—it could be considered the ultimate in single-issue movements—and surveys have shown that female elected officials differ significantly from their male counterparts in their attitudes toward many political goals. Nevertheless, the precise effect of a gender-based electoral formation remains untested. The failure to adopt the Equal Rights Amendment, which had been proposed in the 1970s, suggests that causes distinctive to women may be too narrow a base for a viable party.

Typically, third parties are a response to 'Me-Too-ism', the proclivity of the main parties to take nearly identical positions in their effort to stake out that vast middle ground where dwells the uncommitted voter. An indication of the size of the uncommitted middle may be gleaned from polls in which almost a third of voters classify themselves as 'independent'. No doubt many of these respondents pride themselves on their independence of mind while exhibiting a suspiciously consistent pattern of voting for the same party in every election. But it is fairly clear that the voter of no fixed affiliation, the voter who switches parties unpredictably from one election to the next, often decides presidential contests.

There is a large body of citizens whose political inclinations are unknown since they do not bother to trudge to the polling booths to register their views. In a presidential election more than 40 per cent of those eligible normally do not vote; in congressional elections the abstainers may be a majority. According to the 'good citizen' theory of democracy, the apathy of so many signals danger, but some political sociologists have argued that those who do not vote are those with 'low commitment to democratic norms', that is people who might support a dictator if given the chance. Their failure to vote is a sign of contentment with democracy, the argument runs; their active participation in politics would be the real danger signal. Another theory is that those who fail to vote are caught between 'cross-pressures'. They may have one reason, such as ethnicity, for voting for one party, and another reason, such as economic status, for voting for the other party. They resolve their dilemma by staying home on election day.

Yet another theory posits a more practical reason for non-voting: the failure to become registered in advance. The participation rate of registered voters is relatively high, yet only about 65 percent of those eligible to vote manage to register in advance. The implication is that non-voting is not deliberate abstention but inadvertent disenfranchisement; on the other hand, those states that have loosened their registration requirements in recent decades have seen no startling upsurge in voting.

Registration was designed to avoid irregularities, such as voting more than once in any election or voting by non-residents. (Curiously, voting by resident non-citizens is allowed in some elections of purely local officials, such as town councillor.) But this matter-of-fact prerequisite may pose a substantial barrier for some. Strong interest in an election campaign often does not develop until the last few weeks, by which time the state-determined deadline for registration—typically 30 days before the voting—may have expired. Widespread adoption of the 'motor voter' plan, under which a car driver's license is deemed a sufficient credential at the voting booth, could do much to unblock the route to the ballot box, if registration is the main obstacle. Holding elections on a non-work day (Saturday or Sunday) as in many countries with higher participation rates might also increase turnout.

Despite these theories, however, what, if anything, is signified by the failure to vote remains a matter for sheer speculation. If it is difficult to explain the way people vote, it is even more difficult to explain the way they do not vote. About the only cause of non-voting that is patent is the weather; rain on election day is a notorious dampener of civic ardour.

The parties find their expression as national entities in that ultimate electoral spectacle, the presidential campaign. Although winning the election gives the party control only of the executive branch, it symbolizes capturing the reins of government. As much energy and emotion are invested in that contest as in all other elections combined, and the number of people who participate either as delegates to nominating conventions or volunteer campaign workers runs into the hundreds of thousands.

The campaign begins just after the last election with sporadic declarations by the aspirants that they are *not* candidates for the Presidency. So many politicians have disavowed the office and then run for it that no one would be taken seriously unless he declared his non-candidacy early. Early polls, in addition, often reflect more enthusiasm for a challenge to an incumbent president before a specific challenger is mentioned; once the potential opponent is no longer faceless, support may wane, owing to his 'high negatives', a polling status even worse than 'low name recognition'.

In the immediate aftermath of the Persian Gulf war of 1990–1, many early disclaimers turned out to be genuine, for the most prominent Democrats judged that military victory had rendered President Bush invulnerable in 1992. The field was abandoned to a second tier of lesser known candidates. The episode reveals a crucial flaw in the loose style of American party organization: each of a party's leading lights, finding his personal prospects of winning the Presidency bleak, may decide to sit out an election. The cumulative result is that the rank-and-file party members are left rudderless. The opposition leadership is unburdened by any sense of collective responsibility to mount a campaign, especially when the odds are unfavourable.

Two years before the next election, generally speaking, the candidates formally enter the ring. The enormous length of time spent campaigning for the office has been criticized as a waste of effort which does nothing to enlighten the electorate but much to bore it, and politicians generally recognize the importance of having one's campaign 'peak' precisely on election day. Peaking too early means that the slogans have ceased seeming clever and the voter is tired of seeing the candidate's name on car bumpers. Strangely, all but the last two or three months of the campaign is spent in obtaining the nomination, so that often the final showdown between the party nominees seems somehow anticlimactic.

Winning the nomination means persuading a majority of the approximately four thousand delegates to the Democratic National Convention or the two thousand to the Republican National Convention. Conventions are not mentioned in the constitution, which makes no provision at all for nominating presidential candidates, but they are among the most enduring customary institutions. Until recently the delegates to the convention were chosen by the party organization in each state, usually meeting in a state convention. The national convention allowed a consensus on the presidential candidate to develop among state delegations unfamiliar with all the potential contenders. Delegates bargained in 'smoke-filled rooms', and numerous ballots were often required to select the candidate. But now that improved communications have made candidates' names household words, the convention appears to be searching for a new, more relevant function.

Since the old smoke-filled room is no longer a satisfying method of selection, there has been a growing tendency to choose the delegates themselves through state-wide primary conventions or other selection mechanisms that involve more than just party 'regulars'. Typically a state of proposed delegates committed to voting for Candidate X runs against slates committed to Candidates Y and Z. Most primaries are 'closed' in the sense that only registered members of a party can vote for delegates to its national convention. In a few states, the desire to maximize citizen participation has produced 'open' primaries in which a registered party member can 'cross over' to vote in another party's internal struggle. Until the law was changed in 1959, Californians could vote in *both* party primaries, a permissiveness which most politicians could not abide because it encouraged the opposition to 'raid' a primary and saddle them with easily beatable candidates.

The states with primaries, however, supply only part of the convention delegates, so that the nomination ultimately may be decided by the representatives of the non-primary states. But the significance of the primaries goes far beyond the actual voting strength of the delegations so selected. (Some primaries are merely advisory, and some of those that bind the delegates to vote for the primary winner bind them only on the first convention ballot.) For the primaries give presidential aspirants, most of whom have successfully campaigned only within their own states as governors or senators, a chance to demonstrate their appeal as a national candidate.

In many instances, primary victories have been immensely persuasive. John F. Kennedy, then a senator from Massachusetts, was able, by winning the West Virginia primary in 1960, to dispel the fears of many Democratic politicians that a Catholic would be trounced in predominantly Protestant states. At one stroke, he shattered the tenacious myth that a Catholic could never be elected President because of religious prejudice. In another momentous primary, Senator Eugene McCarthy persuaded President Johnson not to run for re-election by rolling up a sizeable second-place vote in New Hampshire in 1968.

It is not necessary, however, for a candidate to run in any primary. A candidate may choose to 'sit out' the primaries and do business on the convention floor, especially if he is a well-known figure who doesn't need the exposure of the ordeal by battle. For primaries pose a definite risk to a candidate. Victories are often inconclusive; they may be written off as idiosyncrasies or the product of peculiar circumstances. Senator Muskie's victory in New Hampshire in 1972 was not considered impressive because he represented a neighbouring state. Defeat in a primary, however, always looks bad, and may prove conclusive. Hubert Humphrey's loss to Kennedy in the West Virginia primary crushed his chances of gaining the nomination in 1960.

Many valid objections to primaries have been raised. The states that hold them, first of all, are not representative of the American electorate as a whole. Much attention is focused on the New Hampshire primary, held in February of the election year, because it is the nation's earliest. Yet no one would argue that a candidate acceptable to tiny New Hampshire, a rather eccentric state, is thereby the obvious choice of voters elsewhere. To increase the significance of primaries, several states can synchronize their elections, providing a broader sample of the electorate.

In March, 1988, 21 states held primaries and caucuses on the same day, inaugurating an event dubbed 'Super Tuesday'. Many of the Super Tuesday states were in the south, so that it amounted to a regional primary for that section of the country. Hundreds of delegates were at stake for each party.

Although it provided a larger sample of the electorate, Super Tuesday magnified another objection to primaries: the critical role played by expenditure. It is captured pithily in the saying among campaign fund-raisers: 'Money is the first primary.' Before public subsidies began to be provided, in 1976, primaries emphasized the importance of a candidate's personal wealth and that of his associates. Not yet entitled to party financial support, the primary candidate often relied on his personal bank account and on those of his political allies to buy television time, hire staff and pay for the travel of his retinue. The West Virginia primary is again a case in point: in demonstrating the unimportance of a Catholic background to a candidate's acceptability, Kennedy also demonstrated the importance of a family fortune. While Kennedy travelled about the state by air, Humphrey had to make do with a campaign bus.

Even after the provision of public matching funds in primaries, money-raising skills remained a key to success. In Super Tuesday of 1988, electronic outreach across several states necessitated a sudden and intensive investment of seed capital. Those candidates who fared well reaped the rewards of spending perhaps three times as much as those who did poorly. At the beginning of primary season, especially, there may be large financial disparities among the candidates. A year before the 1992 election, one candidate had already raised nearly $800,000; another lagged far behind with less than $50,000. In some years, the leading candidate is millions of dollars ahead of the nearest competitor. Candidates commute between 'the Gold Coasts' (New York and California) to solicit wealthy contributors, even while campaigning in other states. The season of fund-raising get-togethers with celebrity donors from the Southern California entertainment industry has been termed the 'Hollywood primary'. There is something disquieting about watching Presidents, Vice Presidents, senators and governors ignore their official duties while they disport themselves in a marathon of primaries. As the *New York Times* lamented, in an editorial published late in 1975:

> With the national elections still fourteen months away, the country . . . faces the prospect of a President spending one third to one half—and eventually all—of his time crisscrossing the nation by jet plane in an endless round of speechmaking, handshaking, on-the-run news interviews and miscellaneous appearances.

Winning primaries is only part of the candidate's task. He must also woo the delegates from the states which have no primaries. In these states the delegates are frequently chosen by a convention whose members have been selected by neighbourhood-level caucuses. The caucuses have become particularly important as bellwethers of electoral success, giving an early indication of a candidate's 'grassroots' support. Held even earlier than the New Hampshire primary, the Iowa caucuses can transform an overlooked candidate into a major contender. Jimmy Carter's break-through as a presidential campaigner was his performance in the Iowa caucuses in 1976: although little known outside the South, he fared better than more seasoned candidates. In the campaign for the 1992 election, by contrast, Senator Tom Harkin of Iowa, who was an early candidate for the Democratic nomination, could look forward to no significant lift from doing well in Iowa; running in his home state, he presumably had an in-built advantage over outsiders. Any showing less than spectacular, however, could prove fatal.

There are also other, more preliminary contests in which candidates can make their mark. Maine and some other states hold 'straw polls' more than a year before the election, to elicit the presidential preference of key party members. The straw polls have no binding effect, but in the campaign for the 1984 Presidential election four of the main contenders for the Democratic nomination thought it prudent to journey to Maine to appeal personally to the 2000 persons being polled.

In the past, powerful politicians, such as governors, senators and mayors, often controlled the state conventions and therefore the delegations chosen by them. Control by local strongmen is no longer as prevalent, but prominent politicians still influence the composition of delegations and provide much of their leadership. The diligent candidate, consequently, must tour the country, trying to convince the state leaders of his soundness on the issues and of his ability to win the election if chosen. As he listens to requests for his support, a delegation leader has one consideration uppermost in his mind: if he backs what turns out to be the winning candidate—and the earlier the better—his future access to the White House and the patronage and influence it holds, is assured, thereby strengthening his political position in his own state. But if he picks the loser, then he can expect no gratitude from the winning candidate. Early support of a candidate earns more influence, especially support which comes before it is apparent that he will carry the convention. Some leaders commit their troops early, others lead them into the convention hall as an 'uncommitted delegation', keeping all options open. It is common for a candidate to try to demoralize his opponents by claiming to have many delegates secretly committed to him before the convention, but these claims are usually exaggerated. His purpose is to create a 'bandwagon' effect, a panicky feeling among uncommitted delegates that the tide has turned in his favour and that they had better jump on the bandwagon or get left behind.

As the 1992 election approached, considerable disenchantment with the pre-convention phase of the nominating process was evident. Democrats were particularly apprehensive, having lost the three previous elections, that the fragmented system of primaries and caucuses was prone to manipulation by candidates inherently unsuited to winning the White House.

The Iowa caucuses that had first elevated Jimmy Carter from obscurity were a central concern. Iowa was more liberal than the country as a whole, yet by the 1988 election it had come to exert a disproportionate influence. Visiting candidates, journalists and pollsters had pandered to Iowa caucus attenders, turning them into a legendary breed of 'supervoters', savvy *übermenschen* who turned out in the depths of winter to express their candidate preferences. Many of them were single-issue voters, intensely dedicated to their cause and unmoved by the blandishments of consensus politics. Even if Iowa was not typical, the 'bounce' from a respectable showing there could help propel a candidate to victory in later events.

Although simultaneous March primaries would provide a more representative sample, a decisive winnowing effect seemed far from assured. Unlike the 'retail politics' of single-state primaries, the electioneering of the first Super Tuesday, in 1988, had been distinctly wholesale and carried on entirely by electronic means. Maximizing their free television time, candidates streaked by plane to highly contrived appearances in as many as four states in a single day. These gaudily produced visual occasions met the strict definition of a 'media event'—a happening (the candidate milking cows, perhaps) that is more edifying to watch on television than to attend in person. At some stops, the visiting candidate never left the airport. Vast sums were spent saturating 170 'media markets'—the zones covered by local television broadcasts—with negative commercials. Crude 'attack ads' denigrated an opponent's character and distorted his record.

When Wednesday morning dawned, the ultimate drawback of Super Tuesday was already apparent: the costly and often distasteful spectacle had intensified the contest yet had not been decisive. Despite the effort and money expended, there had been what analysts called a 'failure to die', necessitating further primaries. Remnants of the group of relatively unknown Democrats (nicknamed the 'seven dwarfs') who set off together in Iowa lingered on until their fortieth debate, in the New York primary in April.

The flaws of the system, from the Democratic point of view, were illustrated by the eventual nomination of Governor Dukakis. Dukakis managed to survive Iowa, even after inviting derision by advising traditional bulk sweetcorn growers to switch to trendy delicacies like Belgian endives. He also made it past Super Tuesday by dint of a large media budget, much of it raised from his own ethnic community, the Greek-Americans. Yet, burdened by a chilly demeanour and a feeble style on the stump, Dukakis soon proved himself no match for George Bush, the heir to the Reagan mantle. Dukakis carried only a smattering of states in the general election; his triumphant pre-convention campaign seemed a distant and inexplicable memory. To avoid the nomination of candidates so ill-adapted to a general election, many Democratic professionals came to believe, it would be necessary to hold, in effect, a pre-convention in which party regulars designate a short list of contenders to run in the primaries. Whether voters' choices could be limited in such fashion, however, is in some doubt.

The campaign for the nomination comes to a climax at the summer convention, a boisterous, rowdy convocation of thousands of delegates, party officials, and onlookers, which is the only physical incarnation of the national party. Apart from choosing the presidential nominee, the convention serves a number of symbolic functions. The participants spend several days rousing themselves to a fine partisan fervour, with self-laudatory rhetoric, parades and (well-planned) 'spontaneous demonstrations' in favour of one candidate or another. The spirit thus generated is supposed to energize the party workers as they toil on behalf of the nominee. For many participants the convention is a reward for services rendered to the party; the crowd is swollen by alternate delegates, half-delegates and half-alternates, bespeaking an attempt to get as many as possible in on the revelry. (An alternate is provided in case a delegate is taken ill; half-delegates cast one-half vote and a half-alternate is his understudy.)

When assembled, the participants form a colourful panorama of pluralism, a vast celebration of American diversity. Regional idiosyncrasies are proudly flaunted. Puerto Ricans don tropical straw hats, Hawaiians parade with a flower lei around the neck, and Texans cheer for 'real Texas accents' (a barb directed at George Bush, a native New Englander who migrated to that state). Formal roll call votes stretch on interminably because no state can resist the urge to boast about its scenery, its agricultural produce, its climate or its sports heroes. 'Madame Secretary, the Great State of Kansas, the Wheat State, home of the Jayhawks (basketball team)', intones the delegation chairman as he unsubtly prefaces the tally of his contingent with a tourism commercial. The secretary also hears from the 'Land of the Potato' (Idaho), the 'Home of the Grand Canyon' (Arizona), the 'Big Sky State' (Montana), the 'Productive Piedmont' (North Carolina), and 'America's Breadbasket' (Illinois).

The modern convention has, in fact, been likened to a political theme park, a place for amusement and display but not for transacting serious party business, at least not in public. Acknowledging the drift toward spectacle at the expense of substance, the television networks have abandoned gavel-to-gavel news coverage, substituting a two-hour nightly broadcast that often resembles a variety show. Indeed, consultants from the entertainment industry ensure that the party takes maximum advantage of its prime-time slot. Their influence is recognizable in the choice of pastel colour schemes (patriotic red, white and blue appear garish on television), the abbreviated floor demonstrations (now limited to five minutes) and the elimination of 'stemwinders'—the numbing orations from the rostrum that formerly slowed the pace of the event. Despite the visual intensity of its more compact television format, the convention seems to draw a smaller share of the home viewers than in the past, perhaps because they have already been sated by extensive coverage of the primaries, which alone retain a sense of genuine political drama.

The convention does serve to air and sometimes resolve tensions that have developed within the party. There may be a battle in the credentials committee over which of two delegations from the same state represents the true party, requiring the national party to mediate between the state's warring factions. In 1964, for example, the Democratic credentials committee was faced with the choice of seating either all-white delegations from Alabama and Mississippi or all-black delegations organized by civil rights activists. With the wisdom of Solomon, the committee divided the seats between the competing delegations.

The convention's platform committee holds several days of hearings, to demonstrate the party's openness to new ideas, before formulating each of the 'planks', which when nailed together make a platform. The platform is often vague, so as to alienate as few voters as possible, and quickly forgotten once it has been adopted by the full convention. The battle over the platform can aggravate latent antagonism, however, leading to serious disruption. In 1948 Southern Democrats withdrew from the convention which had adopted a mildly pro-civil rights plank, and ran their own 'Dixiecrat' candidate.

But the main purpose of the convention is to pick the presidential nominee, which it does in one of three ways. If there is an obvious nominee, such as an incumbent President or a Vice President who is his heir apparent, the convention may simply choose him by acclamation. If there is a strong but not quite inevitable candidate, it may take only one ballot to obtain a majority. Single-ballot conventions have become usual in recent years because of the extensive cultivation of delegates beforehand. But in the past nomination has required numerous ballots. In 1924, when party rules called for a two-thirds majority, the Democrats balloted 102 times. Failure to secure a majority on the first ballot may shatter the bandwagon effect a candidate has carefully nurtured and 'stampede' delegates to another candidate. When two or more strong candidates fail to overcome each other after numerous ballots, the party may turn to a 'dark horse', a relatively obscure politician whom all factions can agree upon as a compromise candidate.

When the presidential candidate has been chosen, the convention has one more important piece of business before adjourning: approving his 'running-mate', the nominee for Vice President. Because the Vice President is normally an inconsequential figure (with no important duties), the presidential nominee has usually sought the person who would strengthen the 'ticket', attracting votes by virtue of his personal political following. Whether the vice presidential nominee would also make a good President is a decidedly secondary consideration, which explains why there is always some queasiness when a Vice President succeeds a President; the nation is well aware of how one gets to be Vice President.

Usually the convention attempts to balance the ticket by selecting a vice presidential candidate who is everything that the presidential nominee is not—ideologically, ethnically and geographically. If the presidential candidate is a liberal, then it is considered prudent to select a conservative for Vice President. If he is from the east, then a westerner might be chosen to run for Vice President. If one is a Protestant, the other ought to be a Catholic. Such arrangements assure that there will be something for everyone on the ticket, although perhaps at the cost of knowing what the ticket really represents.

An obvious method of consolidating support for the ticket is to have the presidential nominee choose his leading rival for the nomination as his running mate. Serving as 'standby equipment', as a potential vice presidential candidate once disdainfully put it, may not appeal to the rival, who would rather maintain his current electoral power base. Lyndon Johnson was supposedly reluctant to accept the Democratic vice presidential nomination when offered it by John F. Kennedy in 1960, because, at first blush, Johnson considered himself better off remaining as the Senate majority leader.

A drawback to choosing a former opponent for the Vice Presidential nomination is that he may have to live down harsh words spoken in the heat of battle. As Ronald Reagan's running mate in 1980, George Bush staunchly defended Reagan's fiscal proposals even though, during the campaign for the nomination, he had denounced them memorably as 'voodoo economics'. (When Bush, as President, implemented similar economic policies, they were dubbed 'déjà voodoo'.) For his own running mate, Bush seemed at pains to select a compatible, some said complaisant, politician—Dan Quayle. The unseasoned Indiana senator would not overshadow his chief yet could serve as bridge to the Republican Party's most conservative wing, which still doubted Bush's bona fides as President Reagan's successor. The alacrity with which Quayle sought to echo his leader earned him the sobriquet of 'Bush's Bush'.

In selecting vice presidential candidates, according to custom, long-range considerations of suitability for high office are subordinated to the immediate strategic goal: winning the election. In most instances, the convention does not evaluate the candidate at all: it ratifies whomsoever the presidential nominee desires as a running mate. In 1988, the Democrats obediently put their stamp on a senator from Texas at the behest of a presidential candidate from Massachusetts; recreating the 'Boston-Austin axis' of state capitals—so successful when Kennedy ran with Johnson in 1960—seemed an adequate rationale.

Often the convention, indeed the presidential nominee himself, knows quite little about the choice for the secondary position. In 1984, Walter Mondale surprised the Democratic Party by selecting

Geraldine Ferraro, a member of the House of Representatives from New York. In the excitement over nominating the first gender-balanced ticket, neither Mondale nor anyone else in the party checked thoroughly Ferraro's personal finances or the books of her husband's real estate business. They were later to become a distracting issue in the campaign.

In future conventions, however, the vice presidential slot may be thrown open to debate on the floor, because, for one thing, several Vice Presidents have become Presidents in recent decades. The Twenty-fifth Amendment has demonstrated how much more satisfying it can be to know something about the second-highest official before he is thrust into office. Whenever the Vice Presidency becomes vacant, according to the amendment, the President can nominate a successor, who must be confirmed by both houses of Congress. That provides an opportunity for minute scrutiny of the candidate. When Gerald Ford was designated, his personal life, career, finances, and congressional voting records were examined in detail in the Senate and House of Representatives. Having obtained their bi-partisan imprimatur, Ford was a known quantity, so that when he replaced President Nixon in 1974 there was little of the uneasiness that had attended the succession of some popularly elected Vice Presidents. Unlike them, Ford had not been chosen as an afterthought late one night during a frenzied political convention. (Ford was so well liked as Vice President that Ronald Reagan briefly considered having him as his running mate in 1980, even though Ford had already held the highest office. The plan ultimately foundered because the Republicans failed to devise a role in the new administration that would not demean the dignity of a former chief executive.)

Haphazard selection of Vice Presidents is only one of the flaws in the system of nomination by convention, a tradition which many now consider inherently undemocratic and outdated. The main purpose of the convention had been to provide an indirect method of selecting among candidates who, in the pre-electronic age, were but vague names to most voters. Today, however, a convention is no longer needed to make the faces of presidential contenders familiar. They appear on television for many months before the convention. A democratic alternative would be to select the candidates directly in a single nation-wide primary, but more problems might be created than were solved by any of the options. If all contenders were listed on the ballot, none would be likely to obtain a majority, leading to cumbersome runoff elections and bargaining among the candidates for each others' support—which already takes place at a convention.

Although the convention, for lack of anything better, is thus likely to survive for some time, there are indications that it is evolving into an institution more compatible with modern notions of popular participation. In 1974, the Democrats adopted a party charter which encourages minority group members, women and young voters to join in the delegate selection process. As a result, more of these persons are serving as delegates themselves. The charter also introduced a system of proportional representation, under which each state's delegation contains members supporting a variety of candidates, in proportion to their strength in the primaries or state nominating conventions. No longer are a few state leaders, commanding regiments of delegates personally loyal to them, able to broker the nomination. There is still bargaining, but the bargains are more numerous and each leader's bargaining power more attenuated.

Some Democrats, in fact, argue that there has been an excess of popular participation, leaving decisions crucial to the future of the party in the hands of ephemerally enthusiastic amateurs. In response to this criticism, party members holding elective offices—and thus directly responsible for the party's fortunes on a day-to-day basis—are reclaiming some of their influence by serving as ex officio 'super-delegates'.

Other Democrats contend that the convention is simply the wrong way to choose a candidate; they urge that it become an occasion for anointing a candidate already chosen through the pre-convention primaries and caucuses. New York Governor Mario Cuomo, for one, has insisted that the convention's prime-time television coverage is too valuable to squander on the potentially divisive, unflattering process of selecting a candidate; instead, it should be reserved for putting to the voters the attractive message of a unified party. The implication is that the party must coalesce around a candidate before the convention begins. That would entail a historic shift, deliberately transforming the convention from an 'efficient' to a 'dignified' institution, to adopt the terms used by Walter Bagehot in analyzing the English system. Yet if the convention were nothing but a perfunctory 'coronation' of a pre-determined candidate, it would merit hardly any television news coverage.

During the run-ups to both the 1988 and 1992 campaigns, moreover, many Democrats talked wistfully of an open or 'brokered convention' in which the candidate would emerge from the convention floor by means of old-fashioned bargaining, disregarding pre-convention efforts to lock up delegates. The talk may have been a measure of the dissatisfaction with the desultory primary and caucus process. It may also have been the product of a belief, as columnist Tom Wicker wrote, that 'the rare spectacle of a contested, hard-fought convention might produce high television ratings and a surge of enthusiasm for the ultimate [convention] victor'. Ironically, a candidate regarded as a possible winner in an open convention was Governor Cuomo, who always seemed reluctant to enter the primary fray but ready to accept a 'draft' from the delegates on the floor.

By gaining the nomination at the convention, the presidential candidate acquires control of the national party apparatus: its staff, funds, poll-takers, campaign strategists and field workers. But most important of all, he acquires the party name. Since party identification appears to be a potent influence on voting, the label will account for most of his support. Whether a candidate chooses to emphasize his party affiliation above other attributes is a matter of strategy. In general, since the Democratic Party has more registered members than does the Republican, the Democratic candidate is much more likely to beat the drums of party loyalty, even at the risk of losing some Republican supporters. But the candidate's personality and reputation are critically important. Unlike those who run for lesser offices, presidential candidates are celebrities by the time they emerge from the convention.

The final campaign, which lasts from the beginning of September until early in November, strives to rally the party faithful to the cause and to convert that portion of the electorate which has little or no party identification. Many of these voters make their decision in the two months preceding election day, according to the pollsters, who keep a finger pressed to the public pulse as the campaign progresses. To persuade the uncommitted to decide the right way, it is necessary for the candidate either to turn on his personal charm or to tar the opposition with responsibility for the nation's ills. The latter is an effective line of attack, because voters seem to turn out in unusually large numbers when they wish to vote *against* something; they often neglect to vote for candidates towards whom they feel well-disposed. It is helpful to a candidate for the polls to report that he has a good chance of winning, since Americans do not like voting for certain losers. Here is the bandwagon effect writ large: the voters find it so distasteful to be associated with the losing side that they switch to the predicted winner, thus fulfilling the prediction.

Thanks to time zone differences, eastern voters may even stampede—or render apathetic—voters in the west on election day itself. Shortly after the polls closed about 9 p.m. on the East Coast, President Carter conceded defeat in his 1980 re-election attempt. As a result of his broadcast announcement, many potential Democratic voters on the West Coast, who still had hours to get to the polls, never bothered to cast a ballot—a reaction which hurt the party's candidates for congressional and state offices. (To prevent such incidents, it has been proposed that 'election day' consist of a 24-hour voting period that would be the same for all time zones.)

Candidates assiduously avoid taking strong stands on issues (the party platform has by now been consigned to oblivion) or making specific proposals, since that might alienate uncommitted voters. The presidential campaign of Senator Barry Goldwater in 1964 demonstrates the consequences of ignoring this precept. Rather than concern itself with maximizing votes, the Goldwater campaign organization professed an uncompromising right-wing ideology. To secure purity of doctrine, it purged the Republican party ranks of dissidents. The candidate took strong positions on issues such as race relations and the Vietnam War. Goldwater even went so far as to tell special audiences precisely what they did not want to hear. He opposed Social Security pensions in Florida, where a great many of the nation's pensioners live, and he attacked the

Tennessee Valley Authority as 'creeping socialism' in a speech in Tennessee, which owes much of its prosperity to the authority's hydro-electric generators. All this was to present the electorate, in Goldwater's words, with 'a choice, not an echo'. The voters chose. His opponent, Lyndon Johnson, won a landslide victory, and the Republican Party was so severely wounded that one commentator hailed the emergence of the 'one-and-a-half-party system'.

More typically, candidates assess the problem before them as one of discovering how best to appeal to an electorate which is divided into discrete interest groups. They think of voters in ethnic categories (the Jewish Vote, the Irish Vote), occupational groupings (the Farmers, the Businessmen), geographical compartments (the Eastern Vote, the Midwestern Vote), and demographical categories (the Urban Vote, the Rural Vote). They try to tailor their campaign by mailings, by phone and personal canvassing and by television and newspaper advertisements, so as to appeal to each category separately, gambling that the others are not listening. The same candidate may advertise in rural newspapers, urging higher farm prices, and then appear on television in the cities to decry high food costs.

The use of television by presidential contenders has become pervasive despite the evidence that it can do a great deal of harm by emphasizing the visual appeal of candidates rather than their message. 'Television', Vice President Rockefeller once observed, 'is a very revealing medium,' and often what it reveals is not very attractive. In the televised 'Great Debates' of the 1960 election between Nixon and Kennedy, Nixon made a relatively poor impression because he seemed tense and because his face, defying the best efforts of razor and powder puff, bore ominous shadows. Kennedy's boyish countenance and floppy hair, in contrast, lent him a more pleasing television personality.

President Nixon drew a moral from his unfortunate experience. In his subsequent campaigns Nixon purchased air-time for question-and-answer sessions before audiences selected by his staff, who fed them the questions. In this contrived setting, surrounded by pre-programmed sympathizers, the candidate believed that he best projected statesmanlike qualities.

Recognizing that the debate path is strewn with potholes, all presidential candidates eschewed debates for the 16 years following the Kennedy-Nixon encounter. When debating resumed, in 1976, President Ford's staff took extraordinary precautions; they even secured the water glasses to the podium to prevent an accident that might confirm the Ford reputation for physical clumsiness. Even so, Ford's campaign was damaged by a misstatement on a foreign policy issue in a debate with his challenger, Jimmy Carter. Four years later, it was President Carter's turn to come out second best, in a debate with challenger Ronald Reagan. Carter displayed command of the facts in the 1980 debate but seemed too cold and dispassionate. (The outcome may have been affected by the Reagan camp's advance look at Carter's briefing papers for the debate, which had been purloined.) A 'passion gap' also proved to be the undoing of Governor Dukakis during a 1988 election debate against George Bush. Dukakis (an opponent of the death penalty) emotionally alienated a large segment of the audience by displaying no thirst for vengeance when asked how he would react if his wife became the victim of violent crime. The serious political harm suffered by Ford, Carter and Dukakis in these encounters tends to confirm the fear that debating may be inherently superficial, emphasizing physical appearance, mannerisms and minor gaffes, rather than illuminating each candidate's views.

Format could be the key to a significant debate. The 1988 debate imitated a television chat show: a panel of journalists took turns asking each candidate questions. The format generated a memorable moment, at the Vice Presidential level. Republican candidate Dan Quayle, defending himself against the charge of inexperience, likened himself to President Kennedy, who was elected at a similar age. Quayle's opponent, Texas Senator Lloyd Bentsen, jabbed back: 'You're no Jack Kennedy.' The rejoinder skewered Quayle, who had been dogged by a reputation for shallowness, and loomed as a possible turning point for the Democratic ticket.

It was not, however, and the otherwise insipid interview-style format came to be regarded as a factor contributing to the notorious vacuity of that campaign. Each candidate was allowed to 'grandstand', offering a seemingly scripted response to predictable questions. The event was more of a joint appearance or press conference than a debate in the style of the Oxford Union. Face-to-face encounters, without the mediation of journalists, are one alternative. The networks have proposed simulating parliamentary question time: each candidate would interrogate the other in a series of 90-minute broadcasts. The proposal sprang from a belief that direct confrontation would restore spontaneity and ensure that not every candidate utterance was pre-processed.

At election time, such 'packaging' of political candidates at all levels becomes a boom industry, captained by a new breed of professional campaign consultants and media advisers. Bringing to bear skills acquired during decades of selling deodorant soaps and dog food, these electoral *condottiere* show the candidate how to condense his virtues into a fifteen-second spot commercial. The overt message is as innocuous as a jingle; the real object is subliminal persuasion. Looking relaxed and affable, often with his jacket off and tie loosened, the candidate is portrayed in amiable conversation with voters or surrounded by American flags. The viewer is supposed to receive the impression that here is a man of the people, patriotic, at home with common folk and sensitive to their problems. A popular technique (especially if the opponent is single) is to display the candidate at home, surrounded by his wife, children and pets, so as to convey an aura of domesticity and stability.

Waging political warfare by means of commercials does have the advantage of translating the electoral process into the familiar idiom of a popular culture medium. Fears that slick showmanship may mesmerize the electorate are quite unfounded, since even children, reared on television commercials, understand their ulterior motives and tendency to deceive by half-truths and exaggerated claims. Moreover, many newspapers now critically review political commercials, just as they do other television fare, pointing out inaccuracies or misstatements. A poorly reviewed commercial can leave a candidate hoist with his own canard. But negative commercials, especially those of the Willie Horton variety, do nothing to raise the level of discourse in a campaign, and there is some evidence that they dishearten viewers to the point where they fail to vote at all, thereby exacerbating the already low turnout.

The crass merchandising of presidential candidates may also discourage more reflective persons from seeking the office. After campaigning for the 1976 Democratic nomination for almost a year, Senator Walter F. Mondale, a Minnesota liberal, announced he was withdrawing from the race because he could not force himself to conduct the kind of campaign that was required. Mondale explained:

> Nationally, it's more theatre than the politics I know. I kept getting constant suggestions that I needed to buy different clothes and go to speech instructors and spend two days in Hollywood with a videotape machine. I hated that.

Mondale did, however, suppress his distaste of campaigning long enough to be elected Vice President.

The most daunting aspect of presidential campaigning is the raising of funds. 'Money,' a veteran politician once remarked, 'is the mother's milk of politics', but during the 1960s and the 1970s the candidates' need for this nourishment grew inordinately. In the 1972 election, the Republican candidate spent $61 million and the Democratic $39 million. Requiring such huge sums made candidates dependent on 'fat cats', large contributors who are thus in a position to demand political favours. The possibilities for corruption have not been underexploited. Investigations of the 1972 campaign revealed dozens of clandestine, illegal contributions by corporations; a suitcase stuffed with hundred-dollar bills seemed to be the standard unit of contribution.

Provoked by such blatant examples of cloak-and-dagger campaign financing, Congress enacted in 1974 a reform bill designed to change radically the relationship between private money and electoral politics at the Federal level. The law established limits on contributions to candidates and on campaign expenditures, and it provided a subsidy for the major Presidential contenders. The scope of this reform was substantially narrowed by a 1976 ruling of the Supreme Court (*Buckley v. Valeo*), which invoked the First Amendment's guarantee of freedom of speech—on the theory that money talks. Spending by candidates, the court held, represented a form of 'political communication' that could not be restricted. Thus, expenditure limits for the congressional elections (non-subsidized) were invalidated. The court upheld, however, as a quid pro quo for accepting public funds the limit on spending by presidential candidates. The court also upheld limits on the donor's freedom of speech, in the form of restraints on the amount he could contribute, finding that they were justified by the need for 'preventing corruption and the appearance of corruption'.

Funds are raised by the Federal Election Commission from income tax returns; each taxpayer may earmark one dollar of his taxes for campaigns by checking a box. In the primaries, candidates may qualify for matching Federal subsidies by a demonstration of broad-based financial support: raising at least $5,000 in small contributions ($250 or less) in each of 20 states. Under this system, each candidate in the primaries leading to the 1992 election was supposed to be able to spend up to $27 million (the figure is adjusted periodically for inflation). In the general election, the two major-party candidates are fully subsidized—in 1988 they shared a total of $92.2 million—and prohibited from direct spending beyond that level. The candidates also benefit from indirect spending on their behalf by state and national party committees, who are free to raise money from contributors; this so-called 'soft money' was particularly significant in the 1988 election, where it helped pay for advertising in key states. The availability of the funds has become especially critical now that many of the modern campaign functions, such as computerized mailing of literature and sophisticated polling, are high-tech and capital intensive; platoons of volunteer envelope-lickers can no longer be substituted for paid professional services.

Besides money, the strategy of campaigning is heavily influenced by the fact that technically the President is not elected by direct popular vote, but indirectly through the electoral college. Under Article II of the Constitution, a group of electors, one for each senator and representative in the state's congressional delegation, are chosen in each state to cast ballots for President. When the constitution was first put into practice the electors were actually free agents; they could cast their votes for whoever they chose. Today there are conventionally slates of would-be electors, committed to a particular candidate. If a candidate wins a majority of the popular vote in New York, the entire slate of electors committed to him in that state is thereby selected (although a few states allocate electors among the candidates in proportion to the percentage of the popular vote).

The electoral college is an antique and a far cry from direct democracy. Yet, while it is sometimes compared to the Vatican's college of cardinals or similar oligarchical assemblies, its origins lay not in elitism but in the practical need for compromise on the method of choosing a President. Each of the contending viewpoints at the constitutional convention was placated, according to historian John P. Roche:

> The state legislatures had the right to determine the mode of selection of the electors ... The small states received a bonus ... in the form of a guaranteed minimum of three votes, while the big states got acceptance of the principle of proportional power ... and finally, if no candidate received a majority in the college, the right of decision passed on to [the House of Representatives] with each state exercising equal strength.

The electoral college thus gives considerable weight to population, but, owing to the three-elector minimum, the correspondence between size of population and number of electors is only approximate. In 1988, New York State had 26 times the population of North Dakota but only about 12 times the number of electors.

Despite the bonus awarded to small-population states, the net effect of the prevalent winner-take-all mode of allocation is to magnify the significance of the populous states. If a candidate wins the popular majority in New York by a single vote, he acquires all 37 of the state's electors. If he wins the dozen most populous states, however narrowly, he secures a majority of the 538 electors in the nation. Campaigns naturally tend to concentrate on these pivotal states, which are often won by margins of a fraction of one percent of the ballots cast. A mathematically imaginative team of political scientists calculated in one election that the voters in California, which has the largest population of any state, were '2.92 times as attractive targets' as voters in the least populous states. Natives of heavily populated states are, in fact, desirable as nominees because they presumably start with a pronounced electoral college advantage.

The electoral college system does produce some curious distortions in presidential balloting. It has in the past added leverage to liberals and minority groups, because they congregated in the dense, industrial conurbations that dominated states (generally in the north) with large blocs of electoral votes. Winning sizeable majorities in the cities and their suburbs meant carrying the whole state—an electoral vote bonanza. The prudent candidate cultivated these urbanites and paid special attention to their interests. As population shifted to the sprawling motorway megalopolises in the more conservative 'Sun Belt' states of the south and west—Texas and Florida now rank No. 3 and No. 4 in the census—there was less incentive to curry favour with 'Rust Belt' liberals and minorities, or to succour their (by now decaying) traditional cities.

The electoral system leaves open the possibility that a candidate who gains the majority of popular votes nationally will nevertheless lose the election because he fails to amass a majority of the electoral votes. It happened three times in the nineteenth century, including the election of 1876, when Samuel J. Tilden, who held a 250,000-vote margin in the popular balloting, lost by one electoral-college vote. Such a discrepancy between popular and electoral votes may occur when a candidate wins the populous states by slim margins and loses the sparsely inhabited states by large margins. The narrow victories earn him far more electoral votes than his overall performance warrants. (The disparity between electoral and popular vote totals can be enormous. In 1968, Hubert Humphrey polled 42.7 per cent of the popular vote and 191 electoral votes while his opponent, Richard Nixon, polled 43.4 per cent of the popular vote and 301 electoral votes.)

A similarly undemocratic outcome might result if no candidate gained an absolute majority of the electoral votes, which is theoretically possible when more than two persons run. In the absence of a majority, the constitution provides that the President shall be chosen by the House of Representatives from among the three candidates with the highest electoral totals. But here the principal of sovereign equality of the states reasserts itself, for each state delegation in the House casts a single vote. Sparsely settled Wyoming. in other words, casts one vote, and so does teeming California. A President could therefore be chosen, theoretically, by the delegations of the twenty-six least populated states, representing about 15 per cent of the nation's citizens.

Another worrisome, albeit remote, possibility is that the electors might undo the result of the popular voting by casting their ballots for a candidate other than the one to whom they were nominally committed. Pledging of votes has become customary, but it is not a legally binding obligation. In the presidential elections of 1948, 1964 and 1968, there was one 'faithless' elector. So far such aberrations have not influenced the outcome of a contest.

Several constitutional amendments to forestall undesirable consequences of the electoral system have been proposed. One would abandon the electoral college entirely and elect the President by direct, popular vote. The major obstacle would be the need for a single, national election register. The states, which are constitutionally responsible for determining the qualifications for voting, would be unlikely to acquiesce in such an infringement of their prerogatives. By granting the vote to eighteen-year-olds in every state, however, the Twenty-sixth Amendment, adopted in 1971, set a precedent for overriding state discretion and creating a homogeneous presidential electorate.

Another proposal would modify the electoral college by allocating one electoral vote to each congressional district and permitting the winner-take-all system to operate only within a district. The disparity between popular and electoral vote totals would be reduced, since congressional districts are roughly equal in population, but the presidential outcome might then be merely a reflection of the congressional race. Since the Democrats have fairly consistently held a majority of seats in the House of Representatives, Republicans might well fear the consequences of electing Presidents in a similar manner. (On the other hand, congressional elections might become a reflection of presidential elections, which would be welcome to the Republicans.)

A third proposal would mandate proportional representation, assigning each candidate electoral votes in proportion to his share

of popular votes in each state. It would abolish altogether disparities between the popular and electoral votes. But it would also have
the effect of shifting influence away from the heavily populated
states and towards the small-population states, because the large
electoral blocs of the former would be split among Republicans
and Democrats. The major states thus would be unlikely to
look with favour on proportional representation. Moreover, the
winner-take-all version of the electoral college system is viewed
by many as a cornerstone of political stability, because it virtually
guarantees that a majority of electors will support one of the two
main political parties. Proportional representation might yield a
minor-party candidate enough electoral votes to hold the balance
of power, forcing the main parties to bargain for his support.
Given the lack of consensus on any of the proposed reforms of
the electoral college, the system is likely to continue unchanged
until a serious malfunction arises.

CHAPTER TEN

Man Versus the State

All nations constantly confront the problem of drawing the line between the rights of individuals and the interests of the state. The way in which they do so is often the distinctive mark of their system of government. As Federal Judge Jerome Frank has said, 'The test of the moral quality of a civilization is its treatment of the weak and the powerless.' More than most countries, the United States is imbued with a reverence for civil liberties. The Declaration of Independence spoke of man's 'inalienable rights', and the framers of the constitution designed checks and balances to prevent the federal government from becoming a tyranny. So content were the framers with the basic structure that they saw no need for specific guarantees.

Denouncing the 'injudicious zeal for bills of rights', Alexander Hamilton argued in the *The Federalist* that the 'constitution is itself . . . a Bill of Rights'. Recalling that Magna Carta and the Petition of Right were stipulations by monarchs, Hamilton maintained that a Bill of Rights would ill suit a democratic constitution, in which 'the people surrender nothing'. He contended that a Bill of Rights was less necessary to a constitution 'merely intended to regulate the general political interests of the nation, than to a constitution which has the regulation of every species of personal and private concerns'. Finally, Hamilton warned, a Bill of Rights is more than unnecessary; it is dangerous. The provisions would be construed as exceptions to powers that must by implication exist: 'For why declare that things shall not be done which there is no power to do?' With the wisdom of hindsight, it is obvious that Hamilton underestimated the scope of the powers which the government eventually would exercise and the consequent menace to individual liberty. The provisions of the American Bill of Rights have indeed been construed as mere exceptions to powers. But the authority of government has grown inexorably since Hamilton's time, and were it not for the Bill of Rights there would be no exceptions.

To give him his due, Hamilton was certainly justified in claiming that even without a Bill of Rights the constitution was not devoid of specific prohibitions against the infringement of liberty. Article I, in setting forth the legislative power, forbids suspending the writ of *habeas corpus* or passing bills of attainder and *ex post facto* laws. Article III, the judicial article, provides for the trial of all crimes by jury and lays down strict rules of proof for treason trials. Article IV guarantees 'the citizens of each state shall be entitled to all privileges and immunities of citizens in the several states', and Article VI prohibits imposing a religious test for holding public office. Taken as a whole, however, this catalogue of assorted proscriptions hardly amounts to a comprehensive charter of liberties, and one might legitimately ask: if these specific limits need be spelled out in writing, why not others?

Hamilton's arguments were in vain. To win approval of the proposed constitution, its supporters were obliged to accede to the public demand for a Bill of Rights. Adopted in 1791, two years after ratification, the bill took the form of a package of ten amendments, most of which are negative in tone. They do not say 'the citizen shall have the right to ...' Rather, they are couched in terms of prohibitions against specific kinds of government acts. The Bill of Rights is thus much less sweeping and idealistic than some charters of liberty, such as the United Nations Universal Declaration of Human Rights, which lays down broad positive rights, but it is therefore much more difficult to circumvent. With the Bill of Rights, the early Americans hedged their bet on democracy and majority rule. They declared some measures out of bounds, even if a majority desired them, in order to guarantee that the minority would at least survive the consequences of not being on the winning side. If democracy is defined as pure majoritarianism, then the Bill of Rights is undemocratic; but if democracy is held to subsume the concept of legitimate opposition, then the bill is a fundamental part of the democratic scheme. America is, as Professor Henry J. Abraham has put it, a 'constitutional democracy, based upon a government of limited powers under a written constitution, and a majoritarianism duly checked by carefully guarded minority rights'.

In laying down these protections for dissenting minorities, the Bill of Rights speaks with firmness. A provision which begins 'Congress shall make no law' leaves little doubt that the safeguard is to be unqualified. But specific as well as broadly worded provisions require interpretation in concrete cases, and that is the job of the courts. Whenever anyone believes that the federal or state governments have violated the Bill of Rights, causing him personal harm, he may take his complaint to the judiciary. As the apex of the judicial pyramid, the Supreme Court has become the primary guardian of the rights of Americans.

While the meaning of the Bill of Rights may be altered by judicial interpretation, no provision is made for its abrogation in times of war or 'national emergency' in order to permit summary trials, internment or censorship. The guarantees can be removed only by formally amending them. That the republic has stood so long without ever rescinding its Bill of Rights, even temporarily, may perhaps be taken as a rebuke to all those who believe that civil liberties must be the first casualty of national distress.

On the other hand, the executive and legislative authorities sometimes take whatever steps they deem necessary in time of emergency, secure in the expectation that the court will find no conflict with the Bill of Rights when it later reviews those measures. Japanese-Americans, including native-born citizens, were summarily rounded up on the Pacific Coast and shipped to internment camps during the Second World War upon the orders of President Roosevelt. Although that was a clear infringement of the right to due process of law, when the Japanese Exclusion Order was challenged at the end of the war, the Supreme Court upheld it. Dissenting, Justice Murphy expressed what was probably the real sentiment of the bench when he said that the action 'falls into the ugly abyss of racism'. But in his opinion for the majority, Justice Black, normally an avid libertarian, alluded to the difficulty of judicial review of emergency actions: 'We cannot—by availing ourselves of the calm perspective of hindsight—now say that at that time these actions were unjustified.' Japanese-Americans had to wait almost 50 years for a tangible expression of national remorse. Congress made amends for the injustice by awarding each living survivor of the internment camps $20,000 in reparations, the sum recommended by a special commission. About one billion dollars in all has been paid to persons who were removed from their homes by Executive Order 9066 in 1942 solely because they were of Japanese descent. The reparations bill in the Senate declared bluntly that internment was the result of 'racial prejudice, war hysteria and a failure of political leadership'.

On the whole, civil liberties have been staunchly protected by the courts because of an underlying belief that they are vital to the health of the political order—not idealistic encumbrances on effective government. No better illustration can be found of the nexus between civil liberties and American democracy than the First Amendment, which provides:

> Congress shall make no law respecting an establishment of religion, or prohibiting the free exercise thereof; or abridging the freedom of speech, or of the press; or the right of the people peaceably to assemble, and to petition the Government for a redress of grievances.

The freedoms of religion, speech, press, assembly and petition are called 'preferred freedoms', because they allow that vigorous exchange of ideas upon which, according to classic libertarian theory, democratic government thrives. In balancing the rights of citizens against the needs of the state, the court gives greater weight to the 'preferred freedoms' than to some other civil liberties because ultimately the survival of the democratic form of government depends on their maintenance.

Freedom of religion is included among these because religion, like political belief, is properly a matter of conscience and because religious intolerance has been a traditional cause of persecution. The 'establishment clause' of the First Amendment precludes an identification between church and civil authorities, although it has been argued that the intent was merely to prevent the *federal* government from creating an official church that would compete with those that the states might wish to establish. From the earliest days, America had been a haven for refugees from religious persecution, and although some colonies were known to expel a heretic from time to time, the nation as a whole had to face the fact that it was composed of a multitude of faiths.

An atheist might cast a jaundiced eye upon the history of the establishment clause, since it has not prevented government from promoting and sustaining organized religion. Churches and their property have always been exempted from taxation, undoubtedly a beneficial concession. Reaffirming the validity of this traditional practice, the Supreme Court held in 1970 that by granting tax exemption the government 'simply abstains from demanding that the church support the state'.

Much of the debate over the establishment clause concerns largely symbolic controversies: whether a state legislature may keep a chaplain on the payroll (authorized by the Supreme Court in 1983) or whether a Nativity scene may be put on display at Yuletide in a municipal building. In the case of public ceremonies and symbolism, the court carefully evaluates the context. According to the three-part test enunciated in *Lemon v. Kurtzman* in 1971, the display 'must have a secular purpose', its 'primary effect must be one that neither advances nor inhibits religion', and it must not represent 'excessive entanglement with religion'.

When applied to Christmas displays, the test has produced curious results. The court disapproved a Nativity scene inside a Pittsburgh courthouse, emblazoned with a banner reading 'Gloria in excelsis deo', but it approved a Jewish menorah standing next to a Christmas tree on the street outside, evidently on the ground that the latter were seasonal symbols rather than an endorsement of religion. This standard for evaluating displays has become known as the 'reindeer rule', because the presence of kitsch figures, such as a reindeer, evergreen trees or a Santa Claus, proves the absence of a genuine religious message. The sponsors of Nativity dioramas often find themselves in the ironic position of having to argue that they celebrate a winter solstice folk ritual, devoid of religious significance. The irony distresses a school of constitutional interpreters—the 'nonpreferentialists'—who maintain that the original intent of the establishment clause was to prevent government from preferring a particular sect over others but not to preclude generic 'accommodation' of the people's spiritual yearnings. Ceremonial religiosity should be allowable in public life, according to this view, so long as it is not 'coercive' to nonbelievers. There may be no practical way, however, to distinguish accommodation, implying a passive role for government, from state encouragement of worship. First Amendment historian Leonard Levy contends that in fact the nonpreferentialists 'prefer government sponsorship and subsidy of religion rather than allow it to compete on its merits against irreligion and indifference'.

The relationship between religion and education poses a more prickly question. The court has discerned no breach in the wall of separation between church and state when the latter provides free transportation and textbooks for pupils in church schools as well as state schools. In 1983 the court approved a Minnesota scheme of giving parents tax credits for tuition payments to private schools, even though most of the benefits accrued to schools run by churches. But the court has deemed it a violation of the establishment clause for a state to provide funds to church schools for the salaries of teachers, even teachers of secular subjects. Although the distinction may be difficult to fathom, the principle is that the state must maintain 'neutrality' in matters of religion. It may supply books, bus rides and tax benefits to all pupils; where they use them—in secular or religious schools—is their own choice. But paying teachers is a direct subsidy to the religious institution that employs them and thus impermissible.

The companion to the establishment clause, the free exercise clause, is a less contentious provision except in the case of small sects that claim not only the freedom to believe but the freedom to act according to their beliefs. The Jehovah's Witnesses alone have been at the centre of about forty Supreme Court cases. In most of those the court has upheld their right to behave unconventionally in order to fulfil the tenets of their faith. They are permitted to proselytize aggressively, even when it causes a nuisance to others, and their children are permitted to refuse to salute the flag in school, thus avoiding the sin of idolatry. But again the lines are blurred. Jews may not violate Sunday closing laws even though they close their businesses on a different sabbath, but Seventh Day Adventists are entitled to unemployment benefits when their unemployment results from conscientious refusal to work on Saturdays.

When official policy—such as a closing law—placed a substantial burden on the practice of a religion, the court had generally applied a balancing test that was weighted heavily in favour of the citizen. The government had to show a 'compelling governmental interest' in its policy in order to justify overriding the citizen's right to his religious practices. In the 1990 case of *Oregon v. Smith*, however, the court disavowed that test and substituted an analysis much more favourable to the state. It held that the right of free exercise does not relieve an individual of his obligation to comply with a valid law of general applicability merely because the conduct it prohibits happens to be required by his religious beliefs. That is true, the court said, even when the prohibited practice is central to the religion; it was impractical for the court to attempt to determine which beliefs were essential to a faith. The court acted in the case of Native Americans who were denied unemployment compensation after they were discharged for using peyote—a hallucinogenic substance that is illegal but forms part of the traditional rites of some tribes. Although it seems clear that the court was keen to avoid granting religious exemptions for criminal conduct, particularly to obscure sects, the decision was written in such sweeping terms that even conventional denominations were disturbed by the apparent diminution of the principle of religious toleration.

Even more than freedom of religion, freedom of speech is regarded as vital to the healthy functioning of democracy, because it provides the 'marketplace of ideas' in which the nation shops for public policy. And it assures, as the Continental Congress said in 1774, that 'oppressive officers are shamed or intimidated into more honourable and just modes of conducting affairs'. For these reasons the court has given freedom of speech the greatest possible scope when it involves issues of public concern. Newspapers are constitutionally exempt from prior censorship, and the court has made it quite difficult for a government official to sue successfully for libel or slander, lest such penalties have a 'chilling effect' on the discussion of public issues.

Despite the absolute language of the First Amendment, however, the court has carved out several exceptions to freedom of speech and the press in instances where speech seems to go beyond contributing to the theoretical marketplace. One exception is speech that presents a 'clear and present danger' of producing harmful consequences that the government has a duty to prevent. Using 'fighting words' to harangue a crowd into violent action or reaction and inciting others to violently overthrow the government is not constitutionally protected speech. The court thus allowed the prosecution of the Communist Party as subversive, although the justices ultimately drew a distinction between direct incitement to revolutionary acts and mere 'abstract advocacy and teaching of forcible overthrow'. The court was also notably unwilling to prevent the House Un-American Activities Committee from conducting an inquisition for almost forty years into the political beliefs of those it suspected of communist sympathies. By the time it was abolished in 1975, the committee had subpoenaed and publicly interrogated thousands of 'hostile witnesses', an episode whose chilling effect upon free speech amounted to an Ice Age.

The court has also drawn a careful distinction between pure speech, which is protected, and speech mixed with physical action, which is not. While the citizen is entitled to certain forms of 'symbolic speech' that partake of action, such as carrying a picket sign, he may not claim shelter under the First Amendment for engaging in a disruptive sit-in. The line between symbolic speech and action is exceedingly fine. Burning an American flag as a gesture of protest is permissible, but burning a military draft card is not.

In upholding the right to burn the flag, in 1989, the court reasoned that flamboyant (or in this case, flammable) gestures add impact to political communication, especially in the television age. President Bush's reliance on the flag for gripping electoral imagery in the 1988 campaign proved the point. The flag is often abused, moreover, as a commercial emblem without objection. Nevertheless, the ruling had invalidated laws against flag desecration passed by 48 states and the federal government, and it stimulated a hyper-patriotic movement—led by President Bush, no less—to modify the First Amendment, permitting the national banner to be protected. Libertarians eventually overcame the flag protectionists, by arguing that sheltering a secular icon from innocuous domestic dissidents—an anti-desecration law would not affect demonstrations in Teheran—was a trivial pretext for diluting the First Amendment for the first time in two centuries. Deliberately inserting loopholes in the Bill of Rights to permit suppression of political statements might have set a dangerous precedent indeed.

Another traditional exception to freedom of speech, apart from speech mixed with action, is the publication of material that is deemed obscene. The doctrine that obscenity is not speech protected by the First Amendment has been extremely controversial since it was enunciated in 1957 because it legitimized censorship during a period when social and cultural mores were undergoing a drastic transformation. But the court reasoned, in the words of Justice Brennan, that 'implicit in the history of the First Amendment is the rejection of obscenity as utterly without redeeming social importance', and the justice noted a 'universal judgement that obscenity should be restrained'. No better illustration can be found of the utilitarian concept of the First Amendment than the notion that freedom of expression exists only to fulfil the specific function of enhancing democratic government. That speech might also provide a medium for cultural and artistic expression seems to have been ignored by the court. Nevertheless, the justices found it much easier to outlaw obscenity than to define it, and many books, magazines and films have escaped censorship via the loophole of 'redeeming social importance'. By the early 1970s the court had decided to allow each locality to judge for itself what the prevailing moral sentiments of the community were, a step which relieved the bench of the role of film and book reviewer but which raised the chaotic possibility that a best-selling novel in one city would be banned as pornographic in another.

By a stroke of sheer bathos, the First Amendment, with its broad guarantee of free debate, is followed immediately by an amendment that assures the citizen's right to bear arms. The intent was to allow part-time militias to be maintained, and perhaps to remind the governors what might happen if they lost the consent of the governed. In any event, the Second Amendment helped ensure that today's governors would face a heavily armed population—millions of handguns and rifles are in circulation—whose weaponry would be more commonly used in the commission of mass murder than in the defence of civil liberties. By enshrining Americans' natural attraction to firearms as a fundamental freedom, the Bill of Rights has made it more difficult to restrict even military-style assault weapons, which increase the incidence of fatal violence. Gun control advocates took heart, however, when the Supreme Court in 1983 declined to declare unconstitutional a bold village ordinance in Illinois that forbids the ownership of handguns.

The Third Amendment, which prohibits quartering troops in private homes, testifies to the bad memories left by the compulsory lodging of British troops in the homes of the colonists. But in an era when the Defense Department lavishes billions of dollars upon domestic and foreign bases, the possibility of lodging its divisions in spare bedrooms here and there seems quite remote. The Third Amendment is thus little more than an historical curiosity.

The Fourth Amendment, prohibiting unreasonable searches and seizures, was also a reaction to a British colonial practice, that of issuing general warrants empowering officers to search anywhere on the slightest pretexts. But, unlike the Third Amendment, it has assumed a great importance in modern America. The core of the amendment is the warrant procedure: the police must go before a judge to show that they have probable cause to believe that a crime has been committed, justifying a search. They must also specify where the search is to take place, the names of the suspects, and the evidence sought. The amendment is thus one of the main safeguards against arbitrary police practices, especially since the court early in the 1960s began to apply the 'exclusionary rule' in state as well as federal trials.

A judicial invention dating back to 1915, the exclusionary rule makes any evidence secured by the police in a manner prohibited by the constitution inadmissible in a subsequent trial. Denied the fruits of unconstitutional searches, the police are effectively deterred from carrying them out. Concern about high crime rates has, however, led to pressure to carve out a 'good faith' exception to the rule, which would permit a court to accept evidence obtained by a police officer acting in the 'reasonable belief' that his conduct did not violate the suspect's constitutional rights. The rationale is that the exclusionary rule has little deterrent effect on a policeman who believes, albeit erroneously, that he is complying with the constitution. Supporters of the good-faith exception emphasize the primacy of the 'truth-seeking function' of a trial. In 1984, the court allowed such an exception, in the case of a police officer who relied in good faith on a search warrant that proved to be defective (*US v. Leon*). In that instance, Justice Byron White wrote for the court majority, the 'social costs' of excluding 'inherently trustworthy tangible evidence' outweighed the benefits that might be obtained by deterring unconstitutional police tactics. In 1990, however, the court held that illegally obtained information could not be used to impeach the credibility of a defendant's witnesses at trial (*James v. Illinois*). Justice William Brennan, who wrote the court's opinion, declared: 'The occasional suppression of illegally obtained yet probative evidence has long been considered a necessary cost of preserving overriding constitutional values.' Since Justice White joined the majority in that case, the essence of the exclusionary rule appeared to be forcefully reaffirmed.

Although written at a time when physical entry was the only method of search, the Fourth Amendment has been 'adapted' to meet analogous threats to privacy posed by modern technology. Freed of the shackles of literal interpretation, the Fourth Amendment now protects against wiretapping, eavesdropping and other electronic means of surveillance as well as physical intrusions, and it guards individuals in public places as well as on private premises. The amendment, in fact, supplies the foundation upon which the court has constructed a right of privacy that extends far beyond police investigations, into such matters as contraception and abortion.

An invisible bubble of constitutional entitlement shields the citizen wherever he or she may be, provided that the circumstances would create in the mind of a reasonable person a 'legitimate expectation of privacy'. Under this formula, the privacy shield withdraws when incriminating evidence is left in a dustbin, for example, since dustbins are not normally regarded as secure repositories. The Supreme Court has also held that urinalysis of the government's employees to determine if they use illegal drugs, even at home, does not violate privacy rights, since the expectation of privacy is outweighed by the need to maintain workplace safety.

Since the exclusionary rule remains a major instrument for enforcing the Fourth Amendment, it sometimes seems that only suspected criminals have a right to privacy that is routinely vindicated. Yet it has become quite clear that suspects of a different kind also need protection. The Rockefeller Commission reported in 1975 that the Central Intelligence Agency had for about twenty years engaged in illegal spying upon thousands of Americans. The CIA had tapped phones, planted 'bugs', burglarized homes and intercepted letters without warrants. Since the information was gathered for the purpose of 'counter-espionage'—i.e., disruption of dissident political groups—rather than prosecution, the CIA was undeterred by the exclusionary rule. The Rockefeller Commission recommended that the rights of citizens be protected by closer presidential and congressional oversight of intelligence. The goal has been attained in part by formulating 'charters' that for the first time specify the limits on CIA operations—and by creating oversight committees in Congress whose mission is to be watchdogs rather than lap dogs.

Amendments V, VI, VII and VIII provide for 'due process of law' in judicial proceedings, especially criminal trials. A reaction to the memory of the royal Star Chamber, whose primary method of establishing guilt was to torture the accused into confessing, the amendments assure a defendant the right to indictment by grand jury and to speedy, public trial by jury. He also has the right to be represented by counsel, to confront and cross-examine witnesses against him, and to compel by subpoena the appearance of favourable witnesses. The defendant may not be forced to testify against himself and may not be tried again for the same offence once acquitted. He is protected against 'excessive' bail and fines and 'cruel and unusual punishments'.

Most of these rights were enormously expanded by the court in practical terms during recent decades because of a growing realization that the judicial system operated unfairly against the poor and uneducated. The right to remain silent and to representation by counsel might protect those who knew they could refuse to give the police statements when arrested and who had the means to hire a lawyer. But these rights meant little in practice to the ignorant, impoverished arrestee who neither knew he could keep silent nor had the money to secure representation. Since the police often took advantage of a suspect's ignorance in their zeal to obtain convictions, the court decreed that the police had a duty to inform a suspect of his rights. Similarly, the court held that a defendant enjoys not merely the right to hire a lawyer if he can afford one, but the right to be provided with one at government expense if he cannot. To make the right to counsel even more effective, the court subsequently ruled that a lawyer must be allowed to begin representing his client at the police station immediately after arrest.

This so-called Miranda rule, a product of the liberal Warren court, contracted in some respects under the conservative William Rehnquist, who was elevated to chief justice by President Reagan. The Rehnquist court retreated from the scrupulous policy of regarding trials as irretrievably tainted by the introduction of confessions obtained in violation of the Fifth Amendment. It held that a conviction was valid, even though an inadmissible confession had been presented to the jurors (and may have influenced them), so long as they could reasonably have based a verdict of guilt on the other evidence presented. Nevertheless, the Miranda rule continues to be elaborated. In 1990, for example, a majority of the justices held that, once a suspect had indicated a desire to be advised by counsel, the police could no longer reinitiate questioning without his lawyer being present (*Minnick v. Mississippi*). The ruling ensures that self-incriminating disclosures are truly voluntary and not the result of 'coercive pressures' applied during police custody. Conservative displeasure with the Miranda line of decisions was evident, however, in the dissent by Justice Antonin Scalia (joined by Rehnquist). Scalia denounced the majority decision as 'the latest stage of prophylaxis built upon prophylaxis, producing a veritable fairyland castle of imagined constitutional restriction upon law enforcement'.

Even conservatives, however, deign to take advantage of the Fifth Amendment when they become targets of law enforcement. Most of the principal Iran-Contra conspirators of the Reagan Administration escaped punishment because incriminating evidence stemming from their public testimony before Congress was excluded from the trials. The incident demonstrated that, owing to the constitutional guarantee against compelled self-incrimination, obtaining full public disclosure of governmental misconduct through congressional hearings may effectively rule out prosecuting the wrongdoers.

The court also had to consider whether, in its disproportionate toll of the poor and racial minorities, the death penalty amounted to 'cruel and unusual punishment'. Although capital punishment was not 'unusual' in an historical sense, the court declared in 1972, it was imposed so infrequently and arbitrarily that the few persons executed were being subjected to an extraordinary penalty. The court thus invalidated most of the existing capital punishment laws. But many states responded by laying down more precise standards for meting out the supreme penalty.

A new generation of tenants soon populated Death Row, and executions resumed, with the court's approval, after a hiatus of more than a decade. By 1992, more than 3,800 persons had been sentenced to die, and the sentence had been carried out in more than 155 cases. Each execution entails an odyssey through the state and federal judiciaries, often involving multiple appeals by the condemned person to the Supreme Court. In 1991, for example, an execution took place in Georgia after thirteen years of legal proceedings, culminating with the justices—polled by telephone in the middle of the night—voting 6 to 3 against granting the prisoner a reprieve. The Rehnquist court has sought to avoid such cliffhangers by deterring repeated appeals. A prisoner may, for example, be barred by procedural rules from raising a constitutional issue that was not mentioned in his initial appeal.

Placing obstacles in the way of appeals, opponents of the death penalty argue, is as an unseemly effort to rush convicts to the gas chamber, electric chair or lethal injection—hastiness that is particularly objectionable in a system of justice whose outcomes are, statistically at least, far from evenhanded. About 40 percent of the condemned are black, although blacks represent only 12 percent of the US population. Nearly one third of those executed since the resumption of capital punishment have been blacks convicted of killing whites. In contrast, a white condemned to death for killing a black is a rarity—only one in about every

500 executions since colonial times. This disparity feeds the belief that racial bias influences the imposition of the penalty. Even if not 'cruel and unusual', by this logic, execution of a disproportionate number of blacks amounts to a denial of judicial equality. Nevertheless, the Supreme Court held in 1987 that a statistical pattern was insufficient reason to invalidate a death sentence on constitutional grounds; a convict must prove that the judge and jury in his own trial were motivated by racial prejudice. The court has also found no barrier to imposing the death sentence on persons who were as young as 16 at the time of the crime or who were mentally retarded.

Although most advanced industrial countries have abandoned capital punishment, in the US the 'politics of death' are played at both the state and Federal levels. A former governor of Texas, seeking to be returned to office in a 1990 election, aired a campaign commercial in which he strolled along a macabre gallery of poster-sized photographs—portraits of criminals who were executed during his governorship. 'I made sure they received the ultimate penalty—death,' the candidate boasted, 'and Texas is a safer place for it.' Governor Mario Cuomo of New York suffered under a political handicap because of a conscientious objection to capital punishment. Summing up past electoral defeats, he aptly observed: 'The death penalty killed me.' Congress has considered adding about 50 new capital offences—including murder of a federal poultry inspector—to the federal statute books. Since the court is bent on deferring to the legislative branch, there are likely to be few constitutional impediments to carrying out death sentences.

Despite the general expansion of defendants' rights, in some jurisdictions the right to a 'speedy' trial exists only if a two-year delay can be considered speedy. Judges and courtrooms sufficient to handle the criminal caseload are lacking. The protection against 'excessive' bail is relatively meaningless, moreover, because poor defendants are usually unable to raise even amounts that seem modest to the affluent. As a result, they wait in gaol during the lengthy pre-trial period, diminishing their chances of making an effective defence. So far, the court has found nothing unconstitutional about routine trial delays or a bail system that discriminates against the indigent.

Besides transforming many theoretical rights into practical ones, the court made them effective in both state and federal trials. Here was a classic anomaly of federalism. The Bill of Rights had not been explicitly addressed to the states, and in the case of *Barron v. Baltimore* (1833) the court ruled that state governments were not bound by it. As a result, federal trials were held according to one standard of due process and state trials according to another, usually less favourable to defendants.

The potential for removing this anomaly was created by the Fourteenth Amendment, one of the 'Reconstruction Amendments' enacted after the Civil War to prevent the southern states from mistreating newly freed slaves. Echoing the Fifth Amendment, the Fourteenth prohibited any *state* from depriving a person 'of life, liberty or property without due process of law'. The prohibition in itself did not immediately reform state trials, since the court generally construed 'due process' to mean merely the rudiments of procedural fairness. By the early twentieth century, however, the court began to accept the proposition that providing due process meant adhering to the specific terms of the Bill of Rights. One by one, the bill's provisions were 'incorporated' into the Fourteenth Amendment due process clause by judicial decision and made binding upon the states, vastly enhancing the status of the criminal defendant in state courts.

The Fourteenth Amendment did more than extend the existing provisions of the Bill of Rights to the states; it also created a new right, that of 'equal protection of the laws'. Although intended, like the due process clause, to secure even-handed treatment of blacks in the former slave states, the equal protection clause was soon vitiated by two court rulings. In the *Civil Rights Cases* (1883), it was decided that the amendment outlawed only discriminatory action by state governments, not by private individuals or corporations. The state, in other words, could not enact a law segregating restaurants, but the restaurant owners were free to exclude blacks if they wished. The 'state action' doctrine effectively undermined the amendment, because most discrimination suffered by blacks could be classified as 'private'. Thirteen years later the equal protection clause was diluted further when the court, in *Plessy v. Ferguson*, held that states might segregate public facilities, including schools and transport, by race so long as blacks and whites were provided with equal facilities. The most significant consequence of the 'separate but equal' doctrine was the development of two racially distinct school systems, from elementary school through university, in the southern states.

Together, the 'state action' and 'separate but equal' doctrines precluded any attempt by the federal government to outlaw racial discrimination—even if that were not a political impossibility in Congress—and prevented blacks from challenging discriminatory state legislation in the federal courts on constitutional grounds. Enthusiasm for 'Reconstruction' had waned anyway. The north was content to leave the blacks just where the 'states' rights' advocates would have them.

No basic change occurred in the constitutional status of blacks until the post-Second World War period, when the state action doctrine began to atrophy because the court looked more critically upon the supposed distinction between public and private. So-called 'private' discriminatory activities were found to involve the state sufficiently to put them within reach of the Fourteenth Amendment. The state was held responsible for discrimination when practised by a concessionary restaurant in a municipal car park, or by the officials of the state Republican and Democratic party organizations, or by the signatories of a judicially enforceable real estate covenant excluding black residents from a neighbourhood.

Nevertheless, the state action doctrine still seemed to pose a barrier to direct enforcement of blacks' civil rights by federal statute. In 1968, however, the court found a way of circumventing the state action doctrine. Seeking a constitutional basis for federal legislation prohibiting private discrimination, it turned to the Thirteenth Amendment, which had abolished slavery. That amendment, the court said in *Jones v. Mayer*, empowered Congress to enact statutes to rid blacks of the 'badges and incidents' of slavery, that is, the racial discrimination which was the legacy of their ancestors' servitude. The practical outcome of the case was the resurrection of a long dormant 1866 statute, outlawing discrimination by private individuals in the sale or rental of property—an 'open housing' law from the Reconstruction era.

Congress, however, had already gone off in another direction in search of constitutional authority for civil rights legislation. If there was one theatre in which the federal government exercised virtually unlimited discretion, it was in the regulation of interstate commerce. In 1964, Congress passed a civil rights act that prohibited segregation in all places of public accommodation, such as hotels, restaurants, and transport facilities, giving as its rationale the need to rid interstate commerce of the burden of American-style apartheid. Even the most self-sufficient bistro consumed some commodity, whether food, forks, or flypaper, that had moved in interstate commerce.

Like 'state action', the doctrine of 'separate but equal' came under intense judicial scrutiny in the post-war years, and the court was dissatisfied with what it saw. For the reality of 'separate but equal' contradicted the theory. Schools for blacks were not equal to white schools in either physical plant, textbooks, teacher qualifications, curriculum or funds. The judicial attack on the doctrine began at the level of graduate and professional education, since it was plainly ludicrous for the states to pretend to provide equivalent faculties and facilities for a handful of black graduate students. When Texas established a makeshift law school for blacks rather than let them enter the regular state law school, the court in 1950 noted acerbically: 'It is difficult to believe that one who had a free choice between these law schools would consider the question close.'

Unlike state action, however, 'separate but equal' ultimately came to an abrupt end, unanimously repudiated by the court in one of its most momentous cases, *Brown v. Board of Education* (1954). The justices concluded that no matter how good black schools might become in tangible qualities, 'separate educational facilities are inherently unequal' because racial segregation 'generates a feeling of inferiority' in black students.

Although *Brown* made it impossible for states to require school segregation by law, integrating the schools proved to be a perplexing problem. After two decades of often violent resistance to integration, only about half of black students in the south attended racially mixed schools. Moreover, it became clear soon after *Brown* that segregation was not a southern problem alone.

That decision, in fact, put northern and southern school systems on the same footing. In both, blacks attended black schools and whites attended white schools, not because of any legal requirements but because of patterns of residential segregation. *Brown* spelled the end of *de jure* school segregation, separation by law; it did not reach *de facto* segregation, which results from having all-black and all-white neighbourhoods.

Yet if segregated education is inferior to integrated education, is it not denial of equal protection to permit it to continue, regardless of whether it is mandated by law or perpetuated by residential segregation? With respect to the south, the court has declared that school districts which once were legally segregated have a duty to remedy the residual effects by taking positive steps to put black and white pupils into the same building. The court thus has sanctioned bussing students out of their own neighbourhoods into schools where another race predominates. With respect to the north, the court has taken the position that official policies which reinforce residential segregation, such as the drawing of attendance zones along racial lines, amount to *de jure* school segregation. The court has considered bussing an appropriate remedy for such 'dual school systems'. In the larger metropolitan areas, however, blacks are concentrated within the city school district and the whites in separate suburban school districts. Bussing between districts offers the only possibility for achieving racial balance, but to justify it the court would have to find *de jure* segregation. And to do that would require showing either that the officials of all the districts had participated in fostering segregation or that the state government, which has overall responsibility for education, did so.

A classic case was presented to the court in 1974, involving the city of Detroit. Owing to 'white flight', two thirds of the students in the city proper were black; the 'minority' group was a majority inside the city, making school integration impossible. But surrounding the city was a ring of suburbs whose schools were overwhelmingly white. A federal judge ordered bussing between city and suburban schools, but he was overruled by the Supreme Court, which held that it had not been proven that the suburban districts had followed discriminatory policies. Thus, they could not be compulsorily included in an integration scheme. The court refused to accept the theory of overall state responsibility for demographic patterns. It considered each of the suburban districts a discrete unit, leaving the city limits a virtually impenetrable barrier to bussing.

While it thus seemed to be foreclosing the only practical alternative to northern school segregation, the court nevertheless endorsed the concept of taking 'affirmative action' to promote the recruitment of blacks into universities and professional schools. The practice of giving preferential consideration to black applicants who otherwise might lack the proper credentials for admission had been denounced as 'reverse discrimination' against whites. But in 1978, in the case of *University of California v. Bakke*, the court found that giving some weight to a person's race, to compensate for the effects of social discrimination, did not in principle violate the equal protection clause of the Fourteenth Amendment.

Just as he has been denied equal educational opportunity, despite the Fourteenth Amendment, the black has also been kept until recently from full exercise of the suffrage despite the Fifteenth Amendment's explicit prohibition against denial of the right to vote because of 'race, colour or previous condition of servitude'. The Fifteenth Amendment, the last of the Reconstruction amendments, was intended to prevent the southern states from disenfranchising the former slaves, but the states resorted to several ingenious devices to circumvent the spirit of the amendment: the literacy test, the poll tax, the 'grandfather clause' and the white primary law.

The poll tax was a registration fee for voting, usually payable a considerable time before the election. As the poorest class in the south, blacks were naturally deterred from voting by the fee requirement. Even those who could pay and were willing often found that they had missed the payment deadline, which was much less publicized than the election date. Despite its discriminatory effect, the poll tax was held constitutional by the Supreme Court in 1937, but it was abolished for all federal elections by the Twenty-fourth Amendment in 1964.

The white primary was a mechanism for denying even registered black voters any voice in the selection of candidates. In the south's one-party states, where the Democrats invariably swept the general election, the real contest took place in primary elections within the Democratic party. Acting on the premiss that the party was a 'private association', the Democrats excluded blacks from membership and from the privilege of voting in their primary. In the late 1940s, the Supreme Court held that a primary was an integral stage of the electoral process and that parties were sufficiently imbued with official sanction for their discriminatory acts to be construed as 'state action'. Attempts by the Democrats to evade the ruling by holding 'unofficial' pre-primary elections were also invalidated by the court.

Grandfather clauses typically stipulated that anyone whose ancestors did not have the right to vote in 1860, the year before the Civil War began, must pass a literacy test to qualify for the franchise. Illiterate whites, however, were free to vote. The grandfather clause was invalidated by the Supreme Court in 1915, but the literacy test remained. If a state wished to require a literacy test, it had to require all registrants, regardless of their ancestry, to pass it. However, the test was usually administered in a discriminatory fashion by the registrars. A common test as late as the 1960s asked blacks to read and 'interpret' sections of the constitution; the applicant's interpretation was then declared 'wrong'.

The literacy test remained a formidable barrier to black participation in politics until Congress passed the Voting Rights Act of 1965, under its power to enforce the Fifteenth Amendment. The act authorized federally appointed registrars to be substituted for state registrars in places where only a small proportion of blacks were enrolled voters. Since then, blacks in most southern states have become a sizable minority voting bloc that often can decide the fate of elections. Even formerly staunch segregationists like Governor George Wallace of Alabama were forced to woo black voters. The Voting Rights Act has also cleared the way for blacks to be elected to public office. Before the act, less than 100 blacks held elective offices in the southern states. Since its passage, black officeholders have become common in the south, as in the rest of the country, and blacks have been elected to such major positions as mayor of Atlanta and governor of Virginia. The voting rights law has also prevented the drawing of constituency boundaries so as to prevent blacks from achieving fair representation on city and county councils. Although the bench is normally not thought of as a 'representative' institution, electoral arrangements that deprive blacks of an equal chance to become judges, where they are elected, have also been invalidated.

Blacks are only one of the minority groups that have been able to redress their weak position in the political arena by relying upon the rights guaranteed by the constitution. Various dissident political and religious groups, *avant-garde* cultural movements and other isolated minorities have also successfully leaned on these rights to withstand the majority's pressure towards conformity. By association with such pariahs, constitutional rights often tend to be disparaged in practice. That is, the average person, if asked, might say that he supports the First Amendment and freedom of speech but is opposed to Nazis being allowed to hold a public rally.

Indeed, although Americans are raised within a 'culture of rights', they are apparently confused about the precise origin and nature of those rights. A survey conducted by the American Bar Association during the celebration of the bicentennial of the Bill of Rights in 1991 found that fewer than one person in ten knew that the Bill was adopted to protect citizens against abuse of power by the national government. In a similar survey conducted in 1987, nearly half the respondents agreed with the proposition that somewhere in the constitution was the (Marxist) principle: 'From each according to his ability, to each according to his need.' A large majority also thought that the constitution assures free public education through secondary school, even though the Supreme Court has found no guarantee of access to education at any level.

If these surveys are a reliable guide, many Americans are unfamiliar with the rights they actually possess and at the same time mistakenly assume that the nation's founders ordained a utopian social order. When asked how the Bill of Rights might be amplified, a large number of Americans do, in fact, propose a right to receive a government benefit of some kind. Health care is a popular choice—understandably so in a nation where 35 million persons, including many who are employed, lack medical insurance. The response suggests a desire to convert the Bill of Rights from a political charter to a social charter, from a catalogue of proscribed abuses to a menu of prescribed services. The aspiration perhaps is to make the Bill of Rights succour the ordinary person, not, as it sometimes seems, just malefactors, political and spiritual eccentrics, and elitist freethinkers. Also resonating in the popular imagination may be the Ninth Amendment's cryptic reminder that certain rights are 'retained by the people'. It was left to later generations to fathom what these unenumerated rights might be—a formidable challenge, considering that details as minute as the framers' use of a definite versus indefinite article provokes heated debate among latter-day exegetes.

Given widespread misconceptions and differing perceptions about rights, it is possible that the specifics of the Bill of Rights might not win approval in a referendum if put to the voters today under a less hallowed name. As the flag protection debate illustrates, there is often considerable popular support for qualifying, or at least ignoring, provisions that run counter to the passions of the moment. During the Second World War and the Cold War external threats persuaded Americans to accept what has been called the 'national security constitution' a crisis-tempered interpretation that sometimes subordinated individual rights to the patriotic cause. More recently, internal threats—crime, AIDS and illegal drug use—have convinced many that it would be worth modifying some constitutional rights to fortify the government's instruments of control. The revival of militant evangelism in the 1980s, in addition, left a residue of distaste for 'moral relativism', thereby eroding the spirit of tolerance, and the desire to protect women, children and minorities has prompted efforts to restrict expression that is judged harmful to them or likely to incite bigotry-motivated 'hate-crimes'.

Paradoxically, modern Americans seem to feel less personally threatened by the misuse of power than the framers did, even though the scope of government—and thus the potential for abuse—is infinitely greater today. The bicentennial festivities demonstrated, however, that as an abstraction at least the Bill of Rights is still accorded as much reverence as the body of the constitution. Even if considered bothersome when actually invoked, the Bill's guarantees carry the aura of tradition. No better security for human rights could be imagined.

Constitution of the United States of America

We the people of the United States, in Order to form a more perfect Union, establish Justice, insure domestic Tranquility, provide for the common defence, promote the general Welfare, and secure the Blessings of Liberty to ourselves and our Posterity, do ordain and establish this CONSTITUTION for the United States of America.

ARTICLE I

SECTION 1

All legislative Powers herein granted shall be vested in a Congress of the United States, which shall consist of a Senate and House of Representatives.

SECTION 2

(1) The House of Representatives shall be composed of Members chosen every second Year by the People of the several States, and the Electors in each State shall have the Qualifications requisite for Electors of the most numerous Branch of the State Legislature.

(2) No person shall be a Representative who shall not have attained to the Age of twenty five Years, and been seven Years a Citizen of the United States, and who shall not, when elected, be an inhabitant of that State in which he shall be chosen.

(3) Representatives and direct Taxes shall be apportioned among

the several States which may be included within this Union according to their respective Numbers, which shall be determined by adding to the whole Number of free Persons, including those bound to Service for a Term of Years, and excluding Indians not taxed, three fifths of all other Persons. The actual Enumeration shall be made within three Years after the first Meeting of the Congress of the United States, and within every subsequent Term of ten Years, in such Manner as they shall by Law direct. The Number of Representatives shall not exceed one for every thirty Thousand, but each State shall have at least one Representative; and until such enumeration shall be made, the State of New Hampshire shall be entitled to chuse three, Massachusetts eight, Rhode-Island and Providence Plantations one, Connecticut five, New-York six, New Jersey four, Pennsylvania eight, Delaware one, Maryland six, Virginia ten, North Carolina five, South Carolina five, and Georgia three.

(4) When vacancies happen in the Representation from any State, the Executive Authority thereof shall issue Writs of Election to fill such Vacancies.

(5) The House of Representatives shall chuse their Speaker and other officers; and shall have the sole Power of Impeachment.

SECTION 3

(1) The Senate of the United States shall be composed of two Senators from each State, chosen by the Legislature thereof, for six Years; and each Senator shall have one Vote.

(2) Immediately after they shall be assembled in Consequence of the first Election, they shall be divided as equally as may be into three Classes. The Seats of the Senators of the first Class shall be vacated at the Expiration of the second Year, of the second Class at the Expiration of the fourth Year, and of the third Class at the Expiration of the sixth Year, so that one third may be chosen every second Year; and if Vacancies happen by Registration, or

otherwise, during the Recess of the Legislature of any State, the Executive thereof may make temporary Appointments until the next Meeting of the Legislature, which shall then fill such Vacancies.

(3) No Person shall be a Senator who shall not have attained to the Age of thirty Years, and been nine Years a Citizen of the United States, and who shall not, when elected, be an inhabitant of that State for which he shall be chosen.

(4) The Vice President of the United States shall be President of the Senate, but shall have no Vote, unless they be equally divided.

(5) The Senate shall chuse their other Officers, and also a President pro tempore, in the Absence of the Vice President, or when he shall exercise the Office of President of the United States.

(6) The Senate shall have the sole Power to try all Impeachments. When sitting for that Purpose, they shall be on Oath or Affirmation. When the President of the United States is tried, the Chief Justice shall preside: And no Person shall be convicted without the Concurrence of two thirds of the Members present.

(7) Judgment in Cases of Impeachment shall not extend further than to removal from office, and disqualification to hold and enjoy any Office of honor, Trust or Profit under the United States: but the Party convicted shall nevertheless be liable and subject to Indictment, Trial, Judgment and Punishment, according to Law.

SECTION 4

(1) The Times, Places and Manner of holding Elections for Senators and Representatives, shall be prescribed in each State by the Legislature thereof; but the Congress may at any time by Law make or alter such Regulations, except as to the places of chusing Senators.

(2) The Congress shall assemble at least once in every Year, and such Meeting shall be on the first Monday in December, unless they shall by Law appoint a different Day.

SECTION 5

(1) Each House shall be the Judge of the Elections, Returns and Qualifications of its own Members, and a Majority of each shall constitute a Quorum to do Business; but a smaller Number may adjourn from day to day, and may be authorized to compel the attendance of absent Members, in such Manner, and under such Penalties as each House may provide.

(2) Each House may determine the Rules of its Proceedings, punish its Members for Disorderly Behaviour, and, with the Concurrence of two thirds, expel a Member.

(3) Each House shall keep a Journal of its Proceedings, and from time to time publish the same, excepting such Parts as may in their Judgment require Secrecy; and the Yeas and Nays in the Members of either House on any question shall, at the Desire of one fifth of those Present, be entered on the Journal.

(4) Neither House, during the Session of Congress, shall, without the Consent of the other, adjourn for more than three days, nor to any other Place than that in which the two Houses shall be sitting.

SECTION 6

(1) The Senators and Representatives shall receive a Compensation for their Services, to be ascertained by Law, and paid out of the Treasury of the United States. They shall in all Cases, except Treason, Felony and Breach of the Peace, be privileged from Arrest during their Attendance at the Session of their respective Houses, and in going to and returning from the same; and for any Speech or Debate in either House, they shall not be questioned in any other Place.

(2) No Senator or Representative shall, during the Time for which he was elected, be appointed to any civil Office under the Authority of the United States, which have been encreased during such time; and no Person holding any Office under

the United States, shall be a member of either House during his Continuance in Office.

SECTION 7

(1) All Bills for raising Revenue shall originate in the House of Representatives; but the Senate may propose or concur with Amendments as on other Bills.

(2) Every Bill which will have passed the House of Representatives and the Senate, shall, before it become a Law, be presented to the President of the United States; if he approve he shall sign it, but if not he shall return it, with his Objections to that House in which it shall have originated, who shall enter the Objections at large on their Journal, and proceed to reconsider it. If after such Reconsideration two thirds of that House shall agree to pass the Bill, it shall be sent, together with the Objections, to the other House, by which it shall likewise be reconsidered, and if approved by two thirds of that House, it shall become a Law. But in all such Cases the Votes of both Houses shall be determined by Yeas and Nays, and the Names of the Persons voting for and against the Bill shall be entered on the Journal of each House respectively. If any Bill shall not be returned by the President within ten Days (Sundays excepted) after it shall have been measured to him, the same shall be a Law, in like Manner as if he had signed it, unless the Congress by their Adjournment prevent its Return, in which Case it shall not be a Law.

(3) Every Order, Resolution, or Vote to which the Concurrence of the Senate and House of Representatives may be necessary (except on a question of Adjournment) shall be presented to the President of the United States; and before the same shall take Effect, shall be approved by him, or being disapproved by him, shall be repassed by two thirds of the Senate and House of Representatives, according to the Rules and Limitations prescribed in the Case of a Bill.

SECTION 8
The Congress shall have Power

(1) to lay and collect Taxes, Duties, Imposts and Excises, to pay the Debts and provide for the common Defence and general Welfare of the United States; but all Duties, Imposts and Excises shall be uniform throughout the United States;

(2) To borrow Money on the credit of the United States;

(3) To regulate Commerce with foreign Nations, and among the several States, and with the Indian Tribes;

(4) To establish an uniform Rule of Naturalization, and uniform Laws on the subject of Bankruptcies throughout the United States;

(5) To coin Money, regulate the Value thereof, and of foreign Coin, and fix the Standard of Weights and Measures;

(6) To provide for the Punishment of counterfeiting the Securities and current Coin of the United States;

(7) To establish Post Offices and post Roads;

(8) To promote the Progress of Science and useful Arts, by securing for limited Times to Authors and Inventors the exclusive Right to their respective Writings and Discoveries;

(9) To constitute Tribunals inferior to the supreme Court;

(10) To define and punish Piracies and Felonies committed on the high Seas, and Offences against the Law of Nations;

(11) To declare War, grant Letters of Marque and Reprisal, and make Rules concerning Captures on Land and Water;

(12) To raise and support Armies, but no Appropriation of Money to that Use shall be for a longer Term than two Years;

(13) To provide and maintain a Navy;

(14) To make Rules for the Government and Regulation of the land and naval Forces;

(15) To provide for calling forth the Militia to execute the Laws of the Union, suppress Insurrections and repel invasions;

(16) To provide for organizing, arming, and disciplining, the Militia, and for governing such Part of them as may be employed in the Service of the United States, reserving to the States respectively, the Appointment of the Officers,

and the Authority of training the Militia according to the discipline prescribed by Congress;

(17) To exercise exclusive Legislation in all Cases whatsoever, over such District (not exceeding ten Miles square) as may, by Cession of particular States, and the Acceptance of Congress, become the Seat of the Government of the United States, and to exercise like Authority over all Places purchased by the Consent of the Legislature of the State in which the same shall be, for the Erection of Forts, Magazines, Arsenals, dock-Yards, and other needful Buildings;—And

(18) To make all Laws which shall be necessary and proper for carrying into Execution the foregoing Powers, and all other Powers vested by this Constitution in the Government of the United States, or in any Department or Officer thereof.

SECTION 9

(1) The Migration or Importation of such Persons as any of the States now existing shall think proper to admit, shall not be prohibited by the Congress prior to the Year one thousand eight hundred and eight, but a Tax or duty may be imposed on such Importation, not exceeding ten dollars for each Person.

(2) The Privilege of the Writ of Habeas Corpus shall not be suspended, unless when in Cases of Rebellion or Invasion the public Safety may require it.

(3) No Bill of Attainder or ex post facto Law shall be passed.

(4) No Capitation, or other direct, Tax shall be laid, unless in Proportion to the Census or Enumeration herein before directed to be taken.

(5) No Tax or Duty shall be laid on Articles exported from any State.

(6) No Preference shall be given by any Regulation of Commerce or Revenue to the Ports of one State over those of another: nor shall Vessels bound to, or from, one State, be obliged to enter, clear, or pay Duties in another.

(7) No Money shall be drawn from the Treasury, but in Consequence of Appropriations made by Law; and a regular

Statement and Account of the Receipts and Expenditures of all public Money shall be published from time to time.

(8) No Title of Nobility shall be granted by the United States: And no Person holding any Office or Profit or Trust under them, shall, without the Consent of the Congress, accept of any present, Emolument, Office, or Title, of any kind whatever, from any King, Prince, or foreign State.

SECTION 10

(1) No State shall enter into any Treaty, Alliance, or Confederation; grant Letters of Marque and Reprisal; coin Money; emit Bills of Credit; make any Thing but gold and silver Coin a Tender in Payment of Debts; pass any Bill of Attainder, ex post facto Law, or Law impairing the Obligation of Contracts, or grant any Title of Nobility.

(2) No State shall, without the Consent of the Congress, lay any Imposts or Duties on Imports or Exports, except what may be absolutely necessary for executing its inspection Laws; and the net Produce of all Duties and Imposts, laid by any State on Imports or Exports, shall be for the Use of the Treasury of the United States; and all such Laws shall be subject to the Revision and Control of the Congress.

(3) No State shall, without the Consent of Congress, lay any Duty of Tonnage, keep Troops, or Ships of War in time of Peace, enter into any Agreement or Compact with another State, or with a foreign Power, or engage in War, unless actually invaded, or in such imminent Danger as will not admit of delay.

ARTICLE II

SECTION I

(1) The executive Power shall be vested in a President of the United States of America. He shall hold his office during the Term of four Years, and, together with the Vice President, chosen for the same Term, be elected, as follows.

(2) Each State shall appoint, in such Manner as the Legislature thereof may direct, a Number of Electors, equal to the whole Number of Senators and Representatives to which the State may be entitled in the Congress: but no Senator or Representative, or Person holding an Office of Trust or Profit under the United States, shall be appointed an Elector.

(3) The Electors shall meet in their respective States, and vote by Ballot for two Persons, of whom one at least shall not be an inhabitant of the same State with themselves. And they shall make a List of all the Persons voted for, and of the Number of Votes for each; which List they shall sign and certify, and transmit sealed to the Seat of Government of the United States, directed to the President of the Senate. The President of the Senate shall, in the Presence of the Senate and House of Representatives, open all the Certificates, and the Votes shall then be counted. The Person having the greatest Number of Votes shall be the President, if such Number be a Majority of the whole Number of Electors appointed; and if there be more than one who have such Majority, and have an equal Number of Votes, then the House of Representatives shall immediately chuse by Ballot one of them for President; and if no Person have a Majority, then from the five highest on the List the said House shall in like Manner chuse the President. But in chusing the President, the Votes shall be taken by States, the Representation from each State having one Vote; A quorum for this Purpose shall consist of a Member or Members from two thirds of the States, and a Majority of all the States shall be necessary to a Choice. In every Case, after the Choice of the President, the Person having the greatest Number of Votes of the Electors shall be the Vice President. But if there should remain two or more who have equal Votes, the Senate shall chuse from them by Ballot the Vice President.

(4) The Congress may determine the Time of chusing the Electors, and the Day on which they shall give their Votes; which Day shall be the same throughout the United States.

(5) No Person except a natural born Citizen, or a Citizen of the United States, at the time of the Adoption of this Constitution, shall be eligible to the Office of President; neither shall any

Person be eligible to that Office who shall not have attained to the Age of thirty five Years, and been fourteen Years a Resident within the United States.

(6) In Case of the Removal of the President from Office, or of his Death, Resignation, or Inability to discharge the Powers and Duties of the said Office, the Same shall devolve on the Vice President, and the Congress may by Law provide for the Case of Removal, Death, Resignation, or Inability, both of the President and Vice President, declaring what Officer shall then act as President, and such Officer shall act accordingly, until the Disability be removed, or a President shall be elected.

(7) The President shall, at stated Times, receive for his Services, a Compensation, which shall neither be encreased nor diminished during the Period for which he shall have been elected, and he shall not receive within the Period any other Emolument from the United States, or any of them.

(8) Before he enter on the Execution of his Office, he shall take the following Oath or Affirmation:—'I do solemnly swear (or affirm) that I will faithfully execute the Office of President of the United States, and will to the best of my Ability, preserve, protect and defend the Constitution of the United States.'

SECTION 2

(1) The President shall be Commander in Chief of the Army and Navy of the United States, and of the Militia of the several States, when called into the actual Service of the United States; he may require the Opinion, in writing, of the principal Officer in each of the executive Departments, upon any Subject relating to the Duties of their respective Offices, and he shall have the Power to grant Reprieves and Pardons for Offences against the United States, except in Cases of Impeachment.

(2) He shall have Power, by and with the Advice and Consent of the Senate, to make Treaties, provided two thirds of the Senators present concur; and he shall nominate, and by and with the Advice and Consent of the Senate, shall appoint Ambassadors, other public Ministers and Consuls,

Judges of the supreme Court, and all other Officers of the United States, whose Appointments are not herein otherwise provided for, and which shall be established by law: but the Congress may by law vest the Appointment of such inferior Officers, as they think proper, in the President alone, in the Courts of Law, or in the Heads of Departments.

(3) The President shall have Power to fill up all Vacancies that may happen during the Recess of the Senate, by granting Commissions which shall expire at the End of their next Session.

SECTION 3

He shall from time to time give to the Congress Information of the State of the Union, and recommend to their Consideration such Measures as he shall judge necessary and expedient; he may, on extraordinary Occasions, convene both Houses, or either of them, and in Case of Disagreement between them, with Respect to the Time of Adjournment, he may adjourn them to such Time as he shall think proper; he shall receive Ambassadors and other public Ministers; he shall take Care that the Laws be faithfully executed, and shall Commission all the Officers of the United States.

SECTION 4

The President, Vice President and all civil Officers of the United States, shall be removed from Office on Impeachment for, and Conviction of, Treason, Bribery, or other high Crimes and Misdemeanors.

ARTICLE III

SECTION 1

The Judicial Power of the United States, shall be vested in one supreme Court, and in such inferior Courts as the Congress may from time to time ordain and establish. The Judges, both of the supreme and inferior Courts, shall hold their Offices during good Behaviour, and shall, at stated Times, receive for their Services, a Compensation, which shall not be diminished during their Continuance in Office.

SECTION 2

(1) The Judicial Power shall extend to all Cases, in Law and Equity, arising under this Constitution, the Laws of the United States, and Treaties made, or which shall be made, under their Authority;— to all Cases affecting Ambassadors, other public Ministers and Consuls;— to all Cases of admiralty and maritime Jurisdiction;— to Controversies to which the United States shall be a party;— to Controversies between two or more States;—between a State and Citizens of another State;-- between Citizens of different States;—between Citizens of the same State claiming Lands under Grants of different States, and between a State, or the Citizens thereof, and foreign States, Citizens or Subjects.

(2) In all Cases affecting Ambassadors, other public Ministers and Consuls, and those in which a State shall be Party, the supreme Court shall have original Jurisdiction. In all the other Cases before mentioned, the Supreme Court shall have appellate Jurisdiction, both as to Law and Fact, with such Exceptions, and under such Regulations as the Congress shall make.

(3) The Trial of all Crimes, except in Cases of impeachment, shall be by Jury; and such Trial shall be held in the State where the said Crimes shall have been committed; but when not committed within any State, the Trial shall be at such Place or Places as the Congress may by Law have directed.

SECTION 3

(1) Treason against the United States, shall consist only in levying War against them, or in adhering to their Enemies, giving them Aid and Comfort. No Person shall be convicted of Treason unless on the Testimony of two Witnesses to the same overt Act, or on Confession in open Court.

(2) The Congress shall have Power to declare the Punishment of

Treason, but no Attainder of Treason shall work Corruption of Blood, or Forfeiture except during the life of the Person attained.

ARTICLE IV

SECTION 1

Full Faith and Credit shall be given in each State to the public Acts, Records, and judicial Proceedings of every other State. And the Congress may by general Laws prescribe the Manner in which such Acts, Records and Proceedings shall be proved, and the Effect thereof.

SECTION 2

(1) The Citizens of each State shall be entitled to all Privileges and Immunities of Citizens in the several States.
(2) A Person charged in any State with Treason, Felony, or other Crime, who shall flee from Justice, and be found in another State, shall on Demand of the executive Authority of the State from which he fled, be delivered up, to be removed to the State having Jurisdiction of the Crime.
(3) No Person held to Service or Labour in one State, under the Laws thereof, escaping into another, shall, in Consequence of any Law or Regulation therein, be discharged from such Service or Labour, but shall be delivered up on Claim of the Party to whom such Service or Labour may be due.

SECTION 3

(1) New States may be admitted by the Congress into this Union; but no new State shall be formed or erected within the Jurisdiction of any other States; nor any State be formed by the Junction of two or more States, or Parts of States, without the Consent of the Legislatures of the States concerned as well as of the Congress.

(2) The Congress shall have Power to dispose of and make all
needful Rules and Regulations respecting the Territory or
other Property belonging to the United States; and nothing
in this Constitution shall be so construed as to Prejudice any
Claims of the United States, or of any particular State.

SECTION 4

The United States shall guarantee to every State in this Union
a Republican Form of Government, and shall protect each of
them against Invasion; and on Application of the Legislature,
or of the Executive (when the Legislature cannot be convened)
against domestic Violence.

ARTICLE V

The Congress, whenever two thirds of both Houses shall deem
it necessary, shall propose Amendments to this Constitution, or,
in the Application of the Legislatures of two thirds of the several
States, shall call a Convention for proposing Amendments, which,
in either Case, shall be valid to all Intents and Purposes, as Part of
this Constitution, when ratified by the Legislatures of three fourths
of the several States, or by Conventions in three fourths thereof, as
the one or the other Mode of Ratification may be proposed by the
Congress; Provided that no Amendment which may be made prior
to the Year One thousand eight hundred and eight shall in any
Manner affect the first and fourth Clauses in the Ninth Section
of the first Article; and that no State, without its Consent, shall
be deprived of its equal Suffrage in the Senate.

ARTICLE VI

(1) All Debts contracted and Engagements entered into, before
the Adoption of this Constitution, shall be as valid against
the United States under this Constitution, as under the
Confederation.

(2) This Constitution, and the Laws of the United States which shall be made in Pursuance thereof; and all Treaties made, or which shall be made, under the Authority of the United States, shall be the supreme Law of the Land; and the Judges in every State shall be bound thereby, any Thing in the Constitution or Laws of any State to the Contrary notwithstanding.

(3) The Senators and Representatives before mentioned, and the Members of the several State Legislatures, and all executive and judicial Officers, both of the United States and of the several States, shall be bound by Oath or affirmation, to support this Constitution; but no religious Test shall ever be required as a Qualification to any Office or Public Trust under the United States.

ARTICLE VII

The Ratification of the Conventions of nine States, shall be sufficient for the Establishment of this Constitution between the States so ratifying the Same.

Amendments

AMENDMENT I

Congress shall make no law respecting an establishment of religion, or prohibiting the free exercise thereof; or abridging the freedom of speech, or of the press; or the right of the people peaceably to assemble, and to petition the Government for a redress of grievances.

AMENDMENT II

A well regulated Militia, being necessary to the security of a free State, the right of the people to keep and bear Arms, shall not be infringed.

AMENDMENT III

No Soldier shall, in time of peace be quartered in any house, without the consent of the Owner, nor in time of war, but in a manner to be prescribed by law.

AMENDMENT IV

The right of the people to be secure in their persons, houses, papers, and effects, against unreasonable searches and seizures, shall not be violated, and no Warrants shall issue, but upon probable cause, supported by Oath or affirmation, and particularly describing the place to be searched, and the persons or things to be seized.

AMENDMENT V

No person shall be held to answer for a capital, or otherwise infamous crime, unless on a presentment or indictment of a Grand Jury, except in cases arising in the land or naval forces, or in the Militia, when in actual service in time of War or public danger; nor shall any person be subject for the same offence to be twice put in jeopardy of life or limb; nor shall be compelled in any criminal case to be a witness against himself; nor be deprived of life, liberty, or property, without due process of law; nor shall private property be taken for public use, without just compensation.

AMENDMENT VI

In all criminal prosecutions the accused shall enjoy the right to a speedy and public trial, by an impartial jury of the State and district wherein the crime shall have been committed, which district shall have been previously ascertained by law, and to be informed of the nature and cause of the accusation; to be confronted with the witnesses against him; to have compulsory process for obtaining witnesses in his favor, and to have the Assistance of Counsel for his defence.

AMENDMENT VII

In suits at common law, where the value in controversy shall exceed twenty dollars, the right of trial by jury shall be preserved, and no fact tried by a jury shall be otherwise re-examined in any Court of the United States, than according to the rules of the common law.

AMENDMENT VIII

Excessive bail shall not be required, nor excessive fines imposed, nor cruel and unusual punishments inflicted.

AMENDMENT IX

The enumeration in the Constitution, of certain rights, shall not be construed to deny or disparage others retained by the people.

AMENDMENT X

The powers not delegated to the United States by the Constitution, nor prohibited by it to the States, are reserved to the States respectively, or to the people.

[The first ten Amendments, known as the Bill of Rights, were adopted in 1791.]

AMENDMENT XI

The Judicial power of the United States shall not be construed to extend to any suit in law or equity, commenced or prosecuted against one of the United States by Citizens of another State, or by Citizens or Subjects of any Foreign State. [1798]

AMENDMENT XII

The Electors shall meet in their respective states, and vote by ballot for President and Vice President, one of whom, at least, shall not be an inhabitant of the same state with themselves; they shall name in their ballots the person voted for as President, and in distinct ballots the person voted for as Vice President, and they shall make distinct lists of all persons voted for as President, and of all persons voted for as Vice President, and of the number of votes for each, which lists they shall sign and certify, and transmit sealed to the seat of the government of the United States, directed to the President of the Senate;—The President of the Senate shall, in the presence of the Senate and House of Representatives, open all the certificates and the votes shall then be counted;—The person having the greatest number of votes for

President, shall be the President, if such number be a majority of the whole number of Electors appointed; and if no person have such majority, then from the persons having the highest numbers not exceeding three on the list of those voted for as President, the House of Representatives shall choose immediately, by ballot, the President. But in choosing the President, the votes shall be taken by states, the representation from each state having one vote; a quorum for this purpose shall consist of a member or members from two thirds of the states, and a majority of all the states shall be necessary to a choice. And if the House of Representatives shall not choose a President whenever the right of choice shall devolve upon them, before the fourth day of March next following, then the Vice President shall act as President, as in the case of the death or other constitutional disability of the President.—The person having the greatest number of votes as Vice President, shall be the Vice President, if such number be a majority of the whole number of Electors appointed, and if no person have a majority, then from the two highest numbers on the list, the Senate shall choose the Vice President; a quorum for the purpose shall consist of two thirds of the whole number of Senators, and a majority of the whole number shall be necessary to a choice. But no person constitutionally ineligible to the office of President shall be eligible to that of Vice President of the United States. [1804]

AMENDMENT XIII

SECTION 1

Neither slavery nor involuntary servitude, except as a punishment for crime whereof the party shall have been duly convicted, shall exist within the United States, or any place subject to their jurisdiction.

SECTION 2

Congress shall have power to enforce this article by appropriate legislation. [1865]

AMENDMENT XIV

SECTION 1

All persons born or naturalized in the United States, and subject to the jurisdiction thereof, are citizens of the United States and of the State wherein they reside. No State shall make or enforce any law which shall abridge the privileges or immunities of citizens of the United States; nor shall any State deprive any person of life, liberty, or property, without due process of law; nor deny to any person within its jurisdiction the equal protection of the laws.

SECTION 2

Representatives shall be apportioned among the several States according to their respective numbers, counting the whole number of persons in each State, excluding Indians not taxed. But when the right to vote at any election for the choice of electors for President and Vice President of the United States, Representatives in Congress, the Executive and Judicial officers of a State, or the members of the Legislature thereof, is denied to any of the male inhabitants of such State, being twenty-one years of age, and citizens of the United States, or in any way abridged, except for participation in rebellion, or other crime, the basis of representation therein shall be reduced in the proportion which the number of such male citizens shall bear to the whole number of male citizens twenty-one years of age in such State.

SECTION 3

No person shall be a Senator or Representative in Congress, or elector of President and Vice President, or hold any office, civil or military, under the United States, or under any State, who, having previously taken an oath, as a member of Congress, or as an officer of the United States, or as a member of any State legislature, or as an executive or judicial officer of any State, to support the Constitution of the United States, shall have engaged in insurrection or rebellion against the same, or given aid or comfort to the enemies thereof. But Congress may by a vote of two thirds of each House, remove such disability.

SECTION 4

The validity of the public debt of the United States, authorized by law, including debts incurred for payment of pensions and bounties for services in suppressing insurrection or rebellion, shall not be questioned. But neither the United States nor any State shall assume or pay any debt or obligation incurred in aid of insurrection or rebellion against the United States, or any claim for the loss or emancipation of any slave; but all such debts, obligations and claims shall be held illegal and void.

SECTION 5

The Congress shall have power to enforce, by appropriate legislation, the provisions of this article. [1868]

AMENDMENT XV

SECTION 1

The right of citizens of the United States to vote shall not be denied or abridged by the United States or by any State on account of race, color, or previous condition of servitude.

SECTION 2

The Congress shall have power to enforce this article by appropriate legislation. [1870]

AMENDMENT XVI

The Congress shall have power to lay and collect taxes on incomes, from whatever source derived, without apportionment among the several States, and without regard to any census or enumeration. [1913]

AMENDMENT XVII

The Senate of the United States shall be composed of two Senators from each State, elected by the people thereof, for six years; and each Senator shall have one vote. The electors in each State shall have the qualifications requisite for electors of the most numerous branch of the State legislatures.

When vacancies happen in the representation of any State in the Senate, the executive authority of such State shall issue writs of election to fill such vacancies: *Provided,* That the legislature of any State may empower the executive thereof to make temporary appointments until the people fill the vacancies by election as the legislature may direct.

This amendment shall not be so construed as to affect the election or term of any Senator chosen before it becomes valid as part of the Constitution. [1913]

AMENDMENT XVIII

SECTION 1

After one year from the ratification of this article the manufacture, sale, or transportation of intoxicating liquors within, the importation thereof into, or the exportation thereof from the United States and all territory subject to the jurisdiction thereof for beverage purposes is hereby prohibited.

SECTION 2

The Congress and the several States shall have concurrent power to enforce this article by appropriate legislation.

SECTION 3

This article shall be inoperative unless it shall have been ratified as an amendment to the Constitution by the legislatures of the several States, as provided in the Constitution, within seven years from the date of the submission hereof to the States by the Congress. [1919]

AMENDMENT XIX

The right of citizens of the United States to vote shall not be denied or abridged by the United States or by any State on account of sex.

Congress shall have power to enforce this article by appropriate legislation. [1920]

AMENDMENT XX

SECTION 1

The terms of the President and Vice President shall end at noon at the 20th day of January, and the terms of Senators and Representatives at noon on the 3rd day of January, of the years in which such terms would have ended if this article had not been ratified; and the terms of their successors shall then begin.

SECTION 2

The Congress shall assemble at least once in every year, and such meeting shall begin at noon on the 3rd day of January, unless they shall by law appoint a different day.

SECTION 3

If, at the time fixed for the beginning of the term of the President, the President elect shall have died, the Vice President elect shall become President. If a President shall not have been chosen before the time fixed for the beginning of his term, or if the President elect shall have failed to qualify, then the Vice President elect shall act as President until a President shall have qualified; and the Congress may by law provide for the case wherein neither a President elect nor a Vice President elect shall have qualified, declaring who shall then act as President, or the manner in which one who is to act shall be selected, and such person shall act accordingly until a President or Vice President shall have qualified.

SECTION 4

The Congress may by law provide for the case of the death of any of the persons from whom the House of Representatives may choose a President whenever the right of choice shall have devolved upon them, and for the case of the death of any of the persons from whom the Senate may choose a Vice President whenever the right of choice shall have devolved upon them.

SECTION 5

Sections 1 and 2 shall take effect on the 15th day of October following the ratification of this article.

SECTION 6

This article shall be inoperative unless it shall have been ratified as an amendment to the Constitution by the legislatures of three fourths of the several States within seven years from the date of its submission. [1933]

AMENDMENT XXI

SECTION 1

The eighteenth article of amendment to the Constitution of the United States is hereby repealed.

SECTION 2

The transportation or importation into any State, Territory, or possession of the United States for delivery or use therein of intoxicating liquors, in violation of the laws thereof, is hereby prohibited.

SECTION 3

This article shall be inoperative unless it shall have been ratified as an amendment to the Constitution by conventions in the several States, as provided in the Constitution, within seven years from the date of the submission hereof to the States by the Congress. [1933]

AMENDMENT XXII

SECTION 1

No person shall be elected to the office of the President more than twice, and no person who has held the office of President, or acted as President, for more than two years of a term to which some other person was elected President shall be elected to the office of the President more than once. But this Article shall not apply to any persons holding the office of President when this Article was proposed by the Congress, and shall not prevent any person who may be holding the office of President, or acting as President, during the term within which this Article becomes operative from holding the office of President or acting as President during the remainder of such term.

SECTION 2

This Article shall be inoperative unless it shall have been ratified as an amendment to the Constitution by the legislatures of three fourths of the several States within seven years from the date of its submission to the states by the Congress. [1951]

AMENDMENT XXIII

SECTION 1

The District constituting the seat of Government of the United States shall appoint in such manner as the Congress may direct:
A number of electors of President and Vice President equal to the whole number of Senators and Representatives in Congress to which the District would be entitled if it were a State, but in no event more than the least populous states; they shall be in addition to those appointed by the States, but they shall be considered, for the purposes of the election of President and Vice President, to be electors appointed by a State; and they shall meet in the District and perform such duties as provided by the twelfth article of amendment.

SECTION 2

The Congress shall have power to enforce this article by appropriate legislation. [1961]

AMENDMENT XXIV

SECTION 1

The right of citizens of the United States to vote in any primary or other election for the President or Vice President, for electors for President or Vice President, or for Senator or Representative in Congress, shall not be denied or abridged by the United States or any State by reason of failure to pay poll tax or other tax.

SECTION 2

The Congress shall have power to enforce this article by appropriate legislation. [1964]

AMENDMENT XXV

SECTION 1

In case of the removal of the President from office or of his death or resignation, the Vice President shall become President.

SECTION 2

Whenever there is a vacancy in the office of the Vice President, the President shall nominate a Vice President who shall take office upon confirmation by a majority vote of both Houses of Congress.

SECTION 3

Whenever the President transmit to the President pro tempore of the Senate and the Speaker of the House of Representatives his written declaration that he is unable to discharge the powers and duties of his office, and until he transmit to them a written declaration to the contrary, such powers and duties shall be discharged by the Vice President as Acting President.

SECTION 4

Whenever the Vice President and a majority of either the principal officers of the executive departments or of such other body as Congress may by law provide, transmit to the President pro tempore of the Senate and the Speaker of the House of Representatives their written declaration that the President is unable to discharge the powers and duties of his office, the Vice President shall immediately assume the powers and duties of the office as Acting President.

Thereafter, when the President transmits to the President pro tempore of the Senate and the Speaker of the House of Representatives his written declaration that no inability exists, he shall resume the powers and duties of his office unless the Vice President and a majority of either the principal officers of the executive departments or of such other body as Congress may by law provide, transmit within four days to the President pro tempore of the Senate and the Speaker of the House of Representatives their written declaration that the President is unable to discharge the powers and duties of his office. Thereupon Congress shall decide the issue, assembling within forty-eight hours for that purpose if not in session. If the Congress, within twenty-one days after receipt of the latter written declaration, or if Congress is not in session, within twenty-one days after Congress is required to assemble, determines by two thirds vote of both Houses that the President is unable to discharge the powers and duties of his office, the Vice President shall continue to discharge the same as Acting President; otherwise, the President shall resume the powers and duties of his office. [1967]

AMENDMENT XXVI

SECTION 1

The right of citizens of the United States, who are eighteen years of age or older, to vote shall not be denied or abridged by the United States or by any State on account of age.

SECTION 2

The Congress shall have the power to enforce this article by appropriate legislation. [1971]

Index

(Numerals in bold face represent a chapter/section devoted to the subject entry)